Food Will Win the War

Food Will Win the War

Minnesota Crops, Cooks, and Conservation during World War I

Rae Katherine Eighmey

MINNESOTA HISTORICAL SOCIETY PRESS

www.mhspress.org

The Minnesota Historical Society Press is a member
of the Association of American University Presses.

Manufactured in the United States of America

10 9 8 7 6 5 4 3 2 1

♾ The paper used in this publication meets the minimum requirements
of the American National Standard for Information Sciences—
Permanence for Printed Library Materials, ANSI z39.48-1984.

International Standard Book Number
ISBN-13: 978-0-87351-718-8 (paper)
ISBN-10: 0-87351-718-0 (paper)

Library of Congress Cataloging-in-Publication Data

Eighmey, Rae Katherine.
  Food will win the war : Minnesota crops, cooks, and conservation
during World War I / Rae Katherine Eighmey.
     p.   cm.
  Includes bibliographical references and index.
  ISBN-13: 978-0-87351-718-8 (pbk. : alk. paper)
  ISBN-10: 0-87351-718-0 (pbk. : alk. paper)
  1. Food conservation—Minnesota. 2. Cookery, American.
3. Food habits—Minnesota—History. 4. World War, 1914–1918—
Food supply—Minnesota. I. Title.
            TX357.E45 2010
           394.1'209776—dc22
                                        2009003173

Front cover: Poster by Sidney D. Zuckerman for the
State Council of Defense, ca. 1918, MHS collections
Cover design by Brad Norr.
Book design and composition by Wendy Holdman.
Printed by Sheridan Books, Ann Arbor, Michigan.

To the Minnesotans whose
vision, energy, and sacrifices
built the foundation of our
progressive, successful state.

And for my husband and our
children Liz and John,
their spouses John and Chris,
and our grandchildren Justin and Jack,
whose public service in ways large and small
continue to improve their communities.

You are my foundation and inspiration.

Boy Scouts place American flags at soldiers' graves in an annual appreciation of their service and sacrifices.

Contents

MEMBER OF U. S. FOOD ADMINISTRATION

Food will win the war

We observe Meatless days
Wheatless days - Porkless days

and carry out all conservation rules of the U.S. Food Administration

Observing "wheatless" and "meatless" days, Minnesotans along with most Americans stretched the nation's food resources so European Allies and American soldiers could be fed. Restaurant signs like this both informed people of compliance and encouraged participation in home kitchens.

Appetizer

In my mind's eye I see them—the Minnesotans who did all they could to win the "war to end all wars" during the 19 months of 1917–18 when the United States fought World War I by the side of its European Allies.

Of course, I see Minnesota soldiers—young men eagerly off on the adventure of a lifetime, as well as the husbands and fathers whose lives were upended by the call to service. On the home front there are women in uniform, too, exchanging their fashions for white Red Cross dresses and aprons. I imagine some even wearing the practical, home-sewn "food conservation" outfits as they serve their families lunches without bread and dinners without meat. Dust-covered businessmen stand among shocks of grain they have cut and gathered, harvesting crops for neighboring farmers whose sons are fighting "over there." Children are enthusiastically engaged in the cause: boys, wearing the uniform of the newly organized Boy Scouts of America, harvest potatoes and sell war bonds. Canning-club girls demonstrate the newest way to preserve foods as they stand behind tables at the State Fair singing and shouting chants ending in "Hoover!" I've come to know these Minnesotans and many more over the course of the last five years as I read original papers, diaries, letters, reports, and newspapers in the University of Minnesota Archives and Minnesota Historical Society library and wrote of their accomplishments.

Believing that "food will win the war," President Woodrow Wilson and Herbert Hoover, director of the country's wartime food efforts, put a monumental task before the nation in April 1917: immediately begin conserving food at every American table to be able to feed American soldiers and ship as much as possible to European Allies. After the war, Hoover described the impact of the people's efforts: "At our normal rate of export, the Allies would have starved. . . . The

Before the declaration of war with Germany in April 1917, Minnesotans were engaged in building a progressive, successful state. In rural areas, farmers brought advanced methods to their fields, and in cites, homemakers took advantage of modern appliances, including refrigeration.

organization and expenditure of our food resources contributed no less than the Army and Navy to winning the war." America shipped to Europe an impressive 23 million metric tons of food, including 5 million tons of flour, 10 million tons of grains, 1.3 million tons of pork products, and nearly 2 million tons of sugar.[1]

This was "everyone's war," and accomplishing this task depended upon the good will of informed and enlightened American citizens. It succeeded, thanks to the organized and voluntary efforts of ordinary people meeting in kitchens and classrooms, libraries, theaters, and churches, on street corners and over backyard fences all across the country—sharing information, inspiring cooperation, and creating solutions. The world took note of this astounding demonstration of the values, responsibilities, and practices of American citizenship. And, by war's end, America had become a recognized world power.

Food conservation during World War I was, in effect, the first large-scale, social-networking enterprise of the twentieth century. Before the existence of radio and television broadcasting (or even telephones, in many parts of the country), individuals and groups responded to the call for action not only with "can-do" spirit but with "must-do" drive. Government agencies quickly began "building the buzz" using every avenue of information and persuasion they could imagine or invent. Of course, there were press releases, articles, and even celebrity endorsements in silent films. But in the days long before the Internet, Web pages, and Twitter, agents reached onto Main Street and even next to the stove top, encouraging actions by using everything from mannequin tableaus filling department store windows to Food Conservation reminder cards hanging on kitchen cupboard doors. Service flags or banners were one of the most important household decorations of the day. Hung prominently in the front window, they told all who passed by that a man in the household was in the army, navy, or marines.

Minnesotans moved even faster than the national efforts could be organized. Within days after the declaration of war, individuals up and down the state began gathering information and taking decisive action. Nearly everyone got on the bandwagon, motivated by huge parades and small speeches, garden contests, and Liberty bond drives. Women thought up ways to cook tasty conservation meals and sent directions to friends across the country on the wings of a two-cent stamp. University home economists offered new food-saving recipes to newspapers and gave demonstrations across the state. Throughout Minnesota people looked at the situation, saw their role, and began sharing countless tips for conserving food, getting the most from farm or garden, and other war-winning strategies.

Minnesota is, indeed, an ideal state for understanding the complexity of the war-driven food conservation efforts and successes. In 1917 more than half of the state's residents were farmers. Food production, food processing and transportation businesses, and industries in the major cities—Minneapolis, St. Paul, Rochester, and

Duluth—figured prominently in the nation's efforts to move food from farm to table, here or overseas. Minnesota was a state of immigrants, as well, with significant numbers having German origins. Certainly, there were conflicts, problems, and even injustices associated with the government's effort to engage everyone in the war effort. Historian Carl H. Chrislock documented some of these excesses in his history of the times. But the overwhelming impression, based on the hundreds of contemporary personal accounts I've read, is one of cooperation and even eager participation. That is the aspect of the story I tell in this book.

There are two main ingredients in this recipe for success: persuasive information and the actions put into motion by those social-networking and peer-influence efforts. Although I've focused on describing the complex relationships among crops, cooks, and conservation and the actions taken by a wide range of individuals, another key to understanding this significant time in the growth of America can be found in the war-created foods themselves. I encourage you to make the recipes included in the chapters. Eating Corn and Nut Loaf, Lumberjack's Conservation Cake, Uncle Sam's War Biscuits, Victory Cabbage, or any of the other tasty, healthful, and economical recipes I've adapted for modern kitchens will give you a true flavor of the times.

In the end, it is the people themselves who tell the story best. You will find voices here from urban and rural communities, from homemakers and professors, from farmers and lumberjacks. Soldiers speak here, too. Their letters from stateside camps or from abroad gave meaning to home-front sacrifices. I have been deeply influenced by Minnesotans' generosity of spirit. Simply phrased: "I'll do my part—show me how to help." Their unselfish actions demonstrate the great power of the responsibility and opportunity of American citizenship when each of us does a small thing for the common good.

Food Will Win the War

1

One Soldier's Family

Dear Gray, I am sending you some rocks that I made for you this afternoon. I know, my dear boy, you are burdened with baggage, but I thought you would enjoy them. . . . We've learned you will not be able to cable as soon as you get over, as I asked you to do, but we will get a card from the War Department. I will just think you are going to have a safe trip, and it will not be long before we have you back safe and well. Lovingly, Mother. *June 18, 1918*[1]

Tracy Gray Cassidy never tasted the oatmeal rock cookies his mother baked using scarce sugar and fats in her Minnesota kitchen—but that was due to timing, not something more dire. His troop transport ship sailed for France from New York Harbor in June 1918, the same day she mailed the cookies from Minneapolis. Gray eventually arrived home safely from his tour of duty, and the rocks returned to Minneapolis as well, mailed back by a family friend in New York. On August 5, 1918, Mrs. Cassidy wrote with disappointment, "I am so sorry that you could not have had the big box of rocks. . . . I could hardly decide what to send and while I was trying to decide, you were off for the other side."

Gray's family members wrote frequent letters, and, remarkably, both sides of the correspondence have survived. On the home front, it was easy for families to tie up letters from husbands and sons for safekeeping. Across the ocean, this was more of a challenge, but Gray managed to save letters from his mother and father, his brother, his sister Margaret, and Margaret's daughter, Virginia, an irrepressible 14-year-old.

Gray's letters described conditions in camp and overseas. Notes from his family, written from a two-story frame house on a rise three

ROCK COOKIES

⅔ cup milk
1 teaspoon vinegar
1 cup sugar
¼ teaspoon salt
1 cup fat, melted
2 eggs, lightly beaten
2 cups old-fashioned oatmeal
½ cup raisins, finely chopped
2 cups flour
½ teaspoon baking soda
½ teaspoon cinnamon
½ teaspoon cloves

Preheat the oven to 350° F.
Combine the milk and vinegar
and set aside for the milk to
sour. Mix sugar, salt, melted
fat, and eggs. Add sour milk
and mix well. Stir in oatmeal
and raisins, then add flour,
soda, and spices. Drop from
teaspoons onto lightly greased
cookie sheets and bake rocks
until light brown, about 10–12
minutes. (*The Farmer's Wife,*
September 1917)

blocks from Lake Harriet, vividly describe home-front food conservation efforts and offer an intimate perspective on national policies and programs.

Gray reported for duty in May 1918, the second spring of the war. For more than a year, since late spring 1917, Americans had been gradually adapting their eating habits to meet ever-changing war requests. They had been eating bread made with cornmeal, barley flour, and whole grains instead of white flour, practically eliminating desserts, eating half as much meat as before the war, and in general transforming the way they ate so that important food resources could be shared with Allies in Europe and shifted to feed "our boys in uniform."

On June 5, 1917, two short months after the U.S. Congress voted to declare war with Germany, Gray Cassidy and every other young man between the ages of 21 and 30 had been required to register for the military draft. Some Minnesotans had already volunteered for military service after war began in Europe in 1914, while others had served overseas as neutrals in the volunteer ambulance corps and as nurses in the Red Cross. Before the draft, throughout April and May 1917, newspaper front pages had listed the names of eager volunteers who joined the army, navy, and marines rather than waiting to be called up. New soldiers in Minnesota shipped out to the few existing military bases in the United States equipped to train soldiers for combat. Soon

[ca. July 1, 1918]

Somewhere in England.
(Date as Post Mark.)

Dear Family

Arrived safely at Port of Disembarkation, and in Good Health

Daily Drill, Physical Exercises and Music, all added to the pleasure of a delightful journey.

Will send letter on arrival at Head-Quarters.

Gray

KINDLY NOTE MY MAILING ADDRESS:—

Name and Rank..Pvt. Tracy G. Cassidy

No...Co. A.

Regiment...359. U S. Inf.

American Expeditionary Force,
C/o. Army Post Office, London.

Issued with the War Office approval.—T.H.

Gray Cassidy addressed this cheery "arrival card" before he shipped out from New York, and the army mailed it after his ship docked safely in England.

there would be more camps built for the growing army needed to win what became known as "the war to end all wars."[2]

As in other states, Minnesota's National Guard—three infantry regiments (about 2,000 men each), one field artillery regiment, and a small force of naval militia—stepped into the breach during the first days of America's involvement in the war. In March guardsmen were called up to patrol at strategic sites, including iron mines, railroads and ore docks, flour mills and elevators, foundries, railroad terminals, and bridges. Creation of the large fighting force to win the war "over there" would take planning and time.

The buildup of the American Expeditionary Forces to nearly four million men, including some 118,500 Minnesotans, was an undertaking unlike anything the nation had ever seen. In 1917 the United States had no large, standing national military force. There was not a military industrial complex. There were only young men, like Gray Cassidy, whose draft numbers were randomly drawn. Military training camps had to be built. Empty fields were converted to house, feed, and train as many as 45,000 men at a time.[3]

New soldiers frequently drilled in civilian clothes before receiving uniforms at Camp Dodge near Des Moines, Iowa, and other new army camps.

Ground was broken in July 1917 for the Midwest's Camp Dodge, near Des Moines, Iowa. Every day more than 5,000 men, including 2,000 carpenters, worked on the camp's 1,700 buildings. Less than 12 weeks later, Camp Dodge was ready for thousands of draftees from Minnesota and surrounding states. Each barrack building for 250 soldiers had showers, water closets, and other conveniences. The camp boasted 47 hospital buildings and stables for 14,000 horses and mules, with room for 30,000 animals to supply military posts around the country and in France. Some 25 miles of roads serviced rifle ranges, refrigeration plants, laundries, bakeries, and storehouses. There were water, sewer, and lighting systems. Keeping the residents fed required 100 railroad cars of food each day.[4]

Before the draftees arrived, the U.S. Army needed to staff the camps for specialized tasks, jobs that ranged from cooks and bakers to doctors. In this effort and many others to follow, educational institutions, including the University of Minnesota, led the way. The university's home economics staff taught a special six-week course for mess sergeants in June and July. Students spent half of their time in the kitchens at the first officers' training camp at Fort

Snelling, learning the practical skills necessary to feed battalions of hungry soldiers. Minneapolis's Dunwoody Institute trained cooks and bakers throughout the war.[5]

The nation's first 250,000 draftees were called up on July 20, 1917, but they didn't report for duty until September. The delay allowed the men time to plan for their departure or to seek exemption. It also gave the government time to amass the equipment and uniforms for the men—but not quite enough time to complete the buildings at Camp Dodge.

Soldier John Christopherson described his trip on the troop train: "Left New Ulm at 6 P.M. to go to Mankato, where the ladies of the Baptist church gave us supper in the church basement. Left there at 10:30, picked up a couple of cars in Lake Crystal and Blue Earth. Train had twelve coaches filled with men drafted into the National Army. Arrived in Ames, Iowa . . . and then Camp Dodge." Another soldier first saw the camp after being on the train for 19 hours: "We were all pretty tired out, having slept very little on the way, as the boys were pretty jolly and there was a lot of singing going on." One soldier wrote home: "Don't worry about us; we'll do our bit and Minnesota will be proud of us."[6]

By the time Gray Cassidy's draft number was called the next spring, the process of converting citizens to soldiers and moving them overseas was finely tuned and rapid. Eighteen days after his family waved him off to Camp Dodge, Gray and 500 fellow soldiers boarded a troop train for Texas. Three weeks later, he climbed aboard another train to New York. There he transferred to a ship and sailed to England, where he joined the American Expeditionary Forces and moved on to France.

Along the way Gray described what he did, the sights he saw, and what he ate. Gray's first meal at Camp Dodge was a real feast: "We had a pretty good lunch—roast beef, potatoes, creamed peas, coffee, *white* bread, and jelly. . . . We sure were *hungry*."

A few days later Gray wrote, "For breakfast we had French toast, syrup, bacon, and coffee. For dinner, chicken, mashed potatoes, lettuce, green onions, coffee, ice cream, and chocolate cake. For supper, cheese, creamed corn, fried potatoes, peanut butter, coffee, and chocolate pudding, and we had bread with all the meals. . . . The mess sergeant said at dinner that if anyone didn't get enough to eat, he should put his name on the black board. Everybody laughed. The second day I was here we had macaroni and cheese, and I went after it like it was fried chicken. I feel as if I have put on four or five pounds already." Gray's mother wrote back: "What wonderful things you have to eat—all the luxuries."

No wonder Mrs. Cassidy exclaimed about his food. While the daily calorie ration in army training camps was about 4,000 calories, citizens on the home front who voluntarily observed the strongest wartime restrictions during late winter and spring 1918 consumed just over 2,000 calories. In addition, citizens cooked on a complicated wheat- and meat-conserving regimen: Sunday, evening meal wheatless and one meal meatless; Monday, no wheat all day and one meal meatless; Tuesday, no meat all day and evening meal wheatless; Wednesday, no wheat all day and one meal meatless; Thursday, evening meal wheatless and one meal meatless; Friday, no wheat at dinner and one meal meatless; and Saturday, no pork and evening meal wheatless.[7]

Newsy family letters to Gray described ordinary events in Minneapolis. His teenage niece, Virginia, thought her life humdrum compared to Gray's adventures in camp and abroad. Her first letter set the tone: "You are having quite a new experience, aren't you? Anyhow, you have *white* bread, so you should worry. . . . Have you seen any more of that cute boy that marched beside you when you left? I think he's wonderful. Au revoir, Virginia."

Gray's next letter home highlighted the ongoing difficulties of equipping the new army. After two weeks of marching and training in civilian clothes, he wrote Virginia: "I am not much of a soldier yet, but I have my uniform now and I guess I look a little like one. We have been issued one coat, two pairs of pants, one hat, one pair of shoes size 8E. I can get both feet in one. One shirt with about a size 16 collar band. I wear a 14½ shirt. Four suits of underwear, four pairs of socks, a mess kit which has a plate, cup, knife, fork and spoon. . . . The fellow you spoke of is in the barracks with me, has his bunk just four from me, and is a very nice boy."

Gray described army life on the move, beginning with his train ride from Iowa to San Antonio: "These troop trains can only go 20

Food Schedule

	BREAKFAST	NOON DAY MEAL	EVENING MEAL
Monday	MEATLESS WHEATLESS	Wheatless	Wheatless
Tuesday	MEATLESS	MEATLESS	WHEATLESS MEATLESS
Wed'day	MEATLESS WHEATLESS	Wheatless	Wheatless
Thursday	MEATLESS		Wheatless
Friday	MEATLESS		Wheatless
Saturday	MEATLESS	PORKLESS	WHEATLESS PORKLESS
Sunday	MEATLESS		Wheatless

BREAKFAST, - - 4:00 a. m. to 10:30 a. m.
NOON DAY MEAL, 10:30 a. m. to 4:30 p. m.
EVENING MEAL, 4:30 p. m. to 11:30 p. m.
OPEN HOURS, - 11:30 p. m. to 4:00 a. m.

"Help Win the War"

This card is furnished to the trade to assist them in observing the food regulations. Additional copies may be had by applying to . . . .

The LICENSED RETAIL LIQUOR DEALERS ASS'N.
MINNEAPOLIS, MINN.

FRANK P. KALTENBACH CO. PRINTERS. MPLS

Like many American families, the Cassidys voluntarily followed this stringent food conservation schedule during the early months of 1918.

miles an hour and I understand that we will be on the road five days, and we are traveling in day coaches. There is a baggage car fitted out as a kitchen. At meal time the sergeant sends a detail of five men with one of the corporals in charge into the kitchen car. We bring back the food in pails and dish it out to the men. We eat in our mess kits."

Virginia wrote back about life at home: "I lost the second match in the school tennis tournament. Pretty poor, wasn't it. Well, I had to play on cement courts which I wasn't used to and I had to wear my oxfords. . . . It's been raining pitchforks here lately. I wish it would clear up so I could plant a garden. You can just imagine what kind of garden it will be. Bien bonne nuit. Votre niece, Virginia."

War gardens and tennis games remained secondary to the Cassidy family's pride in their soldier. Gray's sister Margaret wrote: "I simply couldn't wait to tell you that at last we have a service flag. It's a perfectly wonderful one, silk with a white cord with tassels on both ends. We have it hanging right above the Red Cross thing in the front window. It's a great big one. Mother thought that while she was getting it she'd get the biggest one in town."

Gray wrote several letters during his five-day trip to San Antonio. Townspeople greeted the train with free or inexpensive treats, a good thing as the army food was not as expansive as it had been: "This is certainly a great trip and I would hate to have missed it. The only thing bad about it is the food. We have the same thing for every meal—corn beef and beans, jelly, bread and coffee. . . . You lose your appetite when you get the same thing for breakfast, dinner, and supper. . . . This morning about 8 o'clock we saw two aero-planes and since then there have been as many as twelve in the air at one time."

By early June, Gray considered himself a soldier. "We have all been hardened up to it now and don't feel right unless we march five or ten miles and have about two hours of physical drill. I said the food wasn't good, but I meant we didn't have as elaborate meals as at Camp Dodge. We get all we can eat, but it is plain. We don't have butter or sugar. I am getting so I like the coffee without sugar or milk. At first it was awful."

In July 1918, Virginia wrote Gray that even city boys too young for military service had "enlisted." She complained, "Nearly all of my friends have left the city and intend to be gone until the first of August. June Corwin has gone on a farm. You know all the boys over 16 are supposed to work now. . . . This life will be good for these city boys."

After soldiers left the country, communications back home came much more slowly. By the time his family read a letter Gray

Red Cross workers and others greeted soldiers at many railroad stations with treats that supplemented onboard rations of corned beef hash.

wrote from a troop ship in late June, he had spent the Fourth of July in London and landed in France. Virginia described her family's joy at receiving Gray's letter: "Yesterday was a red letter day for us. . . . Mother and I were still in bed and grandmother was dressing when [the family maid] came rushing upstairs two steps at a time. We thought she'd lost her mind she was so excited. You can't imagine how we enjoyed the letter. It had been such a long time since we'd heard from you. Don't fall in love with a pretty little French girl."

The Cassidy family struggled financially when Gray was gone. He had arranged for $15 per month from his soldier's pay to be sent home in addition to the $20 monthly stipend the government provided, but this did not make up for the loss of his bank clerk salary. To make ends meet, the family redecorated his room with new paint and curtains and then took in a roomer. His mother explained, "We only want to take someone that will take the room and have breakfast and Sunday dinners." Luckily they rented Gray's room to a family friend, and Mrs. Cassidy was delighted that they could "leave our doors open just as we always have done."

Gray's sister Margaret had several piano students but, according to Virginia, "There weren't any checks coming in." Margaret played piano for silent movies at a theater, a task she found challenging: "I would rather have been digging ditches for six hours." A neighbor woman gave them eggs from a backyard chicken, and other friends brought the Cassidy family freshly caught fish.

In France, Gray's assignment with the signal corps kept him away from the front lines, and his letters home describe life in the village where he was stationed. On August 3, 1918, he wrote: "It is hard to get anything sweet here. About the only things you can buy are milk, cheese and nuts. . . . French children seem to think a lot of the American soldiers. They are always hanging on your back or sitting in your lap." Ten days later he confided: "We talk about nothing but home. It is certainly going to be a great day when we land in old Minneapolis. . . . The people in the states never will realize this war and life like the people have here in France. They save everything and live on almost nothing."

As American forces advanced toward Germany with battlefield successes, soldiers who were not on the front lines found themselves congratulated by grateful French citizens who "shook hands with us and patted us on the back and said, 'Thank you, Americans, thank you.'" In October Gray and some of his fellow soldiers went to a small restaurant and enjoyed a party, topped off with champagne and cigars.

Other American soldiers were not so fortunate that autumn. As they massed for one last "push over the top," they slept on the ground and ate cold food on the edges of the battlefield under the roar of cannon bombardments.

Then there was silence.

After 19 months of American involvement, the war ended on November 11, 1918. The conflict that had begun in 1914 and consumed the European continent from Paris to Moscow eventually claimed the lives of 20 million people. Soldiers and civilians died

After 19 months of war and sacrifice, crowds filled streets with tumultuous celebration across the state. Cars packed with people banging on kitchen pots and pans commandeered the corner of Nicollet and Sixth streets in Minneapolis.

from wounds, injuries, disease, and starvation. Nearly 8,000 Minnesota soldiers were killed or wounded.[8]

Officials signed the Armistice in a railroad car parked on a siding in a French forest. Within hours, cities in France and England—and in Minnesota—exploded with joy. People streamed onto the streets. The celebration in Minneapolis lasted for two days. Virginia wrote Gray that the cannons at Fort Snelling boomed, the siren in nearby St. Louis Park shrieked loudly, and "every whistle in town was blowing."

The experiences and emotions of the Cassidy family were duplicated across Minnesota from city to farm, lumber camp to creamery. Other soldiers wrote home, telling stories of training camp and battlefield. Other families kept diaries and saved letters sent across the country and around the world. Their modest words document the extraordinary events from April 1917 to November 1918. Across the state and the nation individuals made sacrifices, changed daily routines, pitched in to raise money, knitted socks and sweaters for soldiers and sailors, joined forces for a common cause. Minnesotans, along with the rest of the nation, raised and ate different foods. They reduced waste and conserved at every meal. They shipped sacrifice-created surpluses to feed American soldiers and Allies in Europe.

Citizens and soldiers joined to fight "the war to end all wars" with efforts large and small because it was seen as the right thing to do. Asked to participate in a great national undertaking, individual Americans did not shirk. Minnesotans played a significant role; their voices tell the stories of struggles and successes on the pages that follow.

Isn't it positively wonderfully scrumptious, marvelous and grandiflorous that the war is actually over? At two o'clock in the morning, which was about the time the Armistice was being signed over there, people went downtown. Imagine it! They said that the [Minneapolis] streets were packed at 4 o'clock in the morning. We kids went down about one o'clock in the afternoon, and the streets were just jammed. It was positively rare.
Virginia to Gray Cassidy, November 12, 1918[9]

2

Menu for Success

The terrible things that have happened. Who could have dreamed of so much tragedy years ago, and we were so happy-feeling, so secure in our wonderful crops and prosperity in every line of trade. . . . I fear we are such a peace-loving people that we have become oblivious to the possibility of an attack at our very door. *Emma B. to Mrs. Merrill, February 1918*[1]

On April 2, 1917, people across Minnesota and the nation anxiously awaited President Woodrow Wilson's decision about whether the United States would go to war with Germany. Eager to know before the next day's newspaper arrived at their doors, crowds stood in front of newspaper offices reading headlines and stories posted on bulletin boards. The *St. Paul Pioneer Press* reported that the street had nearly been blocked with people reading and commenting, "That means war all right, all right."

"Say, Germany will have to look out when we get our boys over there."

"You bet."

Such eager statements, urging taking up arms against Germany, would have been unheard of just a few months earlier. For most Americans, the European conflict, begun in 1914 after the assassination of the heir to the Austro-Hungarian imperial throne, was seen as the latest skirmish in age-old battles among warring empires an ocean away. The U.S. government had adopted a deliberately neutral stance. Even after a German submarine sank the British liner *Lusitania* in 1915, killing 128 Americans, U.S. citizens resisted engagement in the conflict overseas. After all, the outcome seemed insignificant to the nation's policies and purpose.

The United States had settled its own civil war 57 years earlier, and in the first decades of the twentieth century, Americans were fully engaged in building a peaceful, prosperous, and progressive nation. A successful economy and modernizing inventions transformed daily life for city and rural residents. Automobiles shared the streets with trolleys and horse-drawn wagons. In Minnesota, homemakers in St. Paul, Duluth, and other large cities could telephone markets for daily grocery delivery. The iceboxes in their kitchens were gradually being replaced by electric refrigerators, invented in 1913. The mailman delivered letters twice a day in cities. And while letters mailed in Europe took more than a week to cross the Atlantic by ship, news from Europe, transmitted under the ocean through one of the many trans-Atlantic cables, arrived in hours and was printed in newspapers and delivered in evening and morning editions.

Farming had entered an era of rapid modernization, too. A few farmers began working their fields with gasoline-powered tractors. More importantly, crop, husbandry, and soils research from leading land-grant universities was making a difference in key farming practices. As A. D. Wilson, director of extension service at the University of Minnesota, wrote: "The changed conditions are placing more and more bright and progressive men and women on our farms, who are not ashamed to study their profession and to put their best efforts into it. As a consequence we . . . are developing a true science of agriculture. We no longer depend on 'chance' or 'good luck' for results in farming, but know the conditions that are necessary to good results."[2]

Yet, some American lives were touched by the war from the beginning, and the nation found ways to help people caught up in the ongoing conflict. In the very first days of the war, Herbert Hoover, a globe-traveling consulting civil engineer, was living in London with his wife when, in the space of four days, Germany declared war on Russia and France and then invaded Belgium and Luxembourg. England then declared war on Germany under terms of a protectionist treaty with Belgium and allied itself with France. All Europe was in chaos as travel and communications were disrupted.

Much of the success of the food conservation efforts rested directly in the hands of homemakers. Nearly 80 percent of the nation's food passed through kitchens like this one in St. Paul.

A wealthy couple, the Hoovers quickly established a volunteer organization to aid other Americans trapped without access to money
or ways to return home in these first war-panicked days of August
1914. In time, this became the private Commission for Relief in
Belgium, which Hoover continued to head as he traveled between
the United States and England during the next three years with humanitarian missions into Belgium, France, and Germany.

Minnesota's farmers and flour millers supported Hoover's relief
efforts. Half the state's citizens lived on farms, with most of them
owning the land they worked. These Minnesotans understood the
plight of "starving Belgians" and others whose lands were in combat
zones and whose struggles were described in scores of newspaper
and magazine articles. William C. Edgar, editor of the Minneapolis-
based weekly *Northwestern Miller*, had headed up one of the first private relief efforts. Working through Hoover's commission, Edgar delivered 7,000 tons of flour valued at $600,000 from the millers of the
northwestern states in January 1915. Accompanying the cargo across
the Atlantic under threat of German submarine attack was not without risk. As Edgar wrote to his wife, "Now that it's over, I don't mind
telling you that the trip to Rotterdam was risky business. . . . In my
satchel I carried a pack of cards . . . on the back was [flour company]
Washburn Crosby's advertisement 'Eventually—Why not now?' So
I sat in the cabin playing solitaire. 'Eventually—Why not now?' kept
running in my mind—whimsically—apropos of mine-hitting."[3]

These humanitarian contributions may not have won the war
"over there," but they provided essential energy to strengthen the
resolve of the embattled European population for three years. With
all of this, there was still the hope that the United States could remain neutral in the conflict.

Many Americans, especially in Minnesota, had personal reasons
for concern as they read the war news and stories of dreadful conditions among the civilian population in Europe. Minnesota was home
to a large number of immigrants and first-generation Americans,
many with family in the war-torn countries. In the early twentieth century, only one-fourth of Minnesota's people had been born
in America to parents who were also born on American soil. More
than one-third of Minnesotans were immigrants; nearly a quarter

of them were from Kaiser Wilhelm's Germany. In the state's 1905 census, Germany was the predominant country of origin, followed by Sweden and Norway. (By 1920, this balance would shift, with about one-quarter of the foreign-born population being born in Sweden and one-eighth in Germany.) German-language newspapers served 19 communities in the state, and students in two-thirds of the parochial schools and many of the one-room rural schools in German areas spoke and learned to read in German.[4]

However, Germany's declaration of unconditional submarine warfare in early 1917 changed the opinion of many Americans on the country's neutral stance. In early 1917, German U-boats had begun aggressively attacking ships—peaceful, neutral, or warships—off the coasts of England and France and in the Mediterranean. U-boats torpedoed 210 ships between February 1, 1917, and the middle of March. Even before the March 21 "torpedoing without warning" of the U.S. steamship *Healdton,* killing 13 American seamen, America's entry into the war was no longer unthinkable. Wilson recognized the challenge and the opportunity in his second inaugural address, delivered on March 5, 1917: "We are provincials no longer. . . . There can be no turning back. Our own fortunes as a nation are involved whether we would have it so or not."[5]

Some Americans began to consider changes the nation would need to make to succeed in the now-probable war. In March, President Wilson and Herbert Hoover had discussed the critical role food would play in the coming months. Hoover convinced President Wilson of the importance both of a food policy and of a national commitment to voluntary participation by all Americans in any war effort. When Wilson next spoke to the nation, he told America that this was to be everybody's war. On April 15, less than two weeks after his initial call to war, Wilson asked all Americans to become citizen-soldiers. "We must supply abundant food for ourselves and for our armies . . . and for a large part of the nations with whom we have now made common cause. . . . Without abundant food the whole great enterprise upon which we have embarked will break down and fail."[6]

Minnesota's German Americans were more hesitant. In Brown County, for example, one of three southern Minnesota counties

Minnesotans anxiously awaited the news told in banner headlines. In April 1917, after years of watching European nations at battle, the United States entered what was called "the war to end all wars."

with the highest concentration of German immigrants (at about 8 percent of the population), nearly 1,000 people gathered in the New Ulm armory on March 30 to hear speeches on the war situation. At the time, the city had nearly 6,000 residents; another 16,000 lived in surrounding Brown County. While the audience supported resolutions affirming their allegiance to the United States, they "denied the existence of any adequate reason for American entry into the war." Just six weeks later, on June 5, Brown County boys signed up for the draft, as did every other male aged 21 to 30. When their

GRANDMOTHER'S BREAD

What is Grandmother's Bread? It is the grinding of dried bread into crumbs and the returning of these crumbs into the next baking. According to Mrs. C. P. Noyes of St. Paul, this is what her family has been doing for the past seven weeks, thereby saving half the wheat flour with every baking and 'solving the Hubby Problem' in food conservation by making waste-saving breads and slipping them onto the family table. (*Minnesota Farm Review,* July 14, 1917)

numbers were called up, they marched off to join the newly established national army and fight for America.[7]

There was a war to be fought on the home front, too. Just as America needed to build an army, the nation also needed to develop a food policy, find a way to explain restrictions, and persuade a willing public. Herbert Hoover's successes in Belgian relief made him an expert on feeding people during war. Organizations and individuals contacted him for his suggestions even before the president appointed him in early May to head conservation efforts and long before Congress could authorize the U.S. Food Administration in August. Hoover agreed to serve but stipulated that, as a private citizen, he not be paid a salary. He felt the position "would carry more moral leadership if he were a volunteer alongside his countrymen in war." Hoover's call to volunteer was effective. By the end of the war, some 8,000 people volunteered full time. Three thousand people worked in paid clerical positions. More than three-quarters of a million people, largely women, worked as unpaid members of committees all across the nation, officially listed as "part-time service." Hoover explained the Food Administration's goals to Minnesota's Edgar in a May letter: "better transportation conditions, economy, and savings of waste in manufacture and consumption, together with stabilizing prices and stimulation of production."[8]

Hoover recommended seven conservation measures: use local foodstuffs to avoid unnecessary transportation of goods; use perishable foods to save staples; eliminate waste in all possible ways;

Herbert Hoover knew from his experience providing food relief in war-torn Europe that "food would win the war." President Wilson named him head of the Food Administration, overseeing the nation's crops, cooks, and conservation.

conserve wheat; conserve meats, fats, and sugars; stimulate the use of milk and milk products; and set forth the principles underlying adequate feeding for health. Experts from four key commodities monitored by the Food Administration—grains, meats, fats, and sugar—would share information and anticipate bottlenecks in order to keep essential breadstuffs, meats, fats, and sugar on the plates of American soldiers and European Allies.[9]

American business leaders quickly understood the enormous shift in resources required to fulfill the war's needs. Just after the declaration of war, J. Ogden Armour of leading meat-packer Armour and Company issued a personal call that made front-page news: "Unless the government takes immediate steps to conserve the food supply of this country and have two or three meatless days for each family a week, in less than six months this country will be as short of foods as many European nations."[10]

Newspapers and magazines took up the cause, writing about the sacrifices to come and the jobs to be done in language everyone could understand. In June, for example, the *Brown County Journal* reported on Britain's food conservation rules—which included one meatless day a week, five ounces of meat for lunch and dinner, and two ounces of meat for breakfast on days when meat was allowed—but suggested that restrictions in the United States would not be as stringent. (Ultimately, U.S. restrictions on food were nearly as rigorous as those envisioned by Armour, although the meatless requirement ended in March 1918.)[11]

In May 1917, *The Farmer's Wife*, a monthly magazine with 750,000 readers, trumpeted: "With the Farm Women of this Country lies the sacred charge of serving their nation in its hour of peril. . . . On farmer's wives and daughters, in large measure, rests the fate of the war and the fate of the nations." The magazine urged women to use the nation's supplies cautiously, to produce vegetables, to raise poultry and eggs, and to preserve surplus supplies.[12]

While women's and farming magazines typically ran articles in summer on preserving food for winter use, the imperative had changed. Now the goal became family self-sufficiency, a new kind of food independence that would release commercially prepared foods for military use.[13]

Congress did not act as swiftly or with such insight. It did not pass the Lever Act authorizing and funding the Food Administration until August 1917. Hoover recognized citizens would need information and even some persuasion to take full advantage of the 1917 growing season. He and his staff worked quickly through the spring and summer with the U.S. Department of Agriculture (USDA) to get a variety of materials into the hands of farmers and city dwellers.

Educators at the University of Minnesota's University Farm and Agricultural Extension Service were ideally situated to fill these communication needs. On April 12, three days before President Wilson's call to the nation's citizen-soldiers, the head of the extension service outlined steps to increase farm yields in a news release sent to newspapers across the state. Professor Archie Dell Wilson, known as A. D. Wilson, suggested, since crops in Minnesota and other northern-tier states had not yet been planted, farmers could still shift to meet new wartime requirements. Minnesota was already a leader in its production of wheat and other small grains as well as a leading dairy state and major producer of eggs. Minnesota farmers were in a good position to increase supply of these substitutes for soon-to-be restricted meats. With their considerable resources and expertise, Minnesotans could contribute to food conservation by increasing production, limiting consumption, changing cooking and eating habits, and eliminating waste.[14]

U.S. Secretary of Agriculture David F. Houston cautioned the nation's homemakers that they "must learn to use such foods as vegetables, beans, peas, and milk products as partial substitutes for meat" and they must see that "nothing nutritious is thrown away or allowed to be wasted. If only a single ounce of edible food, on the average, is allowed to spoil or be thrown away in each of our 20,000,000 homes, over 1,300,000 million pounds of material will be wasted each day. It takes the fruit of many acres and the work of many people to raise, prepare, and distribute 464,000,000 pounds of food a year. Every ounce of food thrown away, therefore, tends to waste the labor of an army of busy citizens."[15]

Leaders in Minnesota government acted quickly, too. In mid-April 1917, immediately after meeting with A. D. Wilson and university president George E. Vincent, Governor J. A. A. Burnquist appointed a 29-member committee to develop methods to increase food production and conservation by surveying supplies and prospects across the state. Meetings such as one in Crookston on April 17–18 began to organize "the thousands who do not enlist [in the army] to serve the nation by helping on farms."[16]

State leaders quickly organized two parallel organizations with somewhat overlapping activities as a result of Wilson's crop suggestions and the governor's fact-finding tour. Following the suggestion of Albert F. Woods, dean of the university's Department

Before radio and television broadcasting, posters placed in schools, libraries, stores, and other public places spread the word with simple suggestions for reducing waste—the first step in food conservation.

of Agriculture, Governor Burnquist established the Committee
on Food Production and Conservation, informally called the Food
Committee. Headed by A. D. Wilson, it first met in April to help
farmers increase crop and livestock production, provide farm labor,
assist in price stability, and help women practice food conservation.
Throughout spring and summer of 1917, Wilson's Food Committee,
working through the Agricultural Extension Service and College of
Agriculture and Home Economics, busily built a network into every
Minnesota county.[17]

At the same time, by request of the governor, the legislature established the Minnesota Commission of Public Safety (MCPS), an
organization with sweeping powers to protect public safety and
property and to apply the state's military, civil, and industrial resources for defense of the state and the nation. Seeking to "cover
the entire State through the counties, towns, and rural communities with such a complete network that every man, woman and child
in Minnesota will be brought into the best possible relation with
all activities of the nation," the MCPS took on war-related responsibilities far beyond food and fuel, including mobilization, loyalty,
and readiness. The MCPS created a Women's Auxiliary, headed by
Alice Ames Winter, who also served as chairman of the Council of
National Defense Women's Committee, a federal appointment.[18]

Officially, Wilson's Food Committee functioned under the auspices
of the MCPS, but as a practical matter, the committee and Winter's
Women's Auxiliary worked independently to develop resources in
every county. Wilson's committee offered assistance to farmers and
gardeners and taught practical classes in rural areas, while Winter's
auxiliary focused more on social services, child welfare, and patriotic
education and provided instruction in food conservation in urban
areas. Winter's Council of National Defense chapter largely worked
at disseminating federal information and reporting activities in the
state to the federal office. There was no shortage of work to be done
and plenty of willing hands. By war's end, the Women's Auxiliary had
some 1,500 members and had secured the cooperation of numerous
women's organizations throughout the state.[19]

The late spring and early summer of 1917 brought a flurry of

The Women's Committee used a variety of public forums, including this booth at the Minnesota State Fair, to educate and encourage participation.

activities throughout Minnesota. In early May, cities and towns held huge Wake Up America patriotic parades and speeches to motivate participation in war and conservation efforts. The Red Cross mobilized to raise money for medical and humanitarian needs. Heavily promoted Liberty Loan bond sales raised money to help fund the war. Congress passed conscription legislation on May 18, and on June 5 men between the ages of 21 and 30 registered for the draft.

The university's Agricultural Extension Service, following its land-grant mission to bring campus research and knowledge to the citizens of the state, provided practical advice to farmers and first-time city gardeners as well as to rural and city homemakers. Under the direction of Josephine T. Berry and, later, Mildred Weigley, university home economists distributed news releases to local papers, gave talks to community groups stressing the vital importance of food conservation, taught food preservation skills, and shared wheat-saving recipes, many developed in the department's test kitchen.

These volunteer women's activities fell neatly in line with Hoover's understanding of the most effective means of winning the war with food: "There can be no force used on production and no force used in consumption. There can be intelligent leadership, and there can be a stimulation of patriotism to effect ends for the common good."[20]

In August 1917 Congress finally enacted the complex legislation creating the U.S. Food Administration. The Food and Fuel Control Act, also known as the Lever Act, provided price guarantees to farmers and included provisions to prevent speculation and hoarding, fix trade margins, eliminate waste in manufacture and distribution, and buy and sell essential foods such as wheat and sugar. The law specified penalties, but Hoover opposed them as likely to put retailers and wholesalers out of business. Penalties were seldom imposed.[21]

Pricing and food-purchasing provisions were critical to winning the *other* war that had involved Americans over the past year—what people labeled the "H. C. L.," or high cost of living. Prices for essentials such as wheat, potatoes, and sugar had increased in 1916 as European nations engaged in a bidding war for scarce commodities, as crop failures created even more scarcity, and as transportation of men and materiel began to take precedence over moving sugar from the East Indies to the United States and Europe.

Hoover and President Wilson sought new guidelines to secure voluntary price controls from processors, wholesalers, middlemen, and others in the food chain. To manage two of the most important food resources, Hoover's Food Administration established two key agencies. The Food Administration Grain Corporation was capitalized on August 14, 1917, at $50 million, with shares held by Hoover "in the name of and for the use and benefit of the United States." The United States Sugar Equalization Board, capitalized at $5 million in July 1918, strengthened the federal Food Administration's control over the distribution and price of sugar. These two agencies essentially controlled the country's entire stock of wheat and sugar. Prices were negotiated between government and the producers in "the best interest of all." By the end of the war, the profit of $60 million from these two agencies more than offset the $8 million expenses of the Food Administration and returned more than $50 million to the U.S. Treasury.[22]

Prices of other foods were also controlled, notably the price of meat. Under Food Administration powers, the profits of the five largest meat producers were held at 2.5 percent on sales of meat. Setting prices for dairy products proved much more difficult. Participants in every part of the milk business complained about rising costs of production and sought mediation from the Food Administration. Some agreements were reached on the selling price of milk on a district-by-district basis. In Minnesota, the MCPS held hearings and set a regulated price for milk sold in the Twin Cities. In the end, individuals and companies at every level responded to Hoover's appeals for voluntary cooperation with the Food Administration.[23]

In farm and city households, a summer of exuberant parades, war gardening, home canning, and casual attention to preventing waste in the kitchen passed into a fall that brought serious realization of the task before the nation. The first wave of men whose numbers had been drawn in July was called into service in September.

The call to war became a charge to change the basic way of life in every household. These changes came rapidly and were carried out, for the most part, voluntarily. Men, women, and children were urged to sacrifice at every meal. They were asked to give up wheat, meat, fats, and sugar so that "our food would feed European Allies and American soldiers." An army of schoolchildren canvassed their neighborhoods asking mothers and neighbors to sign a voluntary statement known as the Food Pledge. It read: "I am glad to join you in the service of food conservation for our nation and I hereby accept membership in the United States Food Administration, pledging myself to carry out the directions and advice of the Food Administrator in my home insofar as my circumstances permit."[24]

The loosely worded Food Pledge allowed maximum flexibility, and that flexibility was essential as the administration continually monitored supplies and demand and shifted its specific requests. Before the war the typical American family included bread and meat at every meal. In October 1917 Hoover called for one meatless meal and one wheatless meal each week. At its most stringent, in February 1918, only 3 of the 21 meals served each week were totally unrestricted. The remaining 19 included 7 meatless, 7 wheatless, and 5 meatless and wheatless meals.

The Food Pledge reflected Hoover's belief that the success of food conservation efforts rested on goodwill and volunteer participation.

Early in the fall of 1917, nearly a quarter of a million Minnesota households signed the voluntary Food Pledge, promising to reduce waste and cooperate with the evolving requests of the Food Administration. (Artist Paul Stahr)

He later wrote, "We knew that, although Americans can be led to make great sacrifices, they do not like to be driven."[25]

People seemed to appreciate his understanding, as suggested in this humorous poem that appeared in the *Northfield Norwegian American* on January 25, 1918:

Hoover's Goin' to Get You!

The great old Hoover Pledge has come to our house to stay;
To frown on breakfast bacon and take our steak away;
It cans our morning waffles, and our sausage, too, it seems,
And dilates on the succulence of corn, and spuds and beans,
So skimp the sugar in your cake and leave the butter out!
Or Hoover's goin' to get you if you Don't . . . Watch . . . Out!

O, gone now are the good old days of hot cakes, thickly spread;
And meatless, wheatless, sweetless days are reigning in their
    stead;
And gone the days of fat rib roasts, and two-inch T-bone steaks,
And doughnuts plump and golden brown, the kind that mother
    makes,
And when it comes to pies and cake, just learn to cut it out.
Or Hoover's goin' to get you if you Don't . . . Watch . . . Out!

So spread your buckwheats sparingly, and peel your taters thin;
And tighten up your belt a notch, and don't forget to grin.
And if, sometimes, your whole soul yearns for shortcake high
    and wide,
And biscuits drenched with honey, and chicken, butter fried,
Remember then that Kaiser Bill is short on sauerkraut.
And Hoover's goin' to get him if we'll All . . . Help . . . Out!

In the northern Minnesota town of Eveleth, the drive to gather signatures for the Food Pledge was typical of events all over the state and nation. It began with a parade. The high school's band led nearly 2,400 schoolchildren and teachers. Students carried banners, and kindergarten children rode in automobiles and delivery trucks. Teachers followed up by canvassing house-to-house to gather signatures. Here, and in other cities, signed pledges were sent into Washington, D.C., and residents who signed could display a Food Conservation Volunteer placard in their window. At first, the plan included follow-up surveys to log how many meals were conservation meals, but very little data was actually recorded.[26]

In Washington, D.C., writer Ida Clark captured the emotional connection between the kitchen and the battleground: "The mother in the kitchen, alone with her conscience and her memories, became a food administrator in her own right. But the fact that 'food will win the war' and that every woman had been drafted into the ranks of the Army of American Housewives sank deeply into the consciousness of every loyal American woman." Minnesota responded heartily to sentiments such as these. A. D. Wilson reported that the state had surpassed its goal by enrolling 235,000 people in just two months.[27]

To boost citizen participation, the Food Administration suggested "kitchen warriors" dress in the Food Administration "uniform of service . . . a practical, trim, and attractive house dress. Made in blue, with white collar and cuffs, the insignia upon the sleeve and upon the front of the cap in red, it is especially charming and carries out the national colors. One of the best points about the costume is that it is very easy to launder."[28]

Despite the war and its domestic shortages and restrictions, many Minnesotans ate away from home, occasionally or regularly. Families visited soldiers in training camps, and vacationers took trips to resorts and famous places. Salesmen traveled their territories, buying meals in railroad dining cars and local eateries along the way. Professionals and clerks ate noontime dinners in restaurants, tearooms, or diners with booths and swivel stools. Farmers and their families came to town on Saturday nights for an evening meal and entertainment.

After the successful pledge drive, anxious to begin specific food conservation activities with a public impact, the Food Administration asked restaurant and hotel owners in major cities to begin

DAILY DIET

Menu for an average person weighing 130–150 pounds for an average day's work.

Breakfast: 600 calories

Apple, orange, or stewed prunes 100
Rolled oats, cream of barley, grits, or cornflakes 100
Cream or milk 150
Toast (3 slices), or barley muffins or griddle cakes (2) 150
Butter (1 tablespoon) 100
Coffee

Lunch: 815 calories

Cream of tomato soup or escalloped corn 250
Oatmeal bread (2 slices) 100
Butter (½ tablespoon) 50
1 cup milk 165
Cake or ice cream (½ cup) 250

Dinner: 975 calories

Roast beef or baked fish 150
Baked potato 100
Buttered carrots or beets 125
Lettuce salad with French dressing 150
Corn bread (3 slices) 150
Butter (1 tablespoon) 100
Fresh fruit with cream and sugar 200

(*Pocket Guide to Food Conservation*, University of Minnesota, May 1918)

changing their menus to reflect food conservation necessities, beginning in October 1917. By early November the request for cooperation had reached into the smallest towns of Minnesota. The *Brown County Journal* reported this letter to local eateries that arrived from the Food Administration: "Please start this week and continue to the best of your ability. . . . War will be won by food and not by bullets. It behooves every one of us, therefore, to do his part faithfully, conscientiously, and enthusiastically in this great nationwide

Casual food conservation policies became a call for serious shifts in the national diet as the first summer of the war turned to fall. Colorful posters pointed the way to less popular proteins: fish, eggs, cheese, and poultry.

movement. Please, therefore, put the suggestions which will from time to time be referred to you in immediate operation."[29]

In New Ulm, "Meatless Tuesday" and "Wheatless Wednesday" signs appeared quickly in dining rooms. By early April 1918, owners and managers of nearly 5,000 restaurants and hotels across the country took a significant step when they pledged to "go entirely upon a wheatless basis until after the harvest." The wheat, meat, fat, and sugar saved from the voluntary restaurant restriction program reportedly represented enough rations for eight million soldiers for a month. While actual food savings from restaurant meals was significant, the notices also reminded the public that food conservation was serious business and that they should conserve food at home.[30]

While people did their best to conserve food, as the months passed they continued to mark and celebrate events as they always had. Organizations like the Minneapolis Club held annual banquets, although the fare was carefully adjusted to address wartime restrictions. The annual dinner of the St. Paul Builders Exchange, held on January 23, 1918, included rye rolls and graham bread. Dessert was vanilla ice cream, served with fatless and wheatless macaroons. The souvenir menu included a long poem naming every man from the organization who had been called up into military service and concluded with a call to sacrifice and to buy Liberty bonds.[31]

Women's study and social clubs also met regularly. Many groups voted to eliminate customary treats from their meetings, sometimes giving money to the Red Cross instead, but on special occasions the clubs might have followed University of Minnesota's home economist Mildred Weigley's suggestions for "war sandwiches" that saved wheat, meats, fats, and sugar yet still afforded dainty service.

Americans soon found their fats and sugars restricted dramatically. Dense, calorie-laden foods like butter and other fats could easily be shipped overseas. Shipping disruptions, caused by the diversion of merchant ships to troop transport and by continuing submarine

---

SANDWICHES FOR DAINTY SERVICE DURING WAR TIME

1. Steamed brown-bread fillings: Walnuts mixed with grated cheeses seasoned with salt. Cottage cheese mixed with finely chopped olives or sweet pickles. Paste of ground raisins moistened with lemon juice to which finely chopped nuts may be added.
2. Oatmeal-bread fillings: Paste of ½ pound dates, ¼ to ½ cup finely chopped nuts, moistened with a small amount of cooked salad dressing or lemon juice. Orange marmalade, raspberry jam, blackberry jam, etc. or maple sugar and chopped nuts.
3. Rye-bread fillings: Cottage cheese mixed with chopped pimento. Ground cheddar cheese mixed with finely chopped dill pickles. Paste of sardines moistened with a small amount of salad dressing. Or salmon, tuna, or other fish flaked and mixed with cooked salad dressing.
4. Corn-bread fillings: Paste of ground figs with or without nuts and moistened with a small amount of salad dressing. Or paste of hard-boiled eggs and small amount of salad dressing.
5. Bakery-bread fillings: Peanut butter mixed with salad dressing. Or peanut butter mixed with finely chopped sweet pickles and small amount of salad dressing. Or any of the above cheese and fruit mixtures.
(*The Farmer*, February 16, 1918)

warfare, had reduced the availability of imported cane sugar from Cuba and Java; the beet sugar harvests in the United States and in France were relatively small. By the summer of 1918 the stock of sugar on American shelves had dwindled, just when it was most needed for home canning. Hoover implemented a tracking system to control purchases for canning above the household limit of three pounds per person per month or the equivalent of three tablespoons a day including cooking and table use.[32]

The essential emphasis of the Food Administration was efficiency and balance, and conservation of foods that could be shipped overseas was the critical goal. Substitution of fresh fruits and vegetables for restricted foods became necessary.[33]

While homegrown foods were an important resource, fresh produce from California, Florida, and other warm-weather farms was shipped throughout the war, assuring that Minnesotans could continue to eat the varied diet they were used to. So while families could get grapefruit, they needed to limit sugar sprinkled on top. Shippers packed freight cars as full and as carefully as possible to make sure food got to its destination with little damage or waste of transportation fuel.

These food conservation efforts were a success. In the first year of the war the United States shipped overseas nine million tons more than before the war, a 250 percent increase. How these successes were achieved and the challenges faced by homemakers, through whose hands 80 percent of the food passed, is a lesson in how different American life was in 1917.[34]

Refrigeration to prevent food from spoiling was an essential first conservation step on the kitchen home front. Food, especially the important leftovers, was stowed away in the icebox, literally a metal-lined wooden box chilled by a block of ice weighing between 25 and 100 pounds, delivered once a week. These small "refrigerators" kept only a limited amount of food cool. In addition to daily emptying of water from the drip pan, they required weekly cleaning "with a vengeance." Instructions for maximizing efficiency included covering the ice with newspaper, never putting hot or warm foods in the box, keeping the door tightly shut, and opening it only briefly.

A typical large icebox made by Manteuffel Refrigerator Company in St. Paul stood 60 inches tall, 40 inches wide, and 24 inches deep. It had one ice chamber and three "provision chambers with wooden shelves." The smallest refrigerator sold by the company was just 42 inches high, 34 inches wide, and 19 inches deep.[35]

Not every homemaker had an icebox for cold storage. In directions for preparing jellied chicken, a reincarnation of leftover chicken and broth into an elegant molded salad, Mrs. Fred Rausch of Howard Lake instructed cooks to "set in cool place over night" for the natural chicken gelatin to firm before unmolding. The commonality of sour milk as an ingredient in recipes of the time also suggests limited reliable refrigeration.[36]

In rural areas where ice was not delivered, wives could follow instructions such as these, published in the *Cloquet Pine Knot,* to keep perishable food "in covered vessels suspended in the well or in the coolest place in your home or cellar." Women might even make an iceless refrigerator as described in *The Farmer's Wife:* "Cover a framework with screening and then sew a heavy cloth such as flannel or burlap to tightly enclose it, leaving a seam that can be opened as a doorway. Place two shelves inside the 'ice box' and a pan of water on top. Drape strips of cloth of the same material as the sides into the water and onto the sides. This wicking will draw the water down the sides where it will cool the box as it evaporates. On dry hot days, a temperature of 50 degrees has been known to be obtained in the cooler."[37]

The ideal kitchen, as illustrated in the era's women's magazines and in the "Home Harmonious" column of the *Minneapolis Journal,* was a large open room featuring a center worktable with wooden pot rack arching over the top, a wall-mounted sink, a "Hoosier" cupboard for dry ingredients, and bowls and utensils with a counter for mixing. Cooking took place on the stove top, in an oven heated by a wood or a coal firebox or, in the city, gas. Modern households that had been electrified might have new electric appliances: hot plate, chafing dish, electric percolator, or toaster. Cooking without constant attention was possible in fireless cookers warmed by metal plates heated on the stove and then placed into a well-insulated box or in up-to-date electric models where "the current is turned on

Home delivery was curtailed from grocery stores like this one in Chisago City,
where Alfred Bloom and Alfred Peterson preside, 1915.

until the required heat is reached. This is accurately determined by a
clock attachment . . . whereupon the heat is turned off and the food
goes on cooking in the old-fashioned way."[38]

City homemakers were accustomed to frequent delivery of perishable food. Because kitchens lacked capacity to hold meats, vegetables, milk, butter, and eggs for more than one or two days in home
iceboxes, many grocery stores and meat markets with cold storage
rooms delivered orders to urban customers practically on demand.

During World War I, the Woman's Club of Minneapolis urged its
members to limit the number of deliveries they requested from local
merchants by appealing to their patriotism. Its January 1918 bulletin suggested, "Do not let a fighting man carry your parcels—save
the manpower for essential service. The large stores are reducing the

number of deliveries, in accordance with the request of the National Council of Defense, but . . . women are still demanding many deliveries a day. In so far, therefore, the women are responsible for a distinctly unpatriotic condition. Please do not ask your grocer and butcher for more than one delivery a day."[39]

Shopping habits were hard to break, and it took time and a government mandate for the "cash and carry" movement to take hold. Discounts of 5 percent to shoppers who paid cash and carried their own groceries home failed to have the effect food conservation officers sought. In August 1918, a representative of the federal Food Administration persuaded grocery stores to "voluntarily agree to eliminate delivery." As the *Brown County Journal* explained, "The suspension of the delivery in New Ulm will release four horse rigs and seven autos and quite a few employees, and will also be quite a savings in horse feed and gasoline. . . . The purchaser of groceries is expected to receive the benefit." The paper reported the results of the first days' effort, noting, "Many little express wagons were seen on the streets filled with groceries and being hauled homeward by little Johnny or Bertha. Many market baskets, some the worse for wear, were also seen to dangle from the arms of those who had no other way to get their daily stock of groceries home."[40]

Farm wives were less affected by these changes. They relied on their own meats, fruits, and vegetables raised on their farms and smoked, canned, or cured with their own hands. While farmers owned more cars or trucks than city dwellers, a trip to town didn't happen every day.

Summer is the busiest season in rural areas, and in Minnesota's Red River Valley, farmers typically devoted an estimated one and one-half hours a day to eating meals, ten hours to raising crops, and another two and one-half hours on chores. Some farm wives had a few labor-saving electric appliances such as water pumps, cream separators, or sewing machines they ran off small gasoline-powered generators, but many more cooked on wood-fired stoves, pumped water by hand, and read by kerosene lamps.[41]

Wherever people lived in Minnesota during the war, special conservation events and new communication networks facilitated the spread of the food conservation gospel. Efforts came both from the federal government at the top and from individual citizens at the bottom.

During these 19 months of intense activity the exchange of information and encouragement of action became virtually viral. People across Minnesota were exposed to important facts and shared emotions. Whether the requests started with the federal government or the encouragement came from neighbors, people caught the fever of food conservation and passed it on.

Federal, state, county, and local governments actively pursued all avenues for information and persuasion. The state and federal food administrations provided material to libraries and churches to be used in displays and newsletters, perhaps even as homily topics. In these years before electronic media, moving picture theaters showed newsreels conveying battlefield and home-front scenes, silent except for the whirr of the projector and, perhaps, the piano playing down in front. Sometimes the movies were preceded by a live presentation from a volunteer speaker. These "Four Minute" talks on food conservation, the Red Cross, or other war-related issues were preselected and the speakers were given an outline of talking points and presentation guidelines. Speakers were offered their own pep-talk directions: "Every talk must be put over with a good, hard punch. . . . We are all a part of a great organization that is striving toward just one end, the achievement of victory."[42]

Small-town and big-city newspapers publicized war cooking classes and featured recipes developed by the Food Administration and local cooks. Artists created illustrations with patriotic themes or scenes of wartime devastation in Europe that became the centerpiece of effective newspaper and magazine ads and posters displayed in storefronts and civic buildings. By the end of the war nearly three million dollars worth of billboard space had been donated across the nation for food conservation and war-related messages. Signs in front of public buildings, handouts, special reading lists in libraries, religious sermons, and department-store windows supported patriotic and food conservation messages. County fairs became venues for publicizing new food rules and demonstrating recipes.[43]

Minnesota's annual State Fair offered an ideal outreach opportunity. Fair Secretary Thomas H. Canfield called the 1917 event a "food training camp." Writing to President Wilson, he noted that draftees were being "concentrated in military training camps because they can be trained more efficiently in that way. . . . It would seem that there is just as much necessity to call the great rank and file of food producers and consumers into central food training camps." Accordingly, the State Fair presented demonstrations on baking new war breads and cold-pack canning methods. It introduced the most productive varieties of animals, grains, forage crops, fruits, and vegetables to the farming public. Newspaper advertisements for the fair showed an army of well-dressed agriculturists marching six abreast from the fairgrounds carrying baskets of produce and being saluted by Uncle Sam.[44]

That metaphorical army was trumped in mid-October by this "sight never to be forgotten" on the training fields at Camp Dodge, printed in the *St. Cloud Times*:

> You've heard a lot about the steady tramp of the German army as it marched through Liege [Belgium]. Well, I've heard the first thunder of the marching feet of our own American army. . . . The dust of the road was marked by the prints of thousands of army shoes. . . . Then we emerged on the brow of the hill. I gasped. Spread out before me was a wonderful picture. Troops in all directions, marching and counter-marching, standing at attention. . . . I looked behind me. Down the hill, through a deep cut, hundreds more were coming. . . . I had witnessed a wonderful thing—the first review of our new national army.[45]

Moved to action, Minnesotans across the state transformed social networks and extended peer pressure as they volunteered for civilian service in the new domestic army. As members of state and local committees, these community soldiers made policies and implemented specific food conservation plans for action. They gathered ideas from Minnesotans who suggested better ways to grow crops, store vegetables, and cook delicious meals following Food

Administration guidelines. Households learned to bake breads with less wheat, grow food in war gardens, eat and put up extra vegetables, stretch meat, consider milk as food, and limit the amount of sugar they ate. Fresh in their minds was President Wilson's warning of April 15, 1917, that "without abundant food, the whole great enterprise upon which we have embarked will break down and fail."

———

Well, Mother, I must close and get some eats. I hope the garden is growing, that the pump is working. Gee, how I would like to be there. Believe me, you don't know how much I want to sit on the kitchen chair while you cook dinner. With heaps of love to all, I am sincerely your son.
Frank Street, April 1918, American Expeditionary Force, somewhere in France[46]

3

The Staff of Life, the Stuff of War

I don't know if I've spoken of the meals here, but they sure
are wonderful. The bread is "like mother used to make"
(years ago). It's made here at the post bakery by enlisted
men and sure tastes like homemade bread. We always
have whole-wheat bread, as well as white, and real butter.
Granville Gutterson, Army Air Corps, March 1918, Texas[1]

B read, which provides a balance of carbohydrates and protein,
especially when spread with a bit of fat, was considered a near
perfect food. Bread was easily distributed and tasty when eaten
without being heated. According to Herbert Hoover, citizens in
countries already at war in April and May 1917 consumed one-half
to two-thirds of their total daily calories as bread.[2]

In the United States, before war had affected food production,
bread was typically served at every meal and represented an estimated one-third of a citizen's total calories. A "menu for healthy
eating" sent to *The Farmer* by Fanny K. of Michigan on April 28,
1917, just as the war began, said that breakfast should include bread,
fruit, cereal, and eggs or a "small amount of meat." The noon meal
should include bread, a hot meat dish, a cold meat or a very heavy
salad and soup, potatoes, and dessert. Her evening meal suggestion
included bread, meat and potatoes, vegetable, and salad.

Wheat is the essential ingredient in bread, and Minnesota farmers could play a key role in stretching the supply. Many farmers across
the nation were already in the fields planting for the 1917 fall harvest
when President Wilson called for war against Germany in April. But in
the northern-tier state of Minnesota, farmers had not yet been able
to put in their crops. A. D. Wilson, director of the university's Agricultural Extension Service, immediately urged farmers to shift from

QUICK WAR BREAD

2 tablespoons vinegar
2 cups milk
½ cup sugar
3 cups graham (whole-wheat)
    flour
1¼ teaspoons baking soda
1 teaspoon salt
1 cup flour
½ cup molasses

Preheat the oven to 325° F.
Put the vinegar in a 2-cup
glass measuring cup. Add
milk to make 2 cups. Stir and
let stand until milk is soured,
about 5 minutes. Combine the
sugar, graham flour, baking
soda, salt, and regular flour.
Add molasses and soured milk;
stir well. Pour mixture into
2 greased and floured 4 × 8 loaf
pans. Bake until firm in the
center, about 50–60 minutes.
(*The Farmer's Wife*, June 1918)

their usual oat, alfalfa, and corn crops to wheat. Mid-April reports of drought-driven failure of Kansas's winter-wheat crop added urgency to the efforts.[3]

State Farm Bureau agents in 16 Minnesota counties quickly responded to a survey sent by F. E. Balmer, chief of the agent program. Some responses were completed on April 4, the day President Wilson declared war, and sent to University Farms by return mail. The agent for St. Louis County in northern Minnesota wrote: "Experimenting with new and untried crops at this stage is out of the question, but by all means grow and cultivate to the fullest extent any crop now known to be safe and reliable." Shipping disruptions, caused by the diversion of merchant ships to troop transport and by continuing submarine warfare, had reduced the availability of imported cane sugar from Cuba and Java.[4]

In addition to giving solid information about which crops were usually planted in Minnesota's counties, the agents were asked how much additional acreage could be cultivated to grow more corn, oats, barley, and spring wheat. Their answers highlighted other war-related problems. Even before men were drafted into the army, farmers in Dakota County, south of St. Paul, had trouble cultivating and harvesting crops: "Average farm in Dakota County about 155 acres. Big labor problem." The Grant County agent in the west central part of the state raised another nagging issue: "Many of our farmers would resent a campaign for larger production unless they

THE PRESIDENT OF THE UNITED STATES TO FARMERS

"By planting and increasing his production in every way possible, every farmer will perform a labor of patriotism for which he will be recognized as a soldier of the commissary, adding his share to the food supply of his people."—President Wilson, April 10, 1917.

SPECIAL APPEAL
═══TO═══
FARMER PATRIOTS

"SOLDIERS OF THE COMMISSARY"

FARMERS MUST FEED THE NATION AND ITS FIGHTING MEN

Posters appealing to farmers' patriotism called for planting better seeds, raising more meat, and marketing more milk and eggs.

can be shown that fair prices are in sight." Closer to the Iowa border, the Faribault agent recommended, "Men who have studied and followed special courses of crop and food production can be of great assistance in obtaining production of the needed food supply. Farmers who have specialized in certain crops could help with training and experience." The means for sharing this information was readily at hand, the Dakota agent suggested, through dozens of rural organizations in the state.

There was much to be accomplished. Farm families met in a number of social and learning groups ready to take up the tasks at hand to do all they could to win the war. Farmers clubs, the Grange, county agent meetings, churches, and schools all offered opportunities to learn and to persuade. On April 21, 1917, A. D. Wilson, as head of the state's Food Conservation Committee, sent out a newspaper release saying that "Minnesota's agricultural industries are being organized as never before, and, perhaps, as no other state's farm work is being organized, for the quick and large increase of food production and conservation." He concluded that by the end of the crop year, it would be apparent that the state "has given its full share of patriotic service to the nation."[5]

Professor Wilson called for careful balancing of crops between human and animal needs and between domestic use and overseas relief. Corn did not store as well as wheat, and European tastes and mills were not equipped to accept corn, he noted. U.S. appetites and mills were more flexible, so America should ship as much wheat and flour overseas as possible. Wilson outlined three ways to increase Minnesota's flour supply: grow more wheat; shift domestic usage to alternative grains such as corn, rye, and barley; and get more flour out of each bushel of wheat by milling whole wheat, instead of refined white flour, and thus increasing volume by as much as 15 to 20 percent. Dr. Harvey Wiley, a leading food authority, concurred with Wilson about the advantages of whole wheat: "Under present methods of milling, there are 18 pounds of waste for every 60 pounds of flour milled." He noted further that the "waste" fed to cows was the most nutritious part of the wheat.[6]

Wilson's suggestions for bringing in a bountiful, war-winning crop underscore the differences between agricultural practices in the World War I era and today. In 1917 there were 175,000 farms in Minnesota, but less than 16,000 tractors in the entire United States. Minnesota farms were home to 950,000 horses and other animals. The 1,200 farms in Rock County, for example, had an average of 36 milk cows and other cattle, 90 hogs, five sheep, and nine horses. Cattle, hogs, and sheep brought money to the farm. Horses were essential not only for transportation but for working the farm. Planting and harvesting grain took animal and human power. Huge steam- and gas-powered threshing machines only helped with the process. Men traveled among their neighbors' farms in the fall to bring in crops, while women kept them fed with table-bending threshers' meals. But the outbreak of war meant that many men would be called off the farm to fight.[7]

In the first days of the war, A. D. Wilson outlined some specific and ambitious steps to increase farm yields: Because the school year was almost complete, dismiss high school boys early to work on farms. Increase wheat acreage at the expense of oats. Increase corn acreage. Use all manure to fertilize the soil. Increase clover and alfalfa acreage to keep livestock productive without eating grain. Break up an estimated 500,000 acres of timothy sod with tractors running 24 hours a day. Plant potatoes. Have every family keep a garden. Can or otherwise preserve fruit and vegetables enough for two years.[8]

C. G. Schultz, Minnesota's superintendent of education, issued a call for the "readjustment of educational, social and industrial relations and activities" to strengthen the public service. Specifically, he said, boys should be excused from school if they enlisted in the military or in war work on the home front. Girls could similarly be excused and, if seniors, engage in nursing or Red Cross work. Schultz called for 100,000 "strong, active, industrious farm laborers" to double Minnesota's production in wheat, corn, and vegetables.[9]

Just six weeks into the war, in late June 1917, University of Minnesota home economist Josephine Berry and other food-administration advisors considered various ideas for cutting the country's wheat consumption, especially in bread, by one quarter. This was a formidable task, summed up in a creamery advertisement in the *Bemidji Daily Pioneer,* "The Foundation of a Good Meal. Koors Bread and Butter."[10]

Governor Burnquist's committee for state food production and conservation emphasized the need to reach all the people of the state, and a report cited "quite effective resources for securing publicity at its command; namely, the farm press, the daily press, the publicity agencies of the Agricultural Colleges and . . . the country press."[11]

Minnesota newspapers quickly got with the program and began publishing recipes and suggestions to help homemakers cook husband-pleasing meals while doing their patriotic duty. In May and June 1917, the university's home economics department sent a series of news releases to Twin Cities and Duluth newspapers containing bread, muffin, and griddle cake recipes using corn, oatmeal, and other flours in combination with wheat flour. They also featured

Save a loaf a week — help win the war

U. S. FOOD ADMINISTRATION

Before the war, bread was a menu mainstay in Minnesota homes, typically served at every meal. But if each home saved just one slice of bread each day, more than 300 million loaves would be saved in a year.

recipes using rice in main dishes as a way to stretch meat and to conserve potatoes and wheat.[12]

University-trained home-economics demonstrators were the first to fan out across the state. They conducted training sessions throughout the summer of 1917, particularly in rural counties already familiar with the dedication and expertise of the extension division. The letters and replies in the files of program directors Josephine Berry and, after she moved up to a federal position in September, Mildred Weigley illustrate some of the challenges faced in spreading information about the best ways to preserve garden bounty, change eating habits, and, in particular, make new "war breads."[13]

One reply to Weigley from the Dakota County coordinator hinted at a somewhat unenthusiastic response to their urgings. "Hastings housewives are somewhat above average I think in their skill in handling and preparation of food. They take it as a reflection on their ability to cope with the present emergency when they are asked to pledge money for a 'new fangled' demonstration to teach them any cooking, even war time cooking." The letter also commented on the whole-wheat flour A. D. Wilson had advocated: "Many [women] do

WAR YEAST BREAD

1 cup milk	6 tablespoons brown sugar
1 cup hot water	1 package dry yeast
1 cup cornmeal	4½ to 5½ cups bread flour
1 cup old-fashioned oatmeal, uncooked	

Scald the milk and add hot water, cornmeal, dry oatmeal, and brown sugar. Stir until well blended and set aside to cool. When mixture has cooled to lukewarm, sprinkle dry yeast on top and stir to blend in. Set aside until mixture begins to look slightly bubbly. Add flour gradually until a stiff dough is formed. Turn out onto floured surface and knead until smooth. Place dough in lightly greased bowl, cover with a damp cloth, and let rise until doubled. Punch down. Form into 3 loaves; place in lightly greased pans or on baking sheets. Let rise until it doubles. Preheat the oven to 350° F. Bake until browned and loaves sound hollow when tapped. (D. Jayne, *War Breads Recipes* [Philadelphia, 1918])

Cooking class at Plainview, about 1917. Home economists trained at the University of Minnesota taught woman throughout the state how to make wheat-saving war breads and meat-saving main dishes and also demonstrated new techniques for canning vegetables.

not like dark flour and seem to feel (from their manner) that no use of dark flour could make it palatable to them."[14]

Despite many recommendations for using dark or whole-wheat flour, few home bakers were receptive to the nutritional advantages of the whole-wheat kernel. Many bakers opposed what they saw as unacceptable roughage in their baked goods. Even *Northwestern Miller* editor William Edgar, who strongly supported citizens doing their part in the war effort, agreed. He editorialized in no uncertain terms: "By whatever sophistry it may be supported, every argument for increased extraction flour, mixed flour, or flour otherwise debased is an argument for a deceptive gain in volume at cost of more than commensurate loss in nutritive value."[15]

Esther Moran, supervisor of domestic services for the St. Paul schools, published one of the few whole-wheat recipes that appeared in popular media in the first year of the war. Her *St. Paul Pioneer Press* cooking column featured chocolate whole-wheat cookies, served for dessert in place of cake or pie.

In July 1917 the government's estimates for the amount of available wheat took a serious hit when it learned of the significant failure of the Argentinean wheat crop. This led to more specific government directives. Reaching out to community opinion leaders to influence as many people as possible, Josephine Berry reported the results of a subsequent Food Administration meeting in Washington to pastors in the Twin Cities. Normal consumption in the United States and Canada, she said, would require 700 million bushels of wheat, and the Allies in Europe needed 550 million bushels. America's granaries held only 43 million bushels, less than a normal month's supply because the U.S. harvest of 636 million bushels was also far below normal.[16]

Edgar of the *Northwestern Miller* summed up the challenge: "We of North America now face the very serious task of being obliged to feed the entire world, an undertaking not beyond our ability." Farms across Belgium and France had been out of production since the war began, and America's wheat crop in 1916 and 1917 was significantly below normal. There was no wheat to spare.[17]

Taking action, the federal government called upon Americans to voluntarily make breads with some proportion of non-wheat flour. In early October 1917, Hoover requested that hotels, restaurants, and patriotic homemakers observe "Wheatless Wednesdays" by not serving any wheat products.[18]

CHOCOLATE WHOLE-WHEAT COOKIES

½ cup melted shortening (or butter)   2 cups whole-wheat flour
2 squares baking chocolate   ½ teaspoon salt
1 cup brown sugar, firmly packed   ½ cup raisins, chopped
1 egg   ½ cup nuts, chopped
½ cup milk

Preheat oven to 350° F. Stir chocolate into melted shortening or butter over low heat until it is melted. Stir into brown sugar and add lightly beaten egg. Stir in milk and then flour and salt. Mix well. Add chopped raisins and nuts. Drop by teaspoon onto lightly greased baking sheets. Bake until just lightly browned, about 8–12 minutes. Remove and cool on wire rack. (*St. Paul Pioneer Press*, December 9, 1917)

The Food Administration had the help of national advertisers in selling tasty, wheat-saving cornbread.

Reconnecting the nation with cornmeal seemed a good place to start the shift away from wheat. Cornmeal, although a traditional American staple, had fallen out of favor by the turn of the twentieth century. In the mainstream *Crisco Cookbook*'s bread chapter, 48 recipes call for white flour but only 16 used any other grain including whole wheat, rye, graham, and cornmeal. Ratios were similar for community cookbooks in Minnesota. Minneapolis's Hennepin Avenue Methodist Episcopal Church cookbook, *Culinary Guide,* is typical, with 30 bread recipes using wheat flour, six using other flours, and none using cornmeal.[19]

While some bakers found recipes for corn muffins, cakes, and waffles from old cookbooks helpful, many of these foods still had a high proportion of wheat flour. In addition, a good loaf of yeast-raised bread was the most difficult to accomplish with limited wheat flour because wheat gluten forms the essential structure to hold the air created by the bubbling yeast. By midsummer 1917, however, food scientists at the university's home economics department began experimenting with ways to replace at least one-fifth of the flour in breads and baked goods with non-wheat grains. Their Minnesota Liberty Breads recipes, which included cornmeal yeast bread, rice bread, and rye muffins, became standards for commercial and home bakers across the nation.[20]

Across the state, many homemakers eagerly sought recipes for conservation foods. In Mankato the conservation committee chair noted, "Our requests for information are far in excess of anything we can take care of," and her Mille Lacs compatriot asked for menu suggestions for "a Hoover restaurant or lunch counter at our county fair." From Becker County came a request in September 1917: "I am to have a public safety exhibit . . . the week of our county fair. If possible will you send me one dozen loaves of 'war bread' for exhibition and sampling. Whatever expense is incurred I will meet. Should like to have the bread by Thursday afternoon if possible." To this request, Mildred Weigley, acting chair of the state food commission, replied: "I am sorry that we cannot furnish you with samples of the loaves which you would like. We are not equipped for turning out bread here. I am sending you, however, copies of the recipe. As to using the recipes, one of the Minneapolis teachers . . . found that so long as she followed the directions carefully, she had good results even with inexperienced classes."[21]

Mrs. C. B. Watkins of Cloquet described extensive activities and the lesson she learned in Carlton County: "We got the Board of Education of Cloquet to hire a teacher for courses in canning and drying. . . . We are now sending her into the county districts and small towns. . . . Thus far the schedule includes Moose Lake, Carlton, Barnum, Mahtowa, Scanlon, Knife Falls, Sawyer, and Fond-du-lac village. The latter are Indian villages and the lessons offered there are request of the Indian agent, whose wife had taken the course in town. At each lesson receipts for meat-substitutes, etc, are also given." Watkins continued with a caution, "We have found that the women simply want the canning and drying, and that they will not turn out when the lesson is on war-bread, meat-substitutes, or anything they can get by following a receipt. So we work these in incidentally."

At summer's end in both 1917 and 1918, the Minnesota State Fair dedicated itself to the food conservation effort. Children in the Boys and Girls Club, an activity coordinated by the university, demonstrated how to bake "War Bread." The Northwestern Yeast Company

Members of the Boys and Girls Club, wearing a version of the official food conservation uniform, shared new recipes for wheat-saving breads during live baking demonstrations at the Minnesota State Fair.

of Chicago praised their efforts in a letter: "Judging from the yeast sales throughout the entire United States, we consider that there was more intelligent use of substitutes combined with regular wheat flour in the homes in Minnesota than in any other state in the Union, due to a large degree to the excellent and constructive work done in the Girls' Bread Clubs."[22]

Despite encouragement, some women remained uncomfortable baking yeast breads. The stakes for bread bakers were high, as one cookbook noted, "Nothing insures the health and contentment of the family as much as good bread. There is no article of food about which there has been more written, more instructions given, or in which more failures have been made. In short, nothing is more rare than a good loaf of bread."[23]

While working with new flours caused some homemakers to throw up their hands, other experimenters had more success. Andelia Swanson of Goodhue County began her article in *Junior Soldiers of the Soil* dramatically quoting her younger brother, "Ugh, I hate that barley bread." She continued, "Mother tried to make it twice, as she had heard it was the most difficult of all the substitute breads to make successfully." After several attempts using "both the short and long methods," Andelia produced a loaf so light and tasty that her brother complained when she didn't make it. Buoyed by success, she organized a bread club to teach her friends and their mothers. "I am happy in the thought that I have been able to help Uncle Sam even in so trifling a manner."[24]

Commercial bakers also stepped up to accommodate the government's recommendations. At the beginning of the war, the most common loaf of bakery bread was a "10 cent loaf" made entirely with white flour. The weight of this standard loaf varied within two ounces of a pound, depending upon the cost of wheat.[25]

In Minnesota most loaves contained 16 ounces of dough, which produced a 14-ounce loaf of bread. Through the spring and summer of 1917, bakers made a fair profit by using up relatively inexpensive flour purchased before the shortage beginning in 1916. But that changed when they began to use more expensive flour from the limited 1917 crop. Now flour accounted for up to three cents of the ten-cent purchase price. Some bakers in the state tried increasing the standard loaf size to reduce handling costs per loaf. In Eveleth, Hendrickson's bakery announced the larger loaf in early August with the headline: "Tomorrow we will put a 15 cent loaf of bread on the market. More bread than you can get for 15 cents in small loaves. It is a good, cheap nutritious food that will solve the wartime food problem for you."[26]

The rising cost of bread became of increasing concern in the Twin Cities by the end of the summer of 1917. In response the Minnesota Commission of Public Safety (MCPS) set up an experimental shop for the sale of bread on the "cash-and-carry plan throughout the Twin Cities, which should save customers more than 3 cents on a 10 cent loaf" by eliminating the costs of transportation from large bakeries to retail stores and from stores to homes. Two one-pound loaves would sell for 13 cents. When the month-long test ended in December 1917, MCPS commissioner John Lind reported that the project "has been eminently successful and has attracted the favorable consideration and comment of the Food Administration in

Washington. Minneapolis today enjoys the cheapest bread of any city in the nation. This is virtually true of the other cities in the state. . . . When we started in on our experiment, the universal price for bread . . . at retail was 10 cents for 14 ounces or less. The price now is 7 cents per pound, or rather 14 cents for the double loaf of two pounds."[27]

Though the MCPS retail experiment was deemed a success, federal regulations trumped state and local innovation in mid-December 1917, as bread ingredients had become commodities controlled for the war effort. The *Brown County Journal* reported the changed situation this way: "Bakeries must have federal licenses. After their licenses are received, they will be furnished with formula for the makings of bread. This means less lard, less cream and milk. Also less sugar. People will find that bread baked under government regulation will not taste just the same as it did before, but there will not be any great difference."[28]

The formula issued just before Christmas was based on a 196-pound barrel of regular white flour. The resulting loaves would have been low fat and low sugar, since bakers could incorporate no more than six pounds of nonfat milk, two pounds of margarine or shortening, and three pounds of sugar. The Food Administration duly noted, "The attention of the bakers is called to the shortage of sugar and they are asked to use less than the maximum amounts."[29]

A week later, the next government-mandated change made front-page news in Minnesota flour-milling communities: "No more white flour to be milled." A new War or Liberty flour would contain more of the wheat kernel. According to one account, this technique would save 16 million bushels of wheat a year. Former miller Charles Ritz wrote later that as the "very brisk" demand for flour overseas continued, the government agreed to extend supplies by moving to "80 percent extraction flour. This made dark bread, of course, and helped the situation, but in 1918 the demand was so great that the government then forced the mills to supply a certain percentage of rye, rice, or corn flour with the wheat flour in order to stretch supplies at home and abroad." Pillsbury and other midwestern millers sold individual kinds of flours made from barley, rice, corn, "entire wheat," graham, and rye. They also produced blends such as "All

Little
AMERICANS
Do your bit

Eat Oatmeal-Corn meal mush-
Hominy - other corn cereals -
and Rice with milk.
Save the wheat for our soldiers.

Leave nothing on your plate

UNITED   STATES   FOOD   ADMINISTRATION

NO. 21

Children were involved in the war efforts, too. Boy Scouts helped sell Liberty bonds. Girls did their part in kitchens. Even the littlest Americans could help by leaving "nothing on your plate." (Artist Cushman Parker)

CORNMEAL AND RICE WAFFLES

1 tablespoon vinegar
1 cup milk
½ cup cornmeal
½ cup flour
½ teaspoon baking soda
¼ teaspoon salt, optional
1 cup boiled rice,
  cooled (not instant or
  converted rice)
1 tablespoon melted
  butter
2 eggs, well beaten

Preheat waffle iron to medium. Put the vinegar in the bottom of a glass measuring cup and add milk to make 1 cup. Stir and let stand for 3–5 minutes until the milk sours. Mix the cornmeal, flour, baking soda, and salt in a medium bowl. Stir in the rice. Add the butter, eggs, and milk and stir well. Pour batter on waffle iron and bake until golden brown. (*Eveleth News*, March 7, 1918)

Ready Rye and Wheat," "White Rye and Wheat," and "Bohemian Style Rye and Wheat."[30]

Larger mills employed bakers to test samples from every batch of flour the mill produced. Every day Rose Holub, who tested flour for International Milling, opened 12 sacks of blended flour and mixed loaves of bread from each one to a standard recipe. The dough was "pulled like taffy 100 times to knead it, put in proofing cabinets to rise," and then baked. "They were grinding rye and they were grinding rice, mixing it with white flour." It "didn't test out as good as all white flour, but we couldn't help that because everybody was doing it." Changing equipment to mill different flours proved to be no small task, because "they couldn't grind grains like barley and rice on rollers that they had for the wheat flour. They had to send the rollers to Minneapolis to have them corrugated."[31]

New government rules in early February 1918 contained stringent requirements for grocers, bakers, and manufacturers of wheat-containing products. Bakers and restaurants could sell only mixed-grain Victory bread. Manufacturers of macaroni, crackers, and other products could only purchase 70 percent of the quantity of wheat they used in 1917. Grocers and wholesalers were required to sell one pound of alternative grain products for every pound of flour under a "50/50 Rule." The Food Administration figured it would be easier to encourage homemakers to use unfamiliar alternatives to wheat flour if they had them in their pantries. So for every pound of flour she bought, a homemaker would have to buy another pound of non-wheat substitutes such as oatmeal, cornmeal, barley, or rye. Restaurants and hotels were limited to serving two ounces of bread to any person at any meal. Newspapers printed photographs showing the proper-sized slices.[32]

Frequent news stories describing wheat-saving successes—and passing along guilt-inducing press releases about enforcement of Lever Act rules against hoarding—encouraged most families to continue eating their mixed-grain breads and wheatless and meatless meals. One 1918 brochure provided ammunition against those who still complained. "Let those who murmur over mixed bread read this bill of fare: Breakfast—acorn coffee, 2 slices of bread made of rye, sawdust, and potato flour. Dinner—soup with small piece of tough beef, coarse turnips and potato. Supper—soup again with two slices of bread. This is the fate of 15 American prisoners of war in Germany. Captured last October and since then have been marched many miles on these rations. Exhibited in villages to show American soldiers no match for Germans."[33]

Some bakers saw the 50/50 rule as an opportunity to expand sales. W. W. Loveless advertised his War Bread in the *Worthington Globe*. "If you find it difficult to use up your cereals which you must buy with flour, buy our War Bread; this will enable you to comply fully with the law. We sell a full 16-ounce loaf at 10 cents—3 for 25 cents." In Duluth, Zinmaster's bakery took a positive tack: "Most people find, that after all, 'War Bread' is no hardship—it is rather a pleasant change from the all-wheat bread of yesterday. Most men think, too, the darker it is the better. We are equipped to offer you delicious 'War Bread' and save us all the trouble of using up the substitutes. Zinmaster's War Bread Makes Better Toast!"[34]

In Bemidji, the Koors Brothers bakery employed a patriotic appeal. "First to Fight—Our marines are picked men, chosen for their strength and intelligence. In order to keep them in good physical and mental condition, they must be given plenty of good nourishing food, of which bread must form a large part. See that they have sufficient by economizing on your use of bread and never wasting a crust or crumb."[35]

For homemakers who continued to buy flour to bake their own

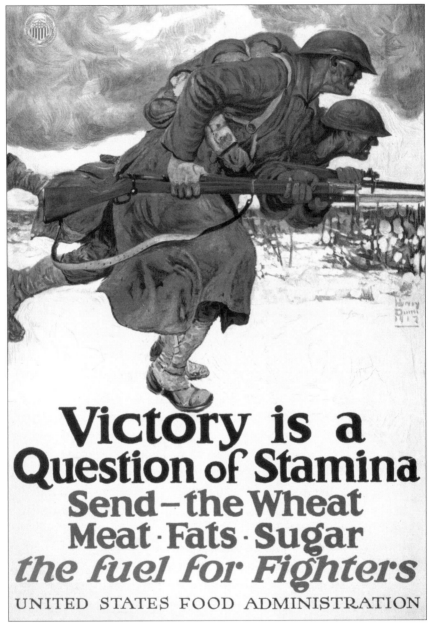

Victory is a Question of Stamina
Send – the Wheat
Meat · Fats · Sugar
the fuel for Fighters
UNITED STATES FOOD ADMINISTRATION

*Emotional posters dramatized the battles to be won and the cost of the war
in terms everyone could understand.*

bread, muffins, and biscuits, the *Le Sueur News* reported on the success of the 50/50 program and outlined ways to use the substitute flour. "Several groceries have stated that their customers who are strictly observing the 11 wheatless meals each week find it necessary to buy substitutes in addition to those ordered under the 50/50 plan." The article then explained complexities in the guidelines. "Some misunderstanding seems to exist on the part of consumers in assuming that with the purchase of wheat flour, one must confine the additional 50 percent purchase to one of the substitutes. If a purchase of 24 pounds of wheat flour is made, a range of substitutes may be selected as follows: cornmeal 8 pounds, corn grits 4 pounds, rice 4 pounds, buckwheat 2 pounds, corn starch 1 pound, hominy 2 pounds, rolled oats 3 pounds." The article concluded with suggestions for using those substitutes as main dishes, breads, and ingredients.[36]

One of the downsides of the new flours was the arrival of unfamiliar pests. For perplexed homemakers, the Food Administration offered a simple solution to prevent flours and grains from becoming infested by insects. It advised homemakers to place these foods in a dripping pan on the upper grate of a coal, wood, gas, gasoline, or kerosene stove and heat them to 185 degrees F. for at least 30 minutes. To assure success, homemakers could even buy small wax capsules to put in the pan. When the wax was melted, the bug eggs and larvae were killed and flour and other grains were safe.[37]

Throughout the war, rules governing use of wheat continued to change, catching even city and county women's organizations off guard when their fund-raising plans confronted tightened rules. It was early January 1918 before the MCPS women's division chapter in Minneapolis had their collection of food conservation recipes ready for sale, but by that time rules about wheat conservation were more stringent than their recipes allowed. Sales were less than anticipated, as the Ramsey County chair explained when she returned the unsold booklets. "I am extremely sorry I was not able to sell more recipes for you, but we have found it difficult inasmuch as the recipes for breads, etc. cannot be used on wheatless days." The Minneapolis chairwoman Mrs. Strong responded, "Of course the situation changes so fast from day to day that I realize that our book is not quite up-to-date."[38]

Mrs. Strong had more work to do. In June 1918 Alice Ames Winter's state council of the national defense office sent an earnest appeal for action. "Reports are continually coming to this office showing that large quantities of substitutes are being wasted in the city for the reason that so many housewives do not understand how to make use of them. We request that you give earnest consideration to the establishment at some central location in Minneapolis of a demonstration kitchen where demonstrations can be given to the women of the various ways of preparing flour substitutes." Within a month Mrs. Strong's committee established a demonstration kitchen which operated through the duration of the war.[39]

Barley flour, one of the first grains to be substituted for wheat in the fall of 1917, remained the most difficult for home bakers to use. It had its defenders, including Christopher Graham, a prominent Rochester physician, who said, "Like corn, it furnishes a balanced ration." To those who said barley was a poor substitute for wheat, the Food Administration responded that problems encountered were due to inexperience of the baker, not to the barley.[40]

White corn flour was touted as a more acceptable alternative in

UNCLE SAM'S WAR RECEIPT FOR BISCUITS

2 cups cornmeal, ground soy beans, or finely ground peanuts, rice flour or other substitute
2 cups white flour
3 tablespoons baking powder
2 teaspoons salt
4 tablespoons shortening
1 to 1½ cups milk, skim milk, or water

Preheat oven to 400° F. Sift dry ingredients twice. Have shortening cold and cut into dry ingredients. Mix quickly with liquid. (If peanuts are used, the roasted and shelled nuts should be finely crushed with a rolling pin and then added after the other ingredients are combined.) Turn dough on floured board, roll into sheet not over ½ inch thick, cut into rounds, place on lightly greased sheet, and bake until light brown, about 10–12 minutes. (*The Farmer's Wife*, October 1917) the *Minneapolis Journal*. "White corn flour deals knockout to new barley bread," headlined one story. Yellow cornmeal was not a popular alternative, according to another article. Corn bread "must be hot or it is fit only for chickens or hogs." It noted further that the yellow cornmeal available in northern states could not match the southern states' hominy, which finds a place on every breakfast table. But, the *Journal* reported, bread made from the newly milled white corn flour was scarcely distinguishable from bread made from wheat flour.[41]

Targeting the slackers who did not join the wheat-saving mission wholeheartedly, the Food Administration passed out ammunition in the form of brochures with emotional messages such as this one:

> We have promised to "grub-stake" the Allies. We said: "You need not farm—you fight!"
>
> And they did not farm, but how they did fight.
>
> Winter is coming on. There were few for the sowing, and there are fewer now for the harvest. The pinch has come. In France they are looking across the sea and saying: "How about that 'grub-stake,' Uncle Sam; how about that 'grub-stake!'"
>
> They are not whimpering, the Frenchmen, they are not that kind, but they are hungry, and if we fail them with our "grub-stake" they will S-T-A-R-V-E! Thousands of them—men, women and little children.
>
> It is food that will win the war![42]

In the weeks before the 1918 summer wheat harvest, the Food Administration further limited the amount of wheat allowed to consumers. As the *Erskine Echo* explained, citizens must "cut use of wheat by ½. Ration per person is 1½ pounds. This means not more than 1¾ pounds of [wheat-saving] Victory bread and one-half pound of cooking flour, macaroni, crackers, pastry, pies, cakes, wheat cereal all combined." The *Echo* ended with an encouraging note that "many thousand families throughout the land are now using no wheat products whatever, except for a very small amount for cooking purposes, and are doing so in perfect health and satisfaction."[43]

By midsummer 1918, it was clear that harvesting the year's grain crops would require every available hand. Owners of large steam

The Sever Finbraaten threshing crew on a farm near Appleton. Crews organized under the auspices of the Farm Bureau and worked with county agents to assure a smooth harvest with fair prices and wages for all parties.

threshing machines, which were essential to harvesting small grains, met in counties across the state under the auspices of the Farm Bureau to establish procedures and pricing. They assigned some men to be machine inspectors so that no time would be lost to equipment breakdowns. Threshing foremen set wages for the harvesting: "Pitchers, $3 a day or 30 cents an hour. Firemen, $3.50. Wages of engineer, separator man, and tanker to be guided by experience, paid $5–$6 per day, and $6 for the tanker who furnishes team and wagon. Prices of threshing: 8 cents a bushel for wheat and rye, 6 cents a bushel for oats and barley, twice the usual price of wheat of 16 cents for flax, buckwheat 10 cents, timothy 25 cents, succotash 6 cents for every 40 lbs if heavy, 6 cents for 32 pounds if light."[44]

Even with wages settled for the months ahead, harvesting required neighbors to help neighbors much as they always had. Since many farmers' sons or hired hands were gone to war, businessmen, merchants, students, and women helped bring in the crops across the state. Articles in the *Crookston Times* in mid-August express the urgency, noting that the man in charge of the Crookston "shock troops" had sent out a frantic call for help. "Last evening over 20 gangs of men ranging from 6 to 35 men were sent out to various farms in answer to calls for help. All worked until dark and the amount of grain put in shock was tremendous. [One] crowd . . . shocked 150

Townsmen and -women volunteered to help harvest their neighbors' crops, driving out from town after the close of business to harvest thousands of acres of Minnesota wheat, oats, barley, and corn. (Artist H. Druitt Welsh)

acres of grain before dark. The work is being well done, too. Some of the city chaps have who never shocked before have already become experts. . . . Those who have cars are also asked to bring them as there is likely to be a shortage of transportation facilities. . . . Urge everyone to turn out tonight." Some farmers were able to pay their town helpers. "The rate of pay has been fixed at 35 cents an hour and the farmers are perfectly willing to pay this amount."[45]

Even women worked in the fields, as a *Crookston Times* article headlined: "Local Girls Do Good Work in Harvest Fields. A number of young ladies of the city . . . [are] shocking the Liberty crops and are willing to go wherever called. The girls volunteered for the work and will again answer any call that may be made."[46]

While no comprehensive statistics for the number of volunteer harvesters exist, a 1918 Farm Bureau report hints at the magnitude of the effort. Fifteen county agents who made reports on the "midnight shock troops" estimated almost 3,000 volunteers in eight counties and 33,203 acres harvested across six counties. Wabasha County calculated the value of the volunteer work at $72,000. In Wright County the agent simply reported, "Because of the number of men taken into war service, the labor situation became very serious in July, August and September. . . . The prospects were that a large amount of crops would be lost. . . . Everyone available in the different towns signed up to assist. . . . As a result of this work, the crops were well taken care of."[47]

On troop train, bypassing the box cars labeled 40 hommes et 8 cheveaux [40 men and 8 horses], . . . slept under blankets on a flat car loaded with supply wagons. . . . We realized that we were becoming hungry so naturally our thoughts turned to food. . . . We went to the cooks who, after a little persuasion, gave us some warm hash, bread and coffee. After we had satisfied our appetite we went back to the car and fixed ourselves in a position from which we could best view the landscape on passing by.

Ingvald D. Smith, July 24, 1918[48]

4

Homegrown Vegetables Year-round

Diary, 1917—

May 1 After dinner we went up town to see patriotic parade.

May 2 Went out and had ice cream.

May 3 Spaded up part of the garden.

May 4 Worked in the garden.

May 5 Outdoors nearly all day.

May 7 Worked in garden.

May 8 Worked outdoors all day. Helped Clarence plant potatoes.

May 9 Mother and I at Clarence's. Finished planting.

Maybelle Jacobson[1]

In the spring of 1917, Maybelle Jacobson had just finished teaching in Beltrami and moved back to Crookston to live with her mother and be near her new fiancé, Clarence. A lifelong diarist, 23-year-old Maybelle wrote short notes about her days and what interested her. In 1916 she did not mention gardening, but in 1917 she wrote about it frequently. Her experiences were echoed across the state, where parades and patriotic events popped up like mushrooms. Many Minnesotans had long planted backyard gardens, but during World War I gardening became an important civic act. Governor J. A. A. Burnquist declared, "Every acre, every yard under cultivation will count in Minnesota's patriotic undertaking to make and save food for the nation." The chair of the Minnesota Commission of Public Safety's crops committee urged, "Let the Minnesota slogan be 'A Garden for Every Home.' Special attention should be given to crops that may be canned, preserved, or dried."[2]

Even before Congress voted to enter the war with Germany in early April 1917, home gardens had been seen as an important weapon against the "H. C. L.," or high cost of living. Food prices had increased relentlessly the previous summer and fall, and vegetable gardening had been a topic in many newspapers including the *Crookston Weekly Times* throughout the late winter and early spring. An advertisement from Minneapolis's Northrup King seed company clearly stated the problem and opportunity: "Beans and many other food products are worth more than at any time in the last quarter century. Yet you can raise a large proportion of your family's food in your own garden and keep your table bountifully supplied with all kinds of delicious fresh vegetables at very slight cost."[3]

But garden seeds were expensive, too. In February the *Times* announced "Gardeners to Suffer Here" because "Crookstonites who go in strong for gardening will hardly be pleased with the new recruits that 'General H. C. L.' has attached to his army." Noting increased prices for radish and spinach seed, among others, it blamed the wartime embargo on seeds from Holland, Germany, France, and England.[4]

Expensive seed or not, the desire to plant vegetables blasted ahead when gardens became *war gardens* not just against the H. C. L. but also against the Kaiser. Not only was gardening something everyone could do; it needed to be done right now. In many parts of the country early April is prime gardening season. In the Upper Midwest conditions may be good only for soil preparation and sowing of cold-tolerant crops. Still, the sooner the planning, seed purchasing, and staking out of new garden spaces happened, the sooner kitchen tables throughout the state could be filled with vegetable dishes taking the place of foods that must be conserved for soldiers and allies.

By May 1, patriotic parades began to set the tone across the state. In Crookston, more than 1,000 members of civic groups, churches, the Juvenile and Citizens Bands, and police and fire departments joined the tour of city streets. Ladies of the Red Cross marched "manfully" in a group of 100, with the Spirit of France represented by Miss Lucia Stone, dressed in a coat of mail, carrying a battle sword, and riding a white horse. The Citizens Auxiliary raised an "Awake America" banner, and parochial-school students, led by children

Food *is* Ammunition—
Don't waste it.

UNITED STATES FOOD ADMINISTRATION

In the spring of 1917 Minnesotans, like other Americans, had already started home vegetable gardens in the battle against the high cost of living. Their efforts increased dramatically when homegrown food became a weapon of choice against the forces of Germany's Kaiser Wilhelm.

dressed as Red Cross nurses flanking Uncle Sam, received "salvos of applause." Veterans from the "North and South Now United" marched behind impersonators of General Grant and General Lee riding horses side by side. Northwest School of Agriculture students carried garden tools and signs proclaiming their "desire and willingness to feed the armies of the world."[5]

Even Mother Nature appeared to cooperate with the patriotic activities in Crookston. Although snow fell on the morning of the parade, followed by a hailstorm at noon, the sun broke through just as the march began. The weather held for the rest of the week, so Maybelle Jacobson and others were able to begin their garden chores.

Novice and experienced gardeners alike found more resources than normal available for gardening. Communities that had set aside land for H. C. L. gardening expanded the plots available for war gardens. On the Iron Range in Eveleth, where nearly 6,000 flag-carrying citizens marched in the May Day parade witnessed by thousands of spectators, the Commercial Club took the lead in securing land for gardens. Suggesting that "few residents had sufficient land on their own lots," the club sought state holdings for that purpose and organized efforts to have it divided and tilled. In less than two weeks the city could announce, "Free ground for gardens up to an acre" on four sites, including state-owned land at St. Mary's Lake. The city offered to plow the land and provide a watchman, as long as gardeners cleared brush first. The Oliver Iron Mining Company gave garden plots and seed potatoes to 450 mining families at cost. Plans for school gardens developed.[6]

In southwestern Minnesota's Pipestone, the Current Events Club organized a community gardening effort. Individuals with vacant lots within the city limits and land "to rent gratis for gardening purposes" were urged to contact members of the gardening committee, while "those desiring land for gardening may secure same by applying to the committee."[7]

Patriotic vegetable eaters did not need to wait months for the first newly planted crops to come in. The noble onion was in good supply in the spring and early summer of 1917 and ready to serve in meat-stretching preparations. Before the war, magazines and cookbooks typically contained only a few simple vegetable recipes, mostly side dishes. After the war began, University of Minnesota home economists quickly began sending recipes to newspapers across the state, moving vegetables up to the front lines as a main course, beginning with suggestions for the plentiful bulbs. Onion recipes suggested boiling, baking, sautéing, stuffing, mashing, frying, escalloping, covering with cream sauce, basting with butter, and adding bacon.[8]

In early May, half the population of Winona marched in the town's patriotic parade, reportedly 12,000 people stretching along the route three miles long. The march concluded at the post office for a stirring patriotic rally, where the main speaker, Mr. Doherty, focused on the importance that food would play in war efforts. He concluded, "I cannot brand the word 'traitor' too deeply on the man who in this hour of stress will deliberately cause a shortage to exist in a commodity or necessity of general consumption for the purpose of enriching himself."[9]

Larger Minnesota cities had patriotic May Day celebrations, too. In Duluth 17,000 marched in a 35-minute parade. The *Duluth News Tribune* noted that "all participated and only the smallest percentage of Duluth's population took advantage of the half-holiday to use it for petty purposes." At the final rally, Senator George M. Patterson expressed the spirit of the community: "All of us cannot go to war. All should not go

VICTORY CABBAGE

4 cups thinly sliced red cabbage
2 tablespoons butter
1 tablespoon minced onion
½ teaspoon salt
pinch nutmeg
pinch cayenne pepper
2 tablespoons vinegar
1½ teaspoons sugar

Soak the cabbage briefly in cold water. Melt the butter in a large frying pan. Add the onion and seasonings and cook until the onion is transparent, stirring frequently. Drain the cabbage and add to the frying pan carefully, as the water clinging to the shreds will tend to spatter. Cover and cook over low heat until the cabbage is tender, about 10–15 minutes, stirring from time to time. Remove lid, add the vinegar and sugar, stir well, and cook for 5 more minutes. (*The Farmer's Wife*, July 8, 1918) to war. We *can* all successfully carry on war by attention to our farms and work in the factories and mines."[10]

A week after the April declaration of war, Minneapolis department store president L. S. Donaldson offered to provide prizes for the city's public schools' garden program. School superintendent B. B. Jackson suggested that "vegetable gardens [are] an aid to reduce the high cost of living and to increase the food supply of the community." Twenty-nine prizes would be awarded for vegetables, and only nine for flower gardens, with the top two prizes of $200 each. The school board allocated $1,000 to pay for "four or five agricultural men" who could "provide directions for planting and caring for the garden and booklets for keeping records and accounts."[11]

Just as quickly, N. J. Jones of St. Cloud offered several vacant lots for the "patriotic agriculture" gardens of the schoolchildren there. The students in the Crookston beginner and juvenile bands, with the wholehearted support of their director, skipped practice the first Saturday in May to put in their war gardens. Garden fever was spreading all over the state.[12]

Farmers were at the front lines of this battle to increase the food supply, and some of them saw risks in misplaced enthusiasm for backyard vegetable crops. "Disappointment or failure will face the inexperienced gardener," headlined an article in *Farmers Equity News* from Alexandria. The article pointed out that "the average back lot gardener with his complete ignorance of the first essentials of agriculture is doomed to disappointment in his endeavors to enlarge the food supply. . . . The spirit . . . is too valuable to go undirected by the proper expert guidance." The columnist suggested instead that gardeners work closely with the farmers out in the country.[13]

Civic leaders had a different sense of the relationship between farm crops and food on the table. In a proclamation on May 4, the mayor of Erskine, G. S. Walker, suggested that cultivation of vacant lots throughout the village and in individual backyards would "enable farmers to give more of their land to grain crops and stock, thereby increasing the supply of these food products." He also noted a secondary benefit: "The vacant lots if not cultivated will produce weeds, to the annoyance and cost to the whole village."[14]

This version of the American spirit "Columbia" by famed illustrator James Montgomery Flagg joined the work of other American artists donated to the Food Administration's information programs.

Newspapers also set out to harness the fervor of novice gardeners with advice on proper garden planning. The *Erskine Echo* published a nationally syndicated article, "Will you raise a garden this summer and help increase the national food supply?" that quoted Benjamin Albaugh, a national expert on city gardening or "gardenettes." Albaugh advocated "sandwich beds," created by placing a five-inch layer of straw, stable litter, or leaves on the gardening area, then covering this with three inches of stable manure, and soaking with a hose. Finally, gardeners added a layer of street scrapings, "avoiding those which have asphalt in them," or a mixture of "fine river sand, rich garden soil and old fine stable manure." Most Minnesotans probably followed the practice Albaugh identified as being used by "people of foreign birth, who from a desire to effect practical economies, or from an inherited penchant for the work, began industriously spading up small areas of unoccupied ground around their houses." The result would be garden produce that could be sold at "full market price."[15]

Northrup King Company's seed advertisements for 1917 began to include quotations from President Wilson, who urged, "Everyone who cultivates a garden helps greatly to solve the problem of the feeding of the nations." Ads also reassured beginning gardeners that seed packages included "full cultural directions."[16]

Governor Burnquist announced that the Minnesota Commission of Public Safety (MCPS) approved a gardening plan "formulated by the state committee of food production and conservation, the school authorities and the garden clubs." The plan's goal was "adding to the state's food production by intensive cultivation . . . beginning . . . with the publication of a bulletin giving exact directions for planning, planting, and cultivation of a garden."[17]

The MCPS distributed brochures written by the University Farms and Agricultural Extension Service. Professor R. S. Mackintosh's Special Bulletin No. 11, *A Garden for Every Home,* issued in May 1917, cheerfully combined practical information for successful gardening with encouraging examples. On the value of vegetables in the diet he wrote, "Perhaps some will find that a vegetable diet is a blessing. Somebody has said that it is better to eat vegetables than to take patent medicines." Citing the value of large community gardens, he

BAKED STUFFED CUCUMBERS

3 short, stubby cucumbers

½ cup minced ham

2 minced onions

2 tablespoons tomato catsup

1 cup stale bread crumbs

a little soup stock

tomato sauce or milk gravy

Preheat oven to 325° F. Cut cucumbers in half lengthwise; scoop out seeds. Boil the halves in salted water for 10 minutes. Allow one cucumber for each two people. Mix minced ham with onions, catsup, and bread crumbs; moisten with a little soup stock. Place in baking dish with a little hot water and bake until cucumbers are tender and stuffing is browned on top, 20–30 minutes. Serve with tomato sauce or milk gravy containing a little diced ham. (Ida C. Bailey, *Delicious Ham and Bacon Recipes* [Sioux Falls, S.D., 1918])

shared a friend's comment that community gardening in his town had been "a success in every way. Boys often say that they like to hoe and pull weeds."[18]

The special bulletin also recommended 16 "important vegetables" for families to "grow enough for daily needs and to can, dry or preserve for two years." Tomatoes were most important, given the variety of ways they could be used. Others on the list were beans (green, lima, and kidney), beets, cabbage, carrots, parsnips, turnips, lettuce, radishes, onions, peas, pumpkins, squash (summer and winter), spinach, Swiss chard, and potatoes. The professor ended with the sentiment, "Every little seed says: 'I am tiny, but I am willing to do my bit. Please, dear planter, give me good soil in which to grow, protect me from weeds, cultivate to conserve plant food and water in the soil, and at the proper time take me for whatever noble purpose you wish.'"

Professors at the Northwest School of Agriculture in Crookston provided advice to gardeners in that part of the state. Professor T. M. McCall urged home gardeners to raise "enough food for home use and to spare." Recognizing that farm animals needed to be fed something other than grains, he suggested farmers raise mangles (root vegetable similar to sugar beets), stock carrots, and rutabagas that "yield 12 to 20 tons per acre as feed for stock."[19]

**CHEESE AND
GREENS ROLL**

1 pound fresh
   spinach, chard, or
   other greens
1 tablespoon butter
1 cup grated mild
   cheese
½ cup (or more) soft
   bread crumbs

Preheat oven to 350° F.
Wash spinach or other
greens thoroughly.
Shake slightly to
remove excess water
and put into a frying
pan over medium heat.
Cover and cook until
greens are wilted. Drain
well and chop fairly
fine. Add butter and
grated cheese. Then the
bread crumbs. Form
into a loaf shape. Place
in a lightly greased pan
and bake until firm and
browned on top, 20–30
minutes. (*The Farmer,*
April 27, 1918)

Gardeners in the Twin Cities could refer to the Minneapolis Garden Club's handbook, *Vegetable Gardening in Minneapolis,* which included diagrams for a variety of garden sizes. The smallest was 20 by 40 feet. Reports from Albert Lea said that "nearly every family is making some plans to put in a garden," some quite large. "Two or three families are co-operating renting large plots of ground near the city . . . believing they can raise enough vegetables for their entire winter use."[20]

Some gardeners hoped to raise enough for a "cash crop." The Great Northern Railroad turned over to its employees 100,000 acres along its rail lines between St. Paul and Oregon for free gardening. Employees simply applied for the plot of land they wanted to work. The president of the line explained, "The period of use is for the crop season only. . . . Proceeds from the sale of the products will, of course, go to the employees who raise them."[21]

In Red Wing the managers of Red Wing Union Stoneware and Red Wing Sewer-pipe Company supported gardening by distributing seed potatoes to heads of families and others who wanted to raise gardens.[22]

Real estate developers made land available for gardens, too. Minneapolis's T. B. Walker offered up 7,000 unused building lots "for cultivation purposes for the coming season." H. T. Baldwin, agricultural instructor at St. Louis Park High School, coordinated the project. Individual farmers could use up to 40 acres if they had "equipment for handling an amount so large." The American Traction

Company offered preplanted war gardens as incentive for purchasers of their lots in New Garden City, only "30 minutes from the center of Minneapolis. Fertile soil, beautiful lake and bathing beaches. $300. Easy terms." In early May an employee of the Northern Field Seed Company reported on the progress of gardening in the southern half of the state. "In the villages . . . all the lots that formerly furnished their annual crop of weeds are being utilized. In many cases regular gardeners have enlarged backyard farms to acres."[23]

Even traveling salesmen caught the gardening bug, as the *Crookston Times* reported: "Around the hotel lobbies . . . the war talk has been replaced by chats of onions, beets, and the different varieties of potatoes. Each knight of the grip has his little farm at home, and his plans for Saturday and Sunday are always good subject for conversation. At Jackson last week . . . a group of traveling men were leaving town. Each carried a sack under his arm. Investigation revealed that they were from Minneapolis and had discovered a place where they could purchase seed potatoes at a bargain. They had all stocked up and were taking them home to plant."[24]

The editor of the *Mankato Ledger,* who published under the motto, "Keep Doing—You Never Can Tell," found his own plans for crops dashed by an experience that was front-page news. A thief stole more than a peck of his unplanted seed potatoes, "nearly as precious as gold." The editor continued, "As it is something over a mile to a safe deposit vault, and the lots being somewhat isolated," the editor took a chance by hiding the seed potatoes until he could get back to plant after a rainy period. The account concluded, "Good luck to the cuss that got them. Here's hoping that the next man he steals . . . from catches him at it and sickens him with a dose of buck shot."[25]

As spring turned into summer, gardeners shifted their attention to keeping their gardens thriving. Newspapers helpfully printed information on combating garden pests. Dallas Keck, Red Lake County agent in Oklee, took the long view and suggested using bran mash for cut worms: "The more insects you kill this year, the fewer you will have next year." He also offered a recipe for unusual greens: "For those tired of spinach or lettuce . . . the weed commonly known as 'lamb's quarter' makes a very appetizing dish."[26]

Esther Moran, supervisor of domestic science for the St. Paul public schools, similarly suggested eating early greens and wild vegetation. She recommended dandelion greens and beet and radish tops, providing some nutritional context for readers of the *St. Paul Pioneer Press:* "If we are to eat less meat, we must substitute . . . and that extra food may be the perishables, such as the vegetables, really the best things we can eat in the springtime. They furnish the body with minerals. . . . They furnish the bulk required to keep the digestive apparatus in perfect working order. They also have an energy value and in some cases have a muscle building property."[27]

In early summer a writer reported on his garden in the *Mankato Ledger,* noting that "basing our calculations upon the prices paid for a peck of green peas in St. Paul, we are about $2.36 ahead of the game on our pea crop. . . . We paid 15 cents for the seed, and we cheated ourselves out of a lot of loafing time while we were spading the ground, planting and weeding the rows, and the indications are good we will get two or three bushels more before the supply peters out."[28]

Throughout the summer of 1917, schoolchildren recorded the hours spent working in gardens, what they planted, and the value of their harvest. Some groups met weekly with a garden supervisor, prompting 12-year-old St. Cloud student Mildred Chittick to write that her supervisor "had an exhibition at the Commercial Club rooms. I got sixth prize, which was 25 cents on a quart of peas. When they scored the gardens on the first of July, I had the third best garden in the city. . . . We went to the high school and canned vegetables from our gardens. . . . I canned one pint of peas, one pint small carrots and one quart string beans."[29]

In September winners were named for produce grown in Eveleth's school gardens, including best container or bunch of beans, beets, cabbage, carrots, cucumbers, radishes, tomatoes, lettuce, onions, peas, and potatoes. Top prize in each category was a dollar. The *University Farm Press News* reported on Minneapolis's success: "About $50,000 worth of vegetables were raised in the school gardens this year. The value of the produce per acre was $785."[30]

In August the university extension service's Special Bulletin No. 14, *Preparation of Perishables for Market,* helped first-time gardeners who wanted to take their root vegetables, cabbages, and dry

A school class at Pipestone, like others across Minnesota, grew gardens in super-vised summer projects. Many competed for prizes varying from a dollar for the best bunch of radishes in Eveleth to the $200 "best school garden" prize in Minneapolis, where $50,000-worth of vegetables were grown in 1917.

beans to commission agents or sell them at farmer's markets. The eight-page booklet advised, "Proper grading and packing . . . often means the difference between profit and loss." It noted the hard work of harvesting truck garden vegetables. New farmers were cautioned that the vegetables needed to be cleaned and marketed in 140-pound sacks.

More advice came from the Food Administration, which encouraged people to buy fresh vegetables in bulk and explained how to store them. "Farmers . . . often have no furnaces in their cellars and a storeroom for fruits and vegetables is easily set aside there. The town dweller who has a heating plant in his basement and no out-of-door space has a problem. It is often possible to partition off a corner of his basement which has at least one window—two if possible—and to use the enclosure for a store house. Windows are essential to control the temperature of the room that would otherwise be too warm. . . . It is desirable to provide slat racks to hold the containers to insure a free circulation of air and to guard against rats and mice."[31]

Josephine Berry, director of the university's home economics program and an initiator of the state's food-conservation plans, offered advice for keeping garden foods over the winter. In addition to giving instructions on root vegetables, she wrote, "Tomatoes, if pulled up by the vine and hung in the cellar upside down, will ripen and furnish fresh fruit well into the winter."[32]

Homemaking columns began running recipes for using the increased supply of root vegetables. The *Mankato Ledger* featured the syndicated "The Kitchen Cupboard" column by Anna Thompson, which offered simple recipes such as creamed carrots, browned parsnips, creamed turnips, and combinations of dried and root vegetables.

Garden clubs across the state reported gardening successes. The St. Cloud club issued a thorough report in 1917 that 3,000 gardens were planted, but 10 to 15 percent of the gardeners "lost their enthusiasm when weeds got a good start." The remaining 2,500 gardens produced $37,000 of food and intangible benefits as well. "Hundreds of men who had hitherto thought gardening profitless play . . . will continue to have one in the years to come." Around the community, "The most noticeable thing is that hundreds of vacant lots and back yards that have heretofore been eyesores, if not breeders of disease through accumulations of refuse and weeds, have been cleaned out and made attractive as well as productive." As to the lasting impact, the club booklet claimed, "The garden movement nationwide is bound to result in America being less of a meat-eating nation," because a garden "filled with prime vegetables naturally effects the dinner table."[33]

By fall, garden plots along the Great Northern right-of-way produced enough food to fill "two freight trains 100 cars each" for the hundreds of families who used the donated plots, claimed Louis W. Hill, president of the line. Hill reported results from the 200-by-200-foot garden of Mrs. P. McCann of St. Paul. Mr. McCann "works in the . . . railway shops adjoining their home. . . . From five cents worth of pumpkin seeds, they raised 50 good pumpkins enough so that the [seven] McCann children are going to have pumpkin pie all winter long. From five cents worth of squash seeds, 95 squash were raised. From ten cents worth of parsnip seeds, they got one and [a] half bushels of parsnips. From two dozen tomato plants, four bushels of tomatoes were produced."[34]

Managing the harvest, storing the crops, and awarding prizes were not the only things on the minds of garden promoters. Since assuring the viability of the war gardens for the 1918 growing season was important, R. S. Mackintosh of the University Farm in St. Paul provided guidelines: "Every person having a war garden should save some seed this season. The war gardens of this year used up a large part of the surplus of certain kinds of garden seeds. . . . Seed should be saved as plants mature, dried thoroughly, and stored in a dry place where they are safe from mice and other pests. All seeds should be labeled."[35]

On farms, saving seed corn from the current year's crop was seen as critically important. University of Minnesota dairy specialist Arthur McGuire noted on his calendar the days in the fall when he selected the best-looking ears and put them in a cool, dry place so they would be viable in the spring. The extension service sent out 46,000 flyers, *Select Seed Corn to Hasten Peace,* urging careful selection of seed corn to increase yields. "Two days spent in the selecting of seed corn in Seed Corn Time, September 10–20, will mean at least 100 bushels more corn next year on every farm's 20 acres of corn. This will be worth at least $50."[36]

Although federal guidelines urged people to eat locally and put restrictions on nonessential transportation of food, Minnesotans were not limited to eating the vegetables they had put up in jars or down in root cellars with their meatless and wheatless dinners. Menus were not all potatoes, cabbages, carrots, and rutabagas. The Food Administration emphasized efficiency and balance of available resources. Conservation of foods that could be shipped overseas to soldiers and the Allies was the primary goal, and substituting fresh fruits and vegetables for these restricted foods was important. The Food Administration advised that rail shipments from growing areas to consumption centers across the nation required packing freight cars as full and as carefully as possible to make sure food got to its destination with little damage or wasted fuel.[37]

In December 1917, the *Mankato Daily Free Press* reported, "Made

Help for first-time gardeners was all around. Store window displays like this one in St. Paul offered encouragement, newspapers printed how-to articles, and the university published booklets with tips on growing, harvesting, storing, and even selling garden crops.

in America Christmas menus are going to be all the fad this year." The choice of shipped-in fruits and vegetables for Minnesota families included California lemons, navel oranges, celery, and cauliflower; Washington apples; Florida grapefruit; Louisiana greens; and carrots, shallots, head lettuce, hothouse leaf lettuce, radishes, parsley, tomatoes, cucumbers, and nuts from unspecified states.[38]

One of Duluth's largest grocery stores, Duluth Marine Supply, sold the best of homegrown and shipped-in foods. They advertised "Duluth-grown Wax Beans, Young Carrots and Strawberry Beets grown and packed by the Boy Scouts, put up in full quart jars. A trial will convince you that the above goods are of extra fine quality." The store also carried Florida grapefruit and lettuce, apples from New York and out west, and other nonlocal produce on its shelves.[39]

The *Duluth News Tribune*'s Market Basket column provided even more details on the complete range of fruits and vegetables shipped by rail into the northern city: apples and grapes from New York; pears from Colorado, Illinois, and Michigan; cranberries from Wisconsin and New Jersey; celery from Wisconsin, Michigan, and California; tomatoes from California; and onions and potatoes from Minnesota were among the fruits and vegetables identified by state of origin. This variety of fruits and vegetables was available through the winter, and in early spring, greens came from local hothouses.

Grocery-store trade magazines offered ideas to help retailers make the most of fresh produce. "Live Methods Sell Perishables. You must get quick turnover on your fruits and vegetables," advised the *American Grocer.* "Put a price on these goods that will do it. Make an appetizing display with them. They should look clean and attractive. Put your display where anyone coming into your store will be sure of seeing them and getting the appeal to buy. When talking to your customers over the phone suggest the fruit or vegetable that you have a long supply of on that day. Housewives like such hints. . . . Have some special in this department every day."[40]

By the second spring of America's involvement in World War I, German troops were ready to begin another big offensive. Thousands of Minnesota's young men were in military training camps or already fighting in Europe. Newspapers brought battle headlines into living rooms across the state, and once again Minnesotans began to garden to win the war. Northrup King consistently mentioned the need for food crops in its seed advertising to home gardeners and farmers, particularly crops that would keep well over long winters.

Heavy artillery against garden pests captured readers' attention

FRENCH-STYLE PEAS

1 cup coarsely chopped lettuce leaves
3 cups fresh peas
1 teaspoon minced parsley or mint leaves

Put the chopped lettuce in the bottom of a steamer or in a strainer placed over simmering water. Put peas and parsley or mint on top of the lettuce. Cover and steam until peas are tender, 15–20 minutes depending on freshness and size. ("Vegetable Hints," *U.S. Food Administration Bulletin,* June 10, 1918) in illustrated articles released to local papers by the U. S. Department of Agriculture. Pictures of menacing caterpillars and grubs were accompanied by a photo of a pump-action hand sprayer, a "necessary implement in the anti-insect campaign."[41]

Department of Agriculture and Food Administration news releases praised the 1917 bonanza results and encouraged 1918 progress. "It was prophesied that because more was planted last year than could be conveniently cultivated or cared for on maturity, there would be a big slump in the 1918 war gardens. But such is not the case. . . . Seed is scarcer than it was last year and there is none to waste. Study the location and extent of your garden and consider well the fruits and vegetables your family likes best before you buy your seeds."[42]

One of the biggest changes for gardeners, and everyone else, was the introduction of Daylight Saving Time in the spring of 1918, a system designed to help keep "the food supply marching along in time to the tune of America." Poetic license aside, government reports calculated that at least five million home producers would "in 7 months of 26 working days" each gain 352 hours, or more than 32 eight-hour days. "Five million soldiers of the soil will gain 910,000,000 hours, or 113,750,000 days. This is the equivalent of 311,644 years." These hours would "increase the efficiency of "these 'backyard munitions plant' workers by fully 25 percent."[43]

In the northern town of Eveleth, most school gardens were ready for sowing by May 23. War gardens became "Liberty Gardens," with 110 plots of varying size available for students. Three 20-by-40-foot plots were dedicated to supplying the school cafeteria with food grown from free government-inspected seeds. Students, who carried their own gardening tools, reported for duty three times a week and promised to write about their gardening experiences at the end of the growing season.[44]

In St. Cloud, citizens planted gardens on "nearly all the vacant and usable tracts of land." The newspaper noted that "a great deal of potatoes were planted this year" and predicted that they would supply the potato needs of the entire city.[45]

By early May, gardening advisors across the state launched a full-scale campaign to "stop the leaks in food production" caused

Some 1917 war gardens lost the battle to weeds. But after a winter filled with war news and sons and neighbors being called into battle, the 1918 gardening season was even more important and successful. (Artist William McKee)

by plant pests and diseases. University Farm specialists under the direction of Dean E. M. Freeman asked farmers and home gardeners to send samples of diseased plants and pests to the state entomologist, A. G. Ruggles. He quickly received "living specimens of injured plants . . . and thousands of insects . . . sent through the mails in tight wooden boxes to be analyzed." According to the *Minneapolis Journal,* Ruggles sent back advice "that promises to seal the doom of millions of pests."[46]

Continuing the war against food waste, other publications offered advice for how to cook crops that had been left in the garden too long before picking. The USDA's *Tips for Cooking Mature Vegetables* suggested that large, overgrown radishes could be cooked like turnips. Wilted vegetables could be soaked in cold water until they regained crispness, and lettuce that "has grown too old for salad" could be chopped, cooked, and served with a cream sauce.[47]

Encouraging wheat savings, *The Farmer's Wife* printed scientific tips on getting nutrition out of vegetables that were substituted for bread, noting that one dish of lima beans, one-third cup of corn, two tomatoes, three cucumbers, three cups of chopped celery, 18 ounces of lettuce (more than two heads), or five cups of cabbage each had the same energy-producing value as two slices of bread. The article continued, "It should be remembered, however, that when other ingredients are served with these vegetables, they not alone add to the flavor, but they add perceptibly to the amount of food value. To add a few nuts and French dressing to cabbage, for instance, will double its food value. Therefore, the same amount that served plain equals two half-inch pieces of bread when treated in this way becomes equal to three slices."[48]

Farmer's Wife food columnist Pearl Bailey Lyons considered fruits and vegetables important in all areas of food conservation. Green peas and beans such as kidney and lima were fine substitutes for meat. Potatoes, sweet potatoes, and bananas could be grain and wheat substitutes. Sweet potatoes, corn, melons, and fruit could be sugar savers.[49]

By war's end, home gardens had proved to be a hugely popular boost to food conservation across the country. In 1917 and 1918 communities across Minnesota proudly boasted of their successful

The Fruits of Victory

Write for Free Book to

National War Garden Commission

Washington, D.C.

Charles Lathrop Pack, President   P.S. Ridsdale, Secretary

Assuring all of the homegrown bounty could serve as meat and wheat substitutes, state and federal agencies published a wide range of brochures, sent main-dish recipes to newspapers and magazines, and put on local demonstrations of canning and drying. (Artist Geonebel Jacobs) community gardening efforts. Minneapolis's 1918 Liberty Garden, in fact, received national recognition. According to H. U. Nelson, secretary of the Minneapolis Garden Club, more than 10,000 families planted gardens on more than 2,000 acres and grew crops valued at nearly $500,000. "This number is almost 30 percent more than that of its nearest rival and does not include the 1,500 gardens outside the city limits cultivated by Minneapolitans."[50]

National statistics reported that in 1917 Americans added three million new gardens, and in 1918 the number increased to five and one-quarter million. These gardens produced food valued at $525 million. While gardening offered a simple way for people to feel that they were doing their part for a national cause, volunteer gardeners also produced the nutritional equivalent of meat for one million soldiers for 302 days and bread for 248 days, or their entire ration for 142 days.[51]

> Canning was a big factor in making our garden a success. What we couldn't eat, we sold; what we couldn't sell, we canned; what we couldn't can, we fed our poultry, so none of it was wasted. Our summer kitchen was our cannery, and the wash boiler our canner. We put up 221 quarts.
> *Ralph Baerman, State Champion Garden Club Member*[52]

By the time Minnesotans planted their vegetable gardens in the late spring and early summer of 1917, the first fruits from winter-hardy berry patches and orchards were ready to be picked. Conservation-minded gardeners dutifully even "put up" the stalwart rhubarb crop as jam, jelly, and conserve. As the search for food savings spread beyond garden patches, *The Farmer* urged readers to "save wild fruit" and suggested neighbors could gather all they could and make a community project by giving "half a day" to pick and can wild crab apples or berries: "Let none of this food go to waste."[53]

In June 1917, before the federal government had begun producing educational brochures about canning and preserving, Josephine Berry of the university's home economics department gave readers of *The Farmer's Wife* a comprehensive recommendation for storing fruits and vegetables: "Tomatoes, greens, spinach, Swiss chard,

RHUBARB AND RAISIN JAM

4 cups rhubarb cut in ½-inch pieces   1 cup raisins
1 cup sugar   2 cups orange juice

Mix rhubarb and sugar; let stand 4–5 hours. Then bring to a boil over medium heat. Chop raisins, add to rhubarb, lower heat, and cook slowly for about 30 minutes, stirring from time to time, until the mixture is quite thick. Add orange juice and bring back just to boiling. Put in sterilized jars and process according to USDA guidelines, or store in refrigerator for up to a month. (*The Farmer's Wife,* June 1917)

dandelion greens, cauliflower, rhubarb and asparagus should be canned. . . . Canning is the only satisfactory way of keeping berries of all kinds and grapes." Foods that could be dried included "plums, apples, peaches, apricots, cherries, currants and pears, corn, string beans, lima beans, peas, squash and pumpkins. String beans, cucumbers and sweet corn (cooked long enough to set the milk) may be salted down."[54]

City cooks in Minnesota who relied on the bounty of other states to fill their jam and jelly jars needed to scurry, the *Minneapolis Journal* suggested in a front-page article in early May 1917. "Fruit canning housewives who figure frugally on waiting until September when fruit is cheap are in for the surprise of their lives. The government has stepped in and commandeered practically all the California fruit crop for factories which are now being constructed. California cherries are now selling for $2.50 to $3.25 and 35-pound cases at $4.50 to $5. This season will last only four or five days. Georgia peaches will be shipped north green and will be on the market in about 10 days. After that there will be practically no fruit to be had."[55]

Despite these warnings, during the summer some fruit did make it into Minnesota grocery stores. The Model Grocery in New Ulm offered pineapples for canning in July but urged customers to "get them now, as the crop will be short on account of frosts in Florida."[56]

Moved by the urgency to preserve food and by uncertainty about

Whether it was seeing green-striped potato bugs as soldiers in the Kaiser's army or calling your vegetable preservation group the "Can the Kaiser Club," young people and a few adults took advantage of the German emperor's title to inspire food conservation efforts. (Artist J. Paul Verrees)

supplies of proper canning containers, readers wrote farm magazines to share their tips. One woman recommended making do with previously used containers. "I have canned berries in syrup and molasses cans with good success. Also tomatoes and other vegetables can be canned this way. To seal the pails, red sealing wax or rosin and a little lard melted together is good. Sterilize cans and lids perfectly. Put lid on pail as soon as it is filled, and put the boiling hot wax or rosin around the edge. . . . Of course the cans must be perfectly sound and free from rust."[57]

Across Minnesota, county fairs put on canning demonstrations and exhibits along with lessons about baking Liberty Bread. Organizers of the State Fair promised to do everything they could to "encourage food production and conservation." Mildred Weigley of the university's home economics department applied this conservation mandate to the judging of canned goods. Instead of putting the opened jars on display, which would make the food spoil, she had them reprocessed after judging so the food would not be wasted.[58]

The university's extension service, the USDA, and Food Administration strongly promoted a new cold-pack method for canning fruits and vegetables. This process used an item found in practically every home—a wash boiler that held from 15 to 20 gallons of water. Home canners blanched vegetables or fruits by submerging them briefly in boiling water, cooled them in an ice-water bath, and then packed them quickly into hot jars, topped off with hot salt water or

APPLE CATSUP

1 quart unsweetened applesauce
1 teaspoon ginger
1 teaspoon cinnamon
1 teaspoon cloves
2 cups vinegar
1 teaspoon pepper
1 teaspoon ground mustard
1 teaspoon onion extract or juice
2 teaspoons salt

Combine all ingredients in a large, heavy pot. Simmer over medium heat. Cook, stirring frequently, until mixture is thick and reduced by at least half. Put in sterilized jars and process according to USDA guidelines, or store in refrigerator for up to 2 weeks. (*Wallaces' Farmer*, August 22, 1918)

Big cook stoves were just the thing to manage the new cold-pack method for home canning.

syrup for fruits. Canners sealed the jars with rubber gaskets and screw-down zinc lids (or snapped the top wire into place), and then carefully lowered the jars into boiling water, where they cooked from 12 minutes for sliced apples to 90 minutes for lima beans.[59]

This new cold-pack method was considered so simple a child could do it, and many did. Even before the war, Boys and Girls Clubs (a precursor to 4-H Clubs), offered canning classes and contests. After war was declared, T. A. Erickson, director of club work at the university farm in St. Paul, sent a memo recruiting students across Minnesota in garden club and canning club work. At the Minnesota State Fair, Boys and Girls Club members put up jars of vegetables in live demonstrations. The 1917 winner was Elsie McNail of Sleepy Eye. Her work was judged best in skill, speed, and cleanliness, and her product had the best flavor, texture, and appearance. As reported by the *Brown County Journal,* the demonstration was accompanied by "patriotic yells, most of them ending with the name 'Hoover!'" and "crowds gathered to hear club members sing their songs and give their club cheers as they canned." O. H. Benson, a national club leader and the inventor of the cold-pack canning method, was on hand, and he noted, "Minnesota is far ahead of any state in the work."[60]

Many public schools organized their own clubs. During summer, students brought vegetables from their gardens and put them up, with supervision, in demonstration classes. In Nyva Johnson's article about the experience, "How I Helped Win the War by Canning at Home," she wrote, "Most all the girls were of the fifth and sixth grade. Although they were small, they did a very good work for their age. . . . We named our club the Kill the Kaiser Klub. . . . The more we could find out from demonstrating, the better it was for us. . . . I canned a total of 561 quarts of vegetables, fruits, and meats. . . . Next year I will try and can more because I will have an earlier start."[61]

The University of Minnesota organized canning demonstrations for adults as well. It sent demonstration agents across the state in early summer, even before Congress enacted Food Administration funding in August 1917. The timing was crucial. Fruit and vegetable crops were ready for harvest. Food would be wasted if not preserved. Many communities took the initiative. Verna Smollet of Eveleth noted on May 22, 1917, that "the school has purchased a steam pressure canner which will be at the disposal of

CORN RELISH

5 cups sweet corn, cut from the cob (about 15 large ears)
1½ green peppers, chopped into ⅛-inch pieces
1 red pepper, chopped into ⅛-inch pieces
4 cups finely chopped cabbage (1 medium)
½ cup sugar
2 ounces dry mustard
4 cups vinegar
½ cup corn syrup

Chop the vegetables by hand (or in a food processor). Combine the vegetables in a large cooking pot. Add the sugar and mustard, then the vinegar and corn syrup. Stir until well blended. Bring to a boil over medium heat, lower the temperature, and simmer until the vegetables are soft, 15–20 minutes. Ladle mixture into sterilized jars and process according to USDA recommendations, or store in refrigerator for up to 2 weeks. Yield: 7 pints. (*The Farmer's Wife*, September 1918) the ladies of the community during the summer." Mayme Bohlander from Montevideo reported, "Our agricultural instructor has been giving quite a number of canning demonstrations this summer and fall. Quite a good number of people have attended, brought vegetables and have done the work at the school."[62]

Interest in food preservation peaked with the harvest season. A writer in Crow Wing County noted, "Thursday we had a very successful demonstration of string beans and canned 24 quarts and salted down 5 gallons (German method) which we placed at the disposal of the Associated Charities." Sauerkraut, the Midwest's favorite method for preserving cabbage, received a hearty endorsement in an interview with Herbert Hoover, who said, "Turning up the nose at sauerkraut because it smacks of Huns [is] ill advised patriotism. It is good food despite its suspicious name." He continued that "the more of it that is eaten, the more staple foods there will be to send to soldiers abroad." Finally, he humorously assured people that because sauerkraut was more Dutch than German in origin, it "must be classed as a neutral and not enemy dish."[63]

By 1918 Minnesota's cities joined wholeheartedly in the food preservation campaign. In St. Paul, a Community Food Center on East Eighth Street opened its doors in July under the direction of Genevieve Burgan. During the next three months, the center hosted 102 demonstrations for 3,000 people and canned 27,792 quarts of vegetables. Another 186 women trained to teach classes in their neighborhoods to 1,950 people. Some 8,000 pounds of vegetables were dried and sacked at the center.[64]

By the end of 1918, the Boys and Girls Club's annual report also tallied significant accomplishment. About 22,010 quarts of fruit, 109,360 quarts of vegetables, and 7,680 quarts of jams, jellies and preserves had been canned. The value of these goods put up by more than 3,500 members was $70,017.20.[65]

Minnesota's commercial canneries also rose to the food conservation challenge. During the 1917 season they packed more than 5 million cans of corn, 1.5 million cans of peas, and 700,000 cans of sauerkraut. (The kraut figure excluded "large quantities put up in wooden containers.") Much of the state's canned food was already contracted for purchase by the military's "Commissary Department,

PICCALILLI

6 pounds ripe or green tomatoes or mixed
1 cabbage (approximately)
2 large cucumbers, peeled and seeded
½ bunch celery
¼ cup salt

2 cups sugar
¼ ounce mustard seed
⅛ ounce celery seed
1 teaspoon black pepper
2 cups vinegar

Chop all the vegetables very finely. Have an equal amount of cabbage and tomatoes. Combine them with the salt and let stand overnight in a cool place. In the morning, drain off the juices and put the vegetables in a large kettle. Add the remaining ingredients, stir well, and bring to a boil. Lower heat and simmer until vegetables are just tender but still crisp. Pour into sterilized jars and seal according to USDA rules, or store in refrigerator for a week. (Catherine Dean Cummings, *Making Food Conservation Interesting* [Simmons Hardware Company, 1918 (?)])

who are ever on the alert to secure the very best canned foods possible for our armies and navy."[66]

The university's advice for drying produce was particularly well received by teachers at training sessions for home economists in the summer of 1917. Drying had a distinct advantage over canning. Dried food could be stored in any kind of container (which did not need to be sterilized), and it took up far less space than canned food. The university recommended that produce be cleaned, sliced, and placed in a warm place to dehydrate—often on a rack up near the top of the stovepipe. The teachers-in-training found the lessons helpful, and one noted that drying was "one of grandmother's methods of preservation [that] has been dropped by the wayside."[67]

As summer harvests continued, a commercial manufacturer of food grinders suggested one way to address cooks' concerns about the abundance of garden produce. "The zealous war gardener often finds that after his garden begins to produce, there are many vegetables which grow so prolifically that it is impossible to use them all up if served in the ordinary way. . . . There are many delicious relishes and similar dishes which can be made from the war garden surplus and in making them you will find a good food chopper almost indispensable." Pickle relishes and sweet preserves took more preparation time but less processing time. A large quantity of chopped, pickled vegetables could fit into one jar, and the sharp or sweet flavors added an enjoyable zest to winter meals.[68]

By the late summer of 1918, strategies for saving fruit, and at the same time saving sugar, became a serious focus. As reported in *Minnesota at War,* the bulletin of the MCPS, sugar supplies for commercial use had been cut in half. While home-canning allotments of up to ten pounds per household (enough for about 20 pints of jelly) were available, home cooks were urged to save sugar by simply putting up the strained fruit juices without sugar and then later making small batches into jelly.[69]

A. D. Wilson, head of the state's food commission, defined the urgency and the responsibility in an appeal to the people of Minnesota. "Vegetables and fruits properly canned and stored now for winter use will greatly reduce the home demand of meat and bread. They will thereby release stores of foodstuffs for the armies which are fighting to give the world liberty and peace and for the people who have been going hungry that such armies might be fed."[70]

My Dearest, I almost forgot to tell you that I went blackberry picking this morning and picked about a quart. I put some sugar on them and had the best meal I've had since we ate together. I suppose it is getting pretty cool in Cloquet. Too cold for blackberries, I'll bet. Remember last fall when we all went after hickory nuts. I only wish we were back there now, but I really don't think it will be so very long 'til we can be back there again. Your loving husband,
David L. Beckman. Somewhere in France [1918].[71]

5

"Meating" the Challenges:
More Meals from Less

I took the final oath to make a sacrifice for my government and received my uniform and took up new quarters on the other side of Paris Island. . . . We have good food but *never any cake or pies*. . . . Tomorrow is Sunday and the regulars know what we'll get but I know they have a special meal. Last Sunday the regulars tell me they had chicken. Our eats are very good and no man in service of Uncle Sam could be treated better than us Marines. *Raymond Brunswick*[1]

As tens of thousands of young men left their Minnesota homes for military service, the food they needed to become a strong fighting force had to shift with them. Prewar home-cooked meals had often included meat three times a day. Breakfast might typically include bacon, sausage, or hash made from leftover meat. Dinners often centered on a substantial meat dish. A third meal, either noon lunch or evening supper, often featured a lighter meat dish, such as sandwiches, croquettes, or soup. While main dishes might be fish, eggs, or cheese, more often than not people cooked beef or pork. Homemakers rarely served chicken.[2]

Early in the war, federal food administrator Herbert Hoover determined how the nation could stretch and shift its meat supply. He focused on four key elements: eliminating waste, increasing meat production, eating unpopular meat varieties, and substituting eggs, cheese, and beans, often in disguised ways, for the meat in familiar recipes. In 1917, hot dishes or casseroles had not found a place in American cuisine, although *Good Housekeeping* had published a few recipes for "meals from the oven," which it claimed were particularly useful on ironing days when the stove needed to be used for heating

the irons. Recipes for casseroles of any kind received little attention. Minneapolis's Hennepin Avenue Methodist Episcopal Church
Culinary Guide, for example, offered only one, "Veal in Casserole."[3]

A recipe booklet issued in 1917 by Wright County's Howard Lake
Library and Improvement Club reflected the restrictions that the
"H. C. L." (high cost of living) and the war placed on everyday kitchens. Most of the 21 recipes in the meat chapter called for ground or
leftover meats used in hash, sauce, or meat loaf. Four use canned
salmon or shrimp. Of the four chicken recipes, Mrs. Murdock's "nice
way to cook a chicken" is the only one that called for chicken on the
bone in recognizable cuts; her instructions, however, suggest that
the specified "young" fowl is no spring chicken, as the recipe says
to cook it "in a little water for an hour" before coating with crumbs
and browning on a griddle.[4]

In the spring of 1917 chickens and eggs were expensive, and they remained so throughout the war. Unlike beef and pork, meats that were
largely managed and processed by five major meat-packers in Chicago,
the nation's chicken supply was raised on "millions of small units
scattered over a wide area," according to a report from the Food Administration. High feed costs in 1916 discouraged some small farmers from
raising poultry for sale, and many who had flocks lost birds or chickens
in harsh weather conditions.[5]

"Egg prices highest known this summer," the *Brown County Journal*
headlined on August 4, 1917. "Farmers have been killing their hens

CREAMED CHICKEN

Meat from one boiled
  chicken
Salt and pepper to taste
1 teaspoon butter
1 teaspoon flour
1 cup cream
1 cup buttered bread
  crumbs

Preheat oven to 325° F.
Cut the chicken meat
medium fine; add salt
and pepper to taste. Put
in a lightly greased bak-
ing dish. Melt the butter
in a small saucepan, stir
in the flour until it bubbles, gradually add the
cream, and stir until the
sauce thickens. Pour the
sauce over the chicken.
Top with buttered bread
crumbs. Bake until nicely
browned. (*Everybody's
Best* [Howard Lake,
Minnesota, 1917], Min-
nesota Historical Society)

because of the high price of feed, and there was a widespread [cold] storage movement last fall by dealers who anticipated a big foreign demand for poultry. This demand never materialized, and dealers now have frozen poultry on their hands for which there is only a limited market. Housewives are loath to purchase it, and frozen stock rarely goes over a market counter. It is said there are fewer eggs in storage at this time of the year than for many years."

Throughout 1917 and 1918, chicken was the most expensive meat for sale in grocery stores and meat markets across the state. It cost more per pound than beef steaks, pork loin, or veal chops and up to three times as much as the cheapest sausages or soup bones. In August 1917, Duluth Meat Supply advertised fresh-dressed broiler chickens at 30 cents a pound, rib roast at 22 cents, veal chops at 20 cents, and ring bologna at 10 cents a pound. Not surprisingly, chicken was not a regular source of protein for Minnesotans. Monthly and weekly planning menus printed in newspapers as well as farm and women's magazines confirm chicken's infrequent place on every-day tables.[6]

In fact, chicken was usually reserved for special dinners, such as a meal for departing soldiers. Some 20,000 people crowded the streets of New Ulm on September 4, 1917, for a parade and speeches by Governor Burnquist and other dignitaries. The event saluted the first men called up in the draft and volunteer enlistees leaving for training at Camp Dodge, Iowa. The banquet that night, held in a "dining room profusely decorated with national colors," featured watermelon cocktail, wafers, spring fried chicken, salad, mashed potatoes, peas, jelly rolls, rye bread, ice cream, cake, coffee, and cigars.[7]

Fancy dinners such as one prepared by a cooking class for the Eveleth school board in mid-March 1917 had become a thing of the past. That five-course dinner began with oyster cocktail and wafers, and tomato bouillon, followed by a main course of roast turkey, mashed potatoes, dressing, buttered peas, asparagus tips and toast, cranberry jelly, stuffed celery, peach pickles, head lettuce with Roquefort cheese, and a frozen pudding dessert with assorted cakes, coffee, and nuts. Showing a sea change in consciousness within a month after the beginning of the war, the *Eveleth News* suggested a dinner recipe to homemakers that combined leftover meat and rice.[8]

Soldiers from St. James depart from festivities at the county fairgrounds. Cities and towns sent their soldiers off to training camp with ceremonies, speeches, and special dinners.

War-driven patriotism stimulated dedication to food conservation measures beginning with reducing every bit of food waste. In
May 1917 the *Brown County Journal* wrote that rich and poor families
had removed phrases such as "Don't like it" and "Won't eat it" from
their language and kept "everything possible out of the garbage
pail." The city of Duluth even inspected garbage during Clean-Up
Week in May 1917. Mrs. J. M. Hickox of the Associated Charities
scolded homemakers, boardinghouse keepers, and society host-
esses when she described the leavings of an extravagant women's
dinner this way: "There were too many courses, an entrée and roast
chicken. . . . I am convinced that when the garbage collector comes
in the morning he will find a considerable portion of the dinner."
She concluded by calling for action: "Sharpen your knives. Get your
housekeeping down to science."[9]

The *Mankato Daily Free Press* similarly urged readers to "Watch
your kitchen waste. Don't throw any leftovers that can be reheated
or combined with other foods to make palatable and nourishing dishes. . . . Every scrap of meat and fish can be combined with

cereals or vegetables for making meat cakes or meat or fish pies and so on, and to add flavor and food value." The newspaper further suggested that "when meat is boiled, the water dissolves out some valuable food and flavoring material. Save such water for soup."[10]

Almost everyone writing about food conservation faulted careless American food-wasting habits and pointed to Europe for inspiration. As Mrs. Hickox in Duluth chided, "A few days in French kitchens would teach the American women how to conserve food."[11]

American cooks began in earnest to develop creative ways of using leftovers. A booklet for the Kleen Kutter meat grinder company by Catherine Dean Cummings read, "Leftovers used to be the housewife's problem. Today they are the solution of a problem." Cummings's recipe for meat cakes, which used leftover meat, stock, and stale bread crumbs, seemed luxurious compared to the plain bread and gravy cakes offered in a *Wallaces' Farmer* recipe. The latter recipe's key to success was the serving suggestion: "It is a good idea to have the supply short, and to preface their entrance with the remark that men who work hard deserve to be fed well, though it does seem like an extravagance."[12]

KLEEN KUTTER MEAT CAKES	WALLACES' FARMER MEAT CAKES
Put any kind of cold cooked meat through Kleen Kutter Food Chopper, using cutter with the smallest holes. Moisten 1 cup bread crumbs with milk or soup stock and mash fine. Add 1 egg well beaten and salt and pepper. Mix with meat, make into flat cakes, and fry in hot butter. (Catherine Dean Cummings, *Making Food Conservation Interesting* [St. Louis, Mo.?, 1918?])	Mix into leftover gravy enough bread crumbs sufficient to absorb the gravy. Let stand until supper time. Stir in a tablespoon flour, a teaspoon baking powder, and 1 egg. A little chopped onion is liked by some. Fry in spoonfuls or bake in ramekins. (*Wallaces' Farmer*, November 9, 1917)

The *Wallaces' Farmer* writer raised the standard for camouflage cookery. "An artist in camouflaging gets no laurels—she does her work so skillfully that her family never finds out. The sign that one has achieved the artist stage is the suggestion on the part of a family member that Hoover is asking for economy and conservation. Then the camouflage cook proudly hugs herself, puts another cup of corn meal in her fruit cake, substitutes coffee for milk, and another tablespoon of corn starch instead of an egg." The article concluded, "Most housekeepers are too sparing of the words which belong to camouflaging. Work up some enthusiasm about the quality of all such dishes, be a little sparing with them, and occasionally serve a really, truly before-the-war dish for variety."[13]

Conservation and restrictions were one path to increasing meat supply. Increasing production was another. People knowledgeable about animal husbandry quickly urged simple steps, such as the agricultural teacher at Thief River Falls high school who suggested giving boys hogs, beef cattle, and lambs to raise for six months, exhibit for prizes, and then sell for slaughter.[14]

The problem of increasing meat production was far from simple because in 1917 livestock production was almost as seasonal as growing vegetables. Calves, usually born in early spring, were weaned and marketed as veal before fall. If fed through the winter, they could be sold the next spring, summer, or fall as beef. Similarly, early spring lambs could be used for meat in the summer or kept through the fall and winter to be sold as mutton. If a farmer lacked resources to raise a large number of hogs, brood sows were sent to market in the spring before they bore another litter. Chickens laid more eggs in spring, and if the eggs were allowed to hatch and mature, the new hens would begin laying in the late winter. Chickens could be ready for the frying pan in eight weeks, or they could be sold months later as roasting hens, with more meat on their bones.

In April 1917 K. A. Kirkpatrick, agricultural agent for the more than 30,000 rural residents of Hennepin County, offered suggestions for increasing the county's food supply. "Raise more poultry than ever, as poultry yields quick results in meat. Keep all brood sows, regardless of the temptation to sell them at the present high prices. Add as many cattle as possible to breeding stock now on farms, regardless of the high cost of acquiring such cattle." Alarmed by the "heavy traffic" to the slaughterhouse, the editor of the *Mankato Ledger* similarly urged "the food censor to get on the job with both feet and save the brood sow at any hazard," thereby avoiding reduction of "the supply of purchasable pigs to an alarming extent."[15]

In the following week's paper the *Ledger* editor suggested that Minnesotans could increase food supplies by bringing the farmyard into town if the Mankato city council "did not have such a sensitive set of smelling organs. Those fine smellers are keeping the people . . . out of the privilege of raising and providing themselves with at least 25,000 pounds of pork next winter at a cost not to exceed six cents a pound, even with feed at the price which it now commands," by refusing to suspend enforcement of an ordinance that "rules out the family hog and the home meat supply."[16]

Herbert Hoover shared the Mankato editor's enthusiasm for the humble hog. Hoover sought a 15 percent increase in hog production to provide more pork meat and lard for the Allies. But 1917 had been a bad year for hog farmers. The price of corn, the feed for most farm-raised hogs, had tripled over the previous two years. This resulted in piglets "going to town," farm shorthand for going to the slaughterhouse.[17]

H. A. Wallace, editor of the leading agricultural newspaper *Wallaces' Farmer,* argued that patriotism alone would not guarantee increased hog productions. Farmers needed to be assured some profit. Hoover's Swine Commission studied the problem and quickly responded with a plan to link the price paid farmers for pork to the cost of corn. Hoover announced in November 1917, "We will try and stabilize the price so that the farmer can count on getting for each 100 pounds of hog ready for market, 13 times the average cost of corn fed into the hogs." This successful policy encouraged farmers to raise more hogs. The resulting supply available for meat in the second half of 1918 was 30 percent higher than normal production and made it possible to remove the request for meatless days.[18]

While families across Minnesota consumed similar breads, vegetables, and sweets, their meat choices varied. Rural residents ate more pork, and city dwellers ate more beef. Farm families typically

Lumberjack cooks in the Minnesota north woods made good use of pork raised as a war measure in the camp clearings, as these waiting carcasses suggest.

raised, cured, and smoked their own pork, which they stored in a smokehouse or icehouse. Although neither consumed much chicken, farmers did so slightly more often (about 15 percent of their meat compared to 10 percent for city residents).[19]

An article in the *Erskine Echo* explained the important role chickens played in farm life. "Every farmer should keep enough chickens to supply eggs and meat for family use. . . . The average farm will support a considerable number of fowl on waste products. . . . The flock is the only available supply of fresh meat during the summer for the average farmer, especially if he lives any distance from town. On many farms the proceeds from the sale of eggs during the laying season pays the grocery bill. . . . Chickens can be taken care of by the farmer out of working hours or by the children or old people."[20]

Enterprising patriots offered suggestions and took unusual actions to increase Minnesota's meat supply. The *Crookston Times* printed the strong opinions of Hazen J. Titus, a well-known resident in charge of railroad dining car service on the Northern Pacific Railway. "Cut out the use of veal. There is very little nourishment in veal. . . . Let all the calves grow into cattle. Then raise squirrels and rabbits. Ever eat squirrels? They're fine. There isn't any kind of meat in the world so good as rabbit. . . . Rabbits can be raised with very little trouble and are very prolific."[21]

Titus wasn't the only person considering alternative meat sources. Burt Day of Hutchinson suggested eating muskrats because hunters trapped and killed thousands for fur during the winter. He noted "250 tons of good food will be wasted," adding that a Michigan yacht club hosted "an annual muskrat dinner, and reservations are always at a premium."[22]

Frog legs had some supporters, too. Under the headline "Next year's fish bait is rapidly disappearing," the *Long Prairie Leader* said, "Two enterprising fellows from Chicago were busy in the vicinity of Maple Lake" catching and shipping frog legs. "They are shipping a barrel a day, each shipment amounting to a thousand pair of legs for which they received 12 cents a dozen. Frog legs are considered a delicacy there and find a ready market." These entrepreneurs apparently captured between 3,000 and 4,000 dozen pairs of legs by stretching a screen of cloth too high for the frogs to jump over along the shore. The "little fellows" then attempted to pass around its ends, but "this trait spells their downfall, for at intervals of 20 feet along the barrier, holes of considerable depth are dug, into which the frogs fall. They are later gathered up and dressed for shipment, the latter operation being the only effort required of the men who are in charge of the unusual industry."[23]

According to the Crookston newspaper, men in Morris were able to ship five tons of the desirable amphibians trapped along the shores of Lake Harris after stretching nets for nearly a mile just before freeze-up in the fall. It required 50 tons of legs "to make the required selection of larger ones" and about three days, the length of the season.[24]

Minnesota's lakes and rivers were a logical source of quality protein to substitute for farm-raised meats. Booth Fisheries Company advertised "Fish for Beef" as early as 1913 and touted the

WARTIME DEVILED FISH

Cooked halibut or cod, cut into small, neat pieces, and brushed with
   melted drippings or butter
1 teaspoon chutney
½ teaspoon curry powder
½ teaspoon dry mustard
1 teaspoon anchovy essence
bread crumbs
butter

Preheat oven to 350° F. Finely chop teaspoon of bottled chutney. Spread
with other ingredients on each piece of fish, place on baking dish, sprinkle
with bread crumbs, and dot with butter. Place in oven for 10 minutes.
(*Mankato Ledger,* October 3, 1917)

company's efficiency in transporting fish to market—"guaranteed
to be fresh—not only on certain days of the week, but every day."
Booth handled fish from the Great Lakes, primarily yellow pike,
sturgeon, herring, pickerel, and perch. The dressed fish were packed
in boxes and shipped east in refrigerated carload lots.[25]

Both the state of Minnesota and the federal government actively
promoted and marketed fish. As the *St. Cloud Daily Times* reported,
"A. F. Shira of the U.S. Commerce Department's Bureau of Fisheries
came to speak on Saturday afternoon at a demonstration of the
preparing and preservation of fish as a 'body building food.'" Shira
toured midwestern cities, including St. Louis, Kansas City, Omaha,
Minneapolis, St. Paul, Milwaukee, Chicago, and Indianapolis, to ex-
tol the value of fish, primarily the abundant Mississippi River carp.[26]

In St. Cloud, the hoped-for audience did not materialize. An article in the *Daily Times* observed that the women "did not take the
advantage given them last Saturday in learning a few lessons in food
conservation" and ignored various bulletins on salting and smoking
fish and the value of carp as food.[27]

Nor did Wisconsin women seem to care for carp. The *Duluth Tribune* reported on an Ashland farmer's market in November 1917

Save the
products of the Land
Eat more fish —
they feed themselves.

UNITED STATES FOOD ADMINISTRATION

There were plenty of food resources in Minnesota's lakes and rivers. The state sponsored out-of-season harvests of fish that were then sold at cost in several communities. River-harvested carp were shipped out by the boxcar to discerning diners across the nation. (Artist Charles Livingston Bull) where the previous week's shipment of carp sold out when priced at seven cents a pound. But when the price was raised to nine cents, "less than half the regular shipment of three barrels was sold, even though farmers selling produce and fresh meat did 'a rushing business.'"[28]

People in other regions of the United States, however, did eat Minnesota carp. Carlos Avery, the state's game and fish commissioner, described how the fish were "packed in boxes of a uniform size and shipped in carload lots. Some are even shipped alive . . . in [rail]cars especially constructed for this purpose. . . . Incredible as it seems, as many [as] 17 or 18 ton of fish may be shipped from Minnesota to New York alone in one express car." By mid-June 1918 more than 1.3 million pounds of carp were sold from Minnesota lakes, and in Milwaukee the weekly consumption reached 25,000 pounds.[29]

Minnesota fishermen also brought to market more appealing fish than carp. Under the direction of the game and fish commission and the Minnesota Commission of Public Safety, local fishermen harvested whitefish out of season from Red Lake and sold it at cost to a welcome market. The success of the program made front-page news in Bemidji: "40,000 pounds . . . have been caught under state supervision—chiefly whitefish and tulibees—and distributed to nearly 100 communities of the state and sold at cost of production plus transportation. The state fisheries are contributing materially to the saving of meats and reducing the high cost of living by bringing fish to . . . many communities where they have not been available." A local women's club, the Housewives League of Bemidji, made arrangements for 200 pounds of the fish to be sold for 12 cents a pound without profit by the merchants in late 1917. Weekly sales rotated among merchants of the city. The group reported that they could have sold twice as much, but "it was all we could get."[30]

During the winter Minnesotans could enjoy ocean fish shipped from the coasts, and on February 7, 1918, the *Pipestone Leader* announced, "Schirmer's City Meat Market offers 3,000 pounds of fish for sale. All strictly fresh, frozen stock including black cod, pickerel, pike, herring, ocean pike, superior white fish, salmon, and tulibee." J. O. Melby, proprietor of the Oklee Meat Market, remodeled his shop to create an area for a "more complete stock of salted, smoked

Rather than lose valuable meat substitutes to normal winter kill, Minnesota permitted off-season harvest of fish from shallow waters in January 1918. Once fishing season opened, anglers took full advantage of the bounty free for the catching. This picture was labeled "Two Hours' Catch at Lake of the Woods."

and canned fish and [to] sell the same as follows: Alaska salmon, Alaska trout, cod fish salt, cod fish dry, Norsk flaksild, gafelbitar [spiced herring], cod fish tongue, Mayflower fish cake."[31]

In January 1918 the state tried to outsmart Mother Nature by permitting fishing in shallow waters "where fish are in danger of suffocation" on ice-covered lakes, "instead of complaining about food waste next spring when large quantities of dead fish are washed ashore to make a health menace. Dipnets, tip-ups, seines, spears and almost any kind of fishing equipment may be used." When fishing season opened officially in the spring, the *Eveleth News* editor reported, "Even though the cost of fishing tackle will be much higher this year than in any other season, this did not seem to effect the enthusiastic people who went out to catch a 'mess' of fish on opening day."[32]

Fisherfolk weren't the only people to bring in their dinner from the wild. Hunters across the state took to the woods and fields to supply fresh game for their own tables. Bag limits of 25 prairie

CORN AND NUT LOAF

1 15-ounce can corn kernels
½ cup very finely ground
  English walnuts (2–3 ounces)
1 cup soft rye bread crumbs
1 egg, lightly beaten

1 tablespoon soft butter or other fat
¾ teaspoon salt
⅛ teaspoon pepper
tomato sauce or white sauce
chopped parsley

Preheat oven to 350° F. Drain the corn and then mix with the ingredients in the order given. Put mixture into a lightly greased loaf pan and bake until firm, about 45 minutes. Serve with tomato sauce or white sauce with chopped parsley. (*Suggestions for Meatless Days*, Agricultural Extension Division Leaflet 33 [Iowa State College of Agriculture and Mechanical Arts, 1918], Iowa State University Archives, Ames)

chickens and 30 quail in one season from September 16 to December 1, 1917, brought forth many "red-caped Nimrods." The *Brown County Journal* warned on opening day, "Residents near lakes will be awakened by a discharge of musketry which will make them think they are near Verdun or Vimy Ridge, where the greatest bombardment the world had ever witnessed has taken place." Birds for the taking included wild duck, coot, gallinules, rails, geese, and brant (similar to Canada geese, but smaller). Most families in New Ulm were "now cutting down the high cost of living by eating wild fowl." Hunters also reported success in the deer and moose season that lasted all of November with a limit of one of each animal. In Bemidji, members of the Commercial Club were treated to free venison bagged by E. E. Ashley, a commercial salesman.[33]

In early October 1917, as increasing numbers of Minnesota men were called up for military training, public eating establishments were called to join the battle for increased food conservation. Hoover's Food Administration began with restaurants and called for one day a week to be wheatless and one day to be meatless. The *Bemidji Pioneer* reported that the first restaurants in town to follow the lead of establishments in Duluth, St. Paul, and Minneapolis were the Third Street Café and Gould's Dairy Lunch. Tuesday would be a meatless day and Wednesday would be wheatless. Fish and chicken would substitute for meat. Rules for serving meats stipulated that "no public eating place shall serve to any one patron at any one meal more than one kind of meat," and bacon could not be used as a garnish."[34]

As hotels and restaurants eliminated meat and wheat from some menus, cut down the number of dishes offered, and reduced the size of meat portions, people who ate daily lunches downtown noticed that prices stayed about the same. In part, this reflected the fact that ingredient costs represented only about one-fifth of a restaurant's expenses, but the Food Administration met complaints head on. It suggested that hotels and restaurants add one meat-and-vegetable "club dish" prepared with a larger, more generous portion of vegetables so that patrons would not leave hungry. Combinations of dishes were to change daily. One night's menu might feature a small steak with baked potato, corn fritters, string beans, green peas, and fried tomatoes. The next night might have corned beef and cabbage with turnips, carrots, stewed celery, and radishes. On Friday nights, grilled fish or lobster might be surrounded with liberal helpings of vegetables.[35]

The meatless day per week urged by Hoover in the fall caused some complaints. The *Winona Weekly Leader* noted, "The Hoover commission urges one meatless day per week and some of the railroads have designated Tuesdays as a meatless day on their dining cars. Some hotels have followed suit." The article then explained a concern of some readers: "Now that we are called upon to have one meatless day, they seem to think it a crime to work in unison with the Catholics. Why not have it a meatless Friday and make it uniform. . . . To do otherwise will be to impose two meatless days upon a large percentage of the country which is already from religious motives 'doing its bit' to conserve."[36]

Restaurants and other public eating places were the front line, but home cooks soon joined the battle. The new meatless days meant that homemakers who had just begun to master meat cakes and casseroles, dishes that stretched a pound of meat with rice or other starches to feed a family of five or six, now had to consider one-dish recipes such as dried peas with rice and tomatoes, pimento

Sir

don't waste while your wife saves
Adopt the doctrine of the clean plate
UNITED STATES FOOD ADMINISTRATION   —do your share
No 188

Although Hoover began "wheatless" and "meatless" food conservation measures with the full cooperation of restaurants and hotels, there were still plenty of opportunities for food waste at meals served outside the home. Eating "everything on your plate" was the order of the day. (Artist Crawford Young)

and cottage cheese roast, and baked cowpeas. To help with planning meals, Minnesota food administrator A. D. Wilson suggested this vegetable-generous menu for a meatless day: breakfast—cream of rye with figs, poached egg on toast, toast and butter, coffee; lunch—scalloped cabbage with cream, rye muffins with butter, fruit; and dinner—baked sweet potatoes, buttered beets, spinach with vinegar, oatmeal bread with butter, and raspberry shortcake.[37]

Depending on where people lived in the state, the 1917 holiday season was as good as it could be or a time of scarcity. In Duluth, cooks read the good news that "a large supply of turkeys is ready for Thanksgiving, with quantities in storage this year." In New Ulm, on the other hand, a newspaper headline despaired, "Word has already been passed by the commission agents in large population centers that turkeys will be scarce articles on Thanksgiving tables."[38]

Farm wives could take matters into their own hands, as a *Farmer's Wife* columnist recommended in November 1917. She wrote that a delicious Thanksgiving meal should cover these points: "home production, economy, patriotic food conservation. [It] cannot be as it has been in our family. A great world-event has changed conditions for all of us." She continued, "Just as I came to this decision, my flock of geese waddled past the window and I decided the chief part of my menu, goose. I cannot feed the big birds with expensive grain." Her final menu included roast goose with stuffing made of half bread and half apples, cinnamon apples, browned potatoes, creamed onions, Patriotic bread, pear salad with honey dressing, brownies with coffee or fruit drink, and hickory nuts.[39]

The *Mankato Daily Free Press* reported on an old-fashioned Thanksgiving feast put together for soldiers at home and abroad. "Special officers for the last two weeks have been buying all the available turkeys in the countryside weighing more than 12 pounds. Dinner for those stationed in Paris included soup, turkey, potatoes, turnips, peas, white bread, butter, apple and peach pie, apples, raisins, nuts, figs, dates, and coffee. Individual turkey portions range from a pound and one-quarter to a pound and one-half." The paper further reported that some of the "special chow" had been shipped in a refrigerated vessel from the United States on November 1, including "130,000 pounds turkey, 1,652,500 pounds sweet potatoes, 11,000 pounds mincemeat pies."[40]

In December, a well-known Brown County meat merchant, Andrew Saffert, continued to do an excellent holiday mail-order business. He was "nearly 'snowed' by the orders he received from his customers in St. Paul, and the capitol employees ordered eighty turkeys in addition to bacon, hams, and sausage. The capitol boys know where to get the best Christmas feed."[41]

Since turkeys and chickens were scarce at Camp Cody in New Mexico, where many young Minnesotans were in training, the camp's social director appealed to Minnesota newspapers to invite family members or friends to send a chicken or a cake to their soldier for a special New Year's Eve barbeque dinner. The camp sought local donations, too. Overall, their requests included 100 steers, 500 fowls, 1,000 sheep, 10,000 loaves of bread, and 7,000 pies and cakes. Donations were to be mailed parcel post to the War Service Board "with the name of your soldier boy, company, and regiment enclosed. It will be placed before him on the mile-long table for him and his pals."[42]

HOT POT OF MUTTON AND BARLEY

1 pound mutton   1 teaspoon salt
3 onions, chopped   4 potatoes
½ cup pearled barley   celery tops or other seasoning herbs

Cut the mutton in small pieces and brown with the onion in fat cut from
the meat. This will help make the meat tender and improve the flavor.
Pour this into a large pot with lid. Add 2 quarts of water and the barley.
Simmer for 1½ hours. Add the potatoes cut in quarters, salt, and seasoning
herbs and cook for one half hour longer. (News release, Minnesota Food
Commissioner [1918]), Food Files, Minnesota Historical Society)

In January 1918, after a long and hard evaluation of the food
needs for the army and the Allies, rail and boat shipping capacity, and
animal stocks, Hoover's Food Administration called for Americans
to drastically restrict meat consumption. Minnesota's cooks were
not only to prepare a weekly meatless meal but they were to go
without meat for entire days. From February to July 1918, the war's
most stringent regulations requested "patriotic servers of food in
America" dish up 11 wheatless meals and 9 meatless meals out of
21 per week.

The new restrictions prompted front-page headlines followed by
the complicated details. As the *Pipestone Leader* explained, "Meatless
means without any cattle, hogs, or sheep. On other days use mutton
or lamb in preference to beef or pork. Porkless means without pork,
bacon, ham, lard, or pork products fresh or preserved. Tuesday is a
meatless day, Tuesday and Saturday are porkless days."[43]

Additionally, at meals where meat was allowed, there were further food restrictions. According to the university's home economics
department, Minnesotans were asked to "use one ounce less meat
per person each day." Suggested substitutes were fish (fresh, canned,
or dried), milk (whole or skimmed), cheese (cottage or whole milk),
eggs, dried legumes (beans, split peas, or lentils), and nuts (walnuts
or peanuts). In place of one ounce of beef round, homemakers could
use ⅔ cup whole or skimmed milk, 2 tablespoons cottage cheese,

1 cubic inch American cheese or 1½ tablespoons grated American cheese, 1 small egg, or ½ cup navy beans, split peas, or lentils.[44]

Homemakers across the state went on hunting expeditions for meat substitutes in their own pantries. The University of Minnesota and the Food Administration provided recipes for vegetarian meat-substitutes, many of which were combinations of cornmeal, beans, or potatoes with cheese and nuts formed into a meatlike loaf. Recipes from the Northwest School and Experiment Station in Crookston provided a persuasively written nutritional analysis that suggested, "Nuts, in general, are rich in both protein and fat, and consequently may be used interchangeably with meat in the diet. One and one-fourth cup chopped walnuts, one and one-third cup chopped peanuts, or about one-third of cup of peanut butter will yield as much energy as a pound of beef round. If nuts are made into a nut and bread crumb loaf, two cups of the loaf yield as much energy as one pound of beef. As a source of protein, nuts are much cheaper than meat."[45]

Women sought advice and recipes from friends. Mrs. Merrill of Minneapolis received this letter from a friend, Emma B. in Ohio: "You asked about how to Hooverize and war recipes. I am under the impression that Mr. Hoover wants

MACARONI AND PEANUTS

This takes the place of meat and potatoes, our expensive luxuries today.

1 cup macaroni
2 quarts boiling water
1 tablespoon salt for boiling water
3 tablespoons fat
3 tablespoons flour
2 cups milk
½ pound ground peanuts
¼ teaspoon salt
¼ teaspoon paprika
½ cup buttered crumbs

Preheat oven to 350° F. Boil macaroni in salted water until just tender and drain. Melt fat in a medium saucepan. Add flour and cook over medium heat until bubbly. Stir in the milk and continue to cook until thickened. Add peanuts, salt, and paprika to taste. Combine with cooked macaroni and put in lightly greased casserole. Cover with crumbs. Bake until bubbly and crumbs are browned, about 20 minutes. (*The Farmer's Wife*, September 1917) us to use the things that cannot be shipped overseas, that we must curtail on sugar, flour, bacon, and meats of all kinds that can be sent to our boys in France. We are doing that and have almost changed our diet. We use eggs in place of meat. My meat bill last winter was $18 to $22; now it is $6 per month."[46]

Soldiers' letters helped Minnesotans appreciate the importance of individual conservation efforts. Raymond Brunswick, a marine in training, wrote to his parents in Duluth: "Twelve of our men have to stay for more training, about 8 were sent to cook school. Maybe they'll be able to stir soup better than they swing a rifle. Lately we've been doing *some* eating. Peaches, steak, pancakes and lots of other good things."[47]

Eating was good even on troop transport ships. Andrew Glenn described the food to his parents in St. Paul while he crossed the North Atlantic in late January 1918: "[The food] could not have been improved upon, considering the number fed and the conditions under which they were fed." One meal included "roast beef, potatoes, green peas, tapioca pudding, coffee, and bread and *butter.*"[48]

Letters home from sons and husbands described the lives of European civilians in the war zone, too. Zens Smith wrote home to his parents in March 1918 that "in France the houses, shops, etc. look more like scenes from some play than real human buildings. But the beauty is rather pathetic when one thinks of all that the people are sacrificing. Our wheatless, meatless, and other eatless days make us think we are feeling the pinch of war, but one has to be over here to realize even a tiny part of what this struggle means. America hasn't even begun to awaken to the realization of what War is. I pray God this may all be over before she ever does!"[49]

Overall, the voluntary civilian meat conservation efforts, along with increased farm production, especially of hogs, were so successful in balancing the meat supply with demand that the Food Administration only mandated meatless days for the entire population from early October 1917 through March 1918. By April, Hoover announced a temporary meat surplus and eliminated the meatless dictates for a 30-day period.

Meatless days were never reinstated, but the Food Administration continued to monitor the supply and demand closely. In early May, state food administrator A. D. Wilson passed along a warning from Hoover that Americans would need to export 75 million pounds of meat to Allies and soldiers fighting in France. Before the war the United States had exported only 13 million pounds. Hoover telegrammed, "We are eating three and a quarter pounds of meat per person each week. Americans need to continue to economize, reduce waste and reduce quantities prepared for each meal and reduce quantities purchased in order to avoid the inconvenience which arises in the restrictions from meatless days and will cause less interference in the daily preparation of food."[50]

In Minnesota, A. D. Wilson cited the meat conservation efforts of Minneapolis's Swedish Hospital as an example for other institutions to follow: "The per capita consumption of meat since January 1 was a small fraction under one and one-half pounds a week and yet no one had complained of not getting enough." The hospital dietician and cooks believed they could bring the consumption down to one pound a week.[51]

By the middle of July 1918 the government was again seeking to limit beef consumption through directives to businesses and appeals to homemakers. Food administrator Wilson reminded home cooks to use no more than one and one-quarter pounds of beef per person per week or no more than one and one-half pounds including the bones. Regulations for hotels, restaurants, and public eating places announced by Walter A. Pocock, hotel representative of the Food Administration for Minnesota, a subcommittee of hotel and restaurant operators, were very specific. "Roast beef, whether served hot or cold, is to be served only on Monday at the midday meal; stewed, boiled, or beef hashes are to be served only on Wednesday and Saturday at the midday meal and steaks in any form including in hamburger on Thursday only at the midday meal."[52]

In New Ulm, meat market owner Andrew Saffert suggested a more exotic substitute in his ad in the *Brown County Journal*. He advertised a "choice supply of fresh reindeer meat direct from Alaska for sale at our meat market today at prices ranging from 23 cents to 60 cents a pound according to cut. If reindeer meat proves popular with

---

CURRY OF LAMB

When it seems desirable to have a meat dish instead of a meat substitute, the cheapest cuts should be selected and these from meats which are not required for our own soldiers or their Allies. The neck or breast of lamb is less expensive as a rule.

Cook meat day ahead in water with onion and celery. Skim off fat and set aside to combine with other fats and use when needed. Remove 1 cup of stock you will need for dish and return bones to simmering stock for an hour longer. This will serve as the foundation for barley soup. To make curry, brown a slice of onion in tablespoon of oil and stir in 1 tablespoon curry powder and 1 cup of stock. Cook until hot. Lay in the meat and stand at the side of the stove for 15 minutes. Serve with boiled rice and cold bananas eaten to offset the heat of the curry. This is an East Indian fashion and seldom fails to please. (*Le Sueur News*, June 6, 1918)

---

the people, we shall order additional supplies. We secure it through the Federal Food Administration."[53]

While homemakers worked to conserve meat, the nation's farmers faced one unwavering task: to produce as much as possible and to get it to market efficiently. For Minnesota farmers, the road to the "Big Five" meat processors began in St. Paul, where South St. Paul's Union Stockyards took "cattle, sheep and swine, affording the farmer a market without the necessity of long hauls and unloading in transit." The number of animals processed through the stockyards increased significantly during the war. Every day hundreds of railcars off-loaded tens of thousands of cattle and hogs into holding pens, where they were fed and watered. Some were loaded onto cars for transport east on one of the adjacent rail lines. Others were sold to packers on the spot.[54]

In 1918 more than four million head of cattle, hogs, and sheep from Montana, South Dakota, Minnesota, and Canada passed through the yards. This 16 percent increase over 1917 established a new record, and earnings increased 25 percent. About half of these cattle went to packers and butchers, while nearly all the hogs were processed at the 24-acre Swift's plant.[55]

Given the ready market for hogs and the speed with which they grew to maturity, many Minnesotans tried to raise them. In Eveleth in April 1917, a week after the declaration of war, health commissioner L. F. Huisman published a large ad in the newspaper, warning, "Notice: Do not buy pigs expecting to raise them within the city, as the ordinance prohibiting the keeping of pigs will be strictly enforced this year." A year later, a new city health commissioner thought differently: "Notice: All persons who wish to raise pigs within the city limits must . . . get permission for same. Do not buy pigs expecting to raise them within the city before you get permission."[56]

For farmers, a University of Minnesota assistant professor of animal husbandry, R. C. Ashby, offered advice on the best way to bring hogs to market: "So far as it is now known, feed is the only substance capable of changing a pig into a finished butcher hog." Minnesota had regularly been among the top eight states for producing both hogs and corn, a good combination, but now that people were eating corn instead of giving it to the pigs, Professor Ashby suggested pasture supplemented by commercial concentrate as the best substitute.[57]

The 1918 Northrup King seed catalog had other suggestions. It listed several varieties of rutabagas "valuable not only for stock feeding but for table use as well." It also suggested planting "mangel wurtzels," a root weighing up to 30 pounds used by European farmers for feed. "Every farmer should put in at least an acre of mangels this season. 8 to 10 acres will be much better. They would yield 15 to 20 tons of high quality animal feed an acre at a cost of less than 15 cents a bushel." In addition, "artichoke roots are an extremely valuable food for hogs. . . . They yield very heavily 300 to 350 bushels to the acre . . . If given an opportunity, the hogs will help themselves." For people who preferred to coddle their hogs, the *St. Cloud Daily Times* printed instructions for a Hog Cafeteria that "any boy or any man could build" to shelter the hogs while they dine on "succulent" foods in the backyard or farmyard.[58]

The 57 boys at the Glen Lake Farm School who "found their way into court and out again by way of the farm" raised sheep, milk cows, turkeys, chickens, and hogs. They fed the hogs at their own "soup kitchen, an enclosed patch of ground about eight-feet square situated on the hillside beside the barn. It is sheltered by trees. A huge

Raising more pigs was one of the fastest ways to increase the nation's meat supply. They can be fed on kitchen waste, and they grow to market weight in less than a year. Although some towns allowed backyard piggeries, the real growth market was among farm boys and girls. In "pig clubs" children learned the best ways to raise a healthy hog.

cauldron holding gallons of garbage from the [nearby] sanatorium boils and simmers all day long."[59]

After hogs had been fed during the summer, they could be turned into food. Minnesota food administrator A. D. Wilson reassured home farmers that they could cure meat for their own use and that they would not be charged with hoarding, even if they kept the meat from a whole hog or more. "Any family has the right to put up meat in the fall for winter use as long as they do not keep quantities in excess of normal needs. Meats of all kinds should be salted and stored."[60]

For those who preferred to sell their home- or farm-raised pork, there were local markets. For example, J. O. Melby of Oklee's meat market paid 18 cents a pound for dressed hogs in 1918. The previous spring he advertised that "nice dressed hogs weighing from 125 to 200 pounds will be paid for at 14 cents per pound when delivered to the meat market."[61]

Children living on farms had an impact on the Minnesota meat supply, too. By the end of the war Wilson reported that "the Boys and Girls Clubs of Minnesota, through their pig and calf clubs, have added 540,000 pounds of meat production to the state. One

TAMALE PIE

½ cup cornmeal, uncooked
1½ cups boiling salted water
2 cups tomato sauce
2 cups cooked, chopped meat
1 teaspoon salt

1 small onion, minced
1 green pepper, minced
½ cup cheddar cheese, grated
½ cup chopped olives (optional)

Preheat oven to 350° F. Stir the cornmeal into the boiling water, reduce heat and cook, stirring from time to time, until cornmeal is thick. Combine 1 cup of the tomato sauce with the meat, salt, onion, and pepper. Stir this into the cooked cornmeal. Press mixture into a lightly greased pie pan. Sprinkle top with cheese. Bake until pie is firm and cheese is melted. Serve with remaining tomato sauce. You may add ½ cup chopped olives to the sauce. ("One Piece Meals" [Iowa State College of Agriculture and Mechanical Arts, 1918], Iowa State University Archives, Ames) thousand boys and girls have produced an estimated number of 1,500 pigs representing 300,000 pounds in production and a money value at present market prices of $51,000."[62]

In a continuing waste-reduction effort that went far beyond turning leftovers into molded salads, some municipalities turned garbage into ham. Forty cities used the garbage from more than two million people to raise 15 to 20 million pounds of pork.[63]

A news release from A. D. Wilson suggested a way for cities and farms to come together on the issue of garbage and hogs: "There is an excellent opportunity for the farmers who come to town regularly with loaded wagons to make use of this hog feed by taking with them on their return trip a load of garbage. A tarpaulin will be needed to cover, to be in compliance with local regulations. Otherwise little or no extra equipment is necessary. In cold weather, especially, fresh garbage is not disagreeable to handle nor is injury done to the average farm wagon when it is cleaned promptly after unloading. Many thrifty farmers are adopting this means of securing hog feed at small expense."[64]

The arrival of spring in 1918 also meant more newspaper articles urging people to raise more poultry. A syndicated article reproduced in the *Oklee Herald* gave poultry a full-fledged patriotic boost: "The more poultry and eggs we produce, the more poultry and eggs we will eat. The more of that food we eat, the less beef and pork we will need or want. Thus we do indirectly the thing we can't do directly. . . . Get some good hens. You will help win the war. You will reduce your own cost of living. You will turn waste into food."[65]

For newcomers to this endeavor, the U.S. Department of Agriculture distributed information on housing fowl. "Often there is an unused shed or small outbuilding that can be converted into a chicken house. You need only 3 or 4 square feet. Two piano boxes with the backs removed can be nailed together and a door cut in the end. They should be covered with a roofing paper to keep the insides dry. A portion of the door should be left open and covered with a piece of muslin to provide ventilation."[66]

U. G. Jaasberg, agricultural instructor of Eveleth High School, organized a poultry club for students to raise backyard chickens and ordered an incubator with 200 eggs. He explained that the chickens

Even city residents were urged to raise chickens in their backyards, both for the eggs the hens laid and the dinner they could become after they were done laying. Chickens grow from egg to pan-ready in less than three months.

would need to be carefully monitored while they were young and the food would have to be carefully prepared. After some weeks, though, "scraps that are left over from the table and which were formerly wasted can be fed to them."[67]

Backyard chicken coops and farmyard flocks made tempting targets for thieves. In August 1918 the *Brown County Journal* described the problem and offered suggestions for coping. "Chicken lifters are abroad in the land. Several hen roosts in the city have acquired the disappearing habit. Rural districts are also suffering from the pest. . . . Load up the old shot gun with buckshot and lay awake with one ear open . . . use the gun on 'em." By October 1918 thievery had increased, prompting the paper to write, "Price of chickens is high. . . . Load up old shotguns with salt and be ready. Chickens bring high prices and are tempting bait for those who play at the midnight pastime at the risk of having their rear anatomy filled with salt or buckshot. . . . Rural residents are preparing to give thieves their full dose from the rear end of the ten-gauge." Some thieves apparently advanced the level of technology used for the crime, for farmers in West Newton offered a $300 reward for chicken thieves who listened in on phone lines to find out when farmers were not at home, used lights to signal, and traveled in automobiles.[68]

By war's end in November 1918, as the joy of peace traveled across the state, the end had come for some chicken flocks as well. The *Le Sueur News*'s Thanksgiving War Menu recipe for chicken pie began with this recommendation for the main ingredient: "Get a good fat fowl for this, a rooster or a hen that has done laying."[69]

I went out to eat and dropped into a place for "Ladies & Gentlemen," but neither were present. The place was full of a mixture of what to all appearances were wild and wooly cowboys, Mexican bandits—men who looked like they were millionaire ranchmen 10 years ago and then lost their fortune and are now still wearing the same clothes. . . . In order to get service they would take a chili dish and hit it on the counter, so I did the same and got some soup that burned all the way down from the pepper in it, and also a steak from a Texas steer that must have run wild on the ranges for 20 years or more. After wrestling with it, I finally got the best of it and paid my bill—30 cents. . . . Hamburgers were for 6 for 25 cents—They sure must have some appetites here.
Granville Gutterson, January 6, 1918, Austin, Texas[70]

6

Milk Is Food:
New Meals from Dairy and Coop

> Now that a food shortage and food substitutes stare us in
> the face, we must master the subject of nutrition. There is
> nothing alarming about the work, and yet women flee from
> it as from a monster. *The Farmer's Wife, June 1918*[1]

During the meatless days of 1917 and 1918, Herbert Hoover's Food Administration urged substitution of milk, cheese, and eggs in main courses for scarce and restricted beef, pork, lamb, chicken, and mutton. Milk and its by-products were important sources of nutrition. Butter, for example, was seen as a key "energy-producing food" for American soldiers and hungry Allies.

In 1917 the United States shipped almost 21 million pounds of butter to the United Kingdom, more than three times the prewar average, and another 742,000 pounds to France. During the war, the United States provided more than 306,000 tons of dairy products, including butter, cheese, and condensed milk, an essential food for European children. This evaporated and canned milk needed no refrigeration, and it was sold in the United States as well. Homemakers added water to dilute it back to "fresh from the cow" consistency.[2]

Minnesota was a leading U.S. producer of milk, butter, and cheese. In 1917 each of the state's 135,000 farmers probably had at least one milk cow that produced an average of a gallon of milk a day. Getting milk to market involved a network of independent dairies, local creameries, village stores, and a lot of hard work.[3]

While everybody helped in the food conservation effort, Arthur McGuire's dairy herd (made up of Grace, Stella, Stuffy, Ida, Brindle, and others) included some of the most productive cows in Minnesota.

University of Minnesota dairy specialist Arthur McGuire, shown here in apron and derby hat, traveled the state suggesting ways to improve dairy operations. He led several "silo tours" encouraging farmers to install the feed-producing towers on their farms.

His 28 cows averaged 353 pounds of butterfat from 7,079 pounds of milk (823 gallons) annually, while the state's averages for 1917 were only 162 pounds of butterfat from 4,275 pounds of milk. McGuire's herd had a distinct advantage: McGuire was the University of Minnesota's knowledgeable dairy specialist. He had a lot of work to do, not only in his own dairy barn but also helping dairymen across the state increase their cows' productivity.

McGuire characterized the state's dairy industry and high-lighted some of its challenges in a letter to the university's Board of Regents. "Minnesota has a system of dairying that is quite different from other states. [It] has been built up very largely, almost entirely, around its cooperative creameries, of which it has 646 and doing a business of $25 million a year in the sale of butter alone." He continued, "In many states the cattle are pastured the greater part of the time. In Minnesota the farmer must feed his stock indoors seven months of the year. In many states farmers buy much of their feed and at prices that destroy their profits. In Minnesota farmers profit most by growing their feed. In many states labor is classified in poor society. In Minnesota the farmer who is not a good workman is ashamed of himself."[4]

The farmers weren't the only ones who worked hard to bring milk to consumers. Every day, milkmen from Henry Schroeder's dairy on Rice Street just north of St. Paul delivered milk throughout the city. Twice a day, the Schroeder children and the dairy's immigrant workers milked more than 100 cows housed in two large barns. The first milking started at five o'clock in the morning. One German employee, Joe Mollner, remembered milking 12 to 13 cows an hour. The milk was bottled while it was still warm and delivered by horse-drawn wagon, each wagon carrying 26 cases of milk containing 12 one-quart bottles each. In the summer, canvas awnings shaded the milk and hand-chipped ice rested on top of the bottles to cool them slightly. The dairy kept an ice house with 400-pound blocks of ice that had been harvested from local lakes during the winter.[5]

Most milk sold in stores or delivered to homes was "whole milk." Some was pasteurized, but none was homogenized, as most milk is today. Left to stand in a cool place, it naturally separated, with the cream gradually rising to the top. After a day the "cream line" appeared. In 48 hours the milk separated completely into cream and skim milk. Homemakers typically used the rich cream for special dishes and the skim milk for cooking. Cooks could also buy cream from the milkman already separated.

During the war, the dairy division of the U.S. Department of Agriculture made suggestions for using the separated cream and skim milk. It recommended cooking a cupful of hot cereal in three cupfuls of skim milk instead of water because it "added as much protein as that contained in three eggs." Skim milk's value in vegetable soups was twofold: homemakers could grind and simmer tough vegetables in the milk, capturing their flavor and nutrients in the protein-rich

> ## VEGETABLE MILK SOUP
>
> 1 quart fresh spinach or
> outer leaves of lettuce,
> tops of green onions, or
> celery leaves
> 1 thin slice onion
> 2 slices stale bread
> 1 quart skim milk
>
> Put the spinach and onion
> through a meat grinder,
> followed by the bread, so
> there is no waste. Put into
> a double boiler with milk,
> and cook until the spinach
> is tender. ("How to Use
> Skim Milk," *The Dairy
> Record*, July 4, 1917)

soup base, and then thicken the soup with stale bread. This provided a nutritious but very inexpensive meal, which was important when the cost of living was high.[6]

Home cooks already used more than two-fifths of the milk in the United States, but the government urged people to put more milk in their diet, either as a beverage or used in cooking. One report noted that people living in cities consumed one and one-half cups of milk a day in all uses, while those in small towns had two cups. Individuals living on farms with dairy cows used three cups a day.[7]

Josephine Berry, head of the University of Minnesota's home economics department, distributed food conservation and nutritional information to audiences across the state in the early days of the war. Seeking quick consumer action, she reached out to groups of opinion leaders. In a letter to pastors in the Twin Cities in late July 1917, she emphasized, "Milk is not sufficiently recognized as a relatively cheap food. By many it is regarded as a luxury or as a beverage. Milk at 10 cents a quart is a cheap source of protein and a reasonably cheap source of energy." She also urged wider use of skim milk and buttermilk.

Even before the war, books on care and feeding of children promoted milk as a protein source. One suggested, "With milk freely supplied and an average of one egg a day, there is no call for the introduction of meat into the diet until after a child is seven years old." These books recommended serving milk as an ingredient in cooked porridges, puddings, and other dishes and only secondarily as a beverage.[8]

One reason parents may have been reluctant to rely on uncooked milk for drinking could have been concern about safety and purity.

Direct interaction with shoppers was one way to change opinions about the value of milk as food. Dairy maids set up information booths in Minneapolis department stores Young Quinlan and Dayton's to spread the word that milk was a valuable nutritional source for meatless days.

Today, nearly all milk is pasteurized by heating to 161° F. for 15 seconds to kill disease-causing bacteria. In 1917, pasteurization was available from larger dairies across the state but was by no means universally done. One food source noted, "Infected milk is one of the chief sources of contagion in various diseases" and urged that milk be heated to 155° F. for 30 minutes to "kill those germs which are dangers to the child without destroying the quality of the milk as a food."[9]

The Food Administration saw milk and milk products as affordable sources of nutrients. State food administrator A. D. Wilson offered serving suggestions: "Every child should consume at least one quart of milk a day until his sixth year. Between the ages of six and twelve his diet should include at least a pint of milk a day. Many children have a real aversion to milk as a drink but its food value must go into his diet in soups, junket, blanc-mange, and so on." *The Farmer's Wife* offered similar suggestions for enticing children to consume milk in foods such as "baked custard, junket, tapioca custard, and French ice cream."[10]

While Minnesota's dairy industry worked to keep up with demands in 1917, it was also undergoing changes in both the nature of milk products and the way milk was sold to customers. Producers, processors, and distributors, including stores and milkmen using horse-drawn wagons, confronted new technology and concerns about disease. Newspaper stories suggest the issues. A front-page article in the *Eveleth News* on May 17, 1917, trumpeted the opening of the new Cloverdale Creamery, a "wholesale and retail business supplying the retail trade of the city with pasteurized milk and cream, as well as buying from farmers and churning the extra cream. Owner W. R. Anderson will serve dairy lunches and ice cream in the parlor of the building and will also handle bakery goods."

In the same issue of *Eveleth News,* a prominent notice on page six from the city's health commissioner warned, "Notice to cow owners. All persons in the city owning cows and all persons outside the city owning cows and supplying milk to the residents of Eveleth must have their cows tested at once for tuberculosis at their own expense, which will be $1.00 per head. Any cow-owner failing to comply with this order is liable under city ordinance to imprisonment in the county jail for not more than sixty days or pay a fine of not less than $5.00 or more than $50.00 together with the costs of prosecution."

The kinds of milk and milk products varied from dairy to dairy and milkman to milkman. Minneapolis's Quaker Creamery advertised a full line of milk products on its letterhead: "Our wagons will serve you with the following: pasteurized milk and cream, fresh butter churned daily, whipping cream, buttermilk, Bulgarian buttermilk, inspected and certified milk for babies." Some vendors offered unbottled cream dipped from a large can into any container provided. In Duluth the MacCroft Dairy in Riverside Park advertised "Holstein milk—health, vitality, nutrition," and invited visitors to "come and see for yourself. Pure milk specialists. Investigate us for your children's sake."[11]

Most milk in Minneapolis and St. Paul was marketed through the Twin Cities Milk Producers, a cooperative of more than 2,000 dairymen in the ten-county, 50-mile-radius milk-shed. Organized in March 1917, the producers' cooperative sold pasteurized milk to almost every store or milkman in the Twin Cities. Many of the 200 independent sellers not part of the cooperative sold raw milk, in part because some experts believed that the digestibility of dairy products was negatively affected by pasteurizing. However, as in Eveleth, all milk sold in the Twin Cities came from cows tested for tuberculosis.[12]

In the spring and summer of 1917 it seemed just about everyone was complaining about the high cost of milk. Just after home economist Josephine Berry said milk was a bargain at 10 cents a quart, society women in St. Paul urged boycotting the increased quart price of 14 cents as too expensive.[13]

Dealers worried about prices as well. Wages of milk wagon drivers increased 15 to 20 percent, resulting in an average salary of $90 a month. The average glass milk bottle lasted just 12 days on the milkman's route. Although drivers were partially responsible for the cost of lost or broken bottles, replacing them was still an expense for the dairy. Simply raising the price of milk did not bring automatic profits, since in some areas where the price increased from 8 cents to 10 cents a quart, sales declined 15 percent.[14]

Milk bottles lasted a bit longer in Duluth, but bottle shortages and related costs were of such concern that the *News Tribune* appealed to its readers: "Look over your pantry shelves and pick out the empty bottles. Help Us to Help Hoover. The average life of a milk bottle is 20 trips. Imagine if you can the cost when thousands of bottles are destroyed every day. You can help lower this waste by returning all empty bottles. . . . Will you help us keep the price of milk as low as possible?"[15]

Flora Rose of the University of Minnesota's Agricultural Extension Service took the position that "milk was a cheap food" no matter what consumers believed. As homemakers learned to make breads from oatmeal, cornmeal, and other non-wheat products and main dishes from vegetables, she cautioned, they should not react to increased prices of any particular food by banishing it from

Posters promoting milk as a food source filled classrooms and other places of public influence. It was a hard sell. As one milk producer noted, everyone knows food is something you chew. (Artist Tod Hart)

the "family board" because it may be the "cheapest possible source of some nutritive substance necessary to the health and welfare of the body." Rose ruefully related an incident underscoring the difficulty of persuading people of the nutritional value of milk-based dishes. When a well-known milk company executive was given data showing that a quart of milk had the same nutritional value as a pound of meat, he responded, "That is all very well on paper . . . but you and I know they are just nonsense. Why, a real food is something you have to chew."[16]

Acting as a clearinghouse for public concerns on war issues, the Minnesota Commission of Public Safety invited individuals and groups to write with complaints and suggestions for improving social conditions, regulations, and food conservation. It didn't take long for people to ask the agency to address the increasing price of milk. One lengthy letter sent to Governor Burnquist in July expressed a strong opinion: "I think this milk trust is one that should be investigated . . . and I know or expect the state food commission after investigation will wipe out the milk trust along with others."[17]

The MCPS, with a sweeping charter to protect the public safety and civil resources of the state, centered its hearings on milk pricing in the Twin Cities, home to one-quarter of the state's population. Providing milk to Minnesota families at a price they could afford was one of the first food conservation tasks undertaken by the MCPS.

During the three days of hearings in October 1917, the MCPS

SCALLOPED CHEESE

6 large slices of bread
  cut ¾ inch thick
1 cup grated cheese
2 eggs
2 cups milk
¼ teaspoon dry mustard
1 teaspoon salt
⅛ teaspoon pepper

Preheat oven to 325° F. Cut bread in 1-inch squares. Fill oiled baking dish with alternate layers of bread and cheese. Beat eggs slightly, add to milk with seasonings, and pour over bread and cheese. Bake until the mixture sets and browns on top. (Mrs. Charles Thompson, Social Service Division, Minneapolis General Electric Company, to Mildred Weigley, October 24, 1917, Food Files, Minnesota Historical Society) received information from several perspectives. H. H. Kildee, chairman of dairy husbandry at the University of Minnesota, reported that the annual per-cow costs included $7.75 in feed, labor at 24 cents an hour for 150 hours a year per cow, and $147.02 in annual incidental expenses such as ice, fuel, bedding, interest, depreciation, and bull service.[18]

John O. Lysne, who farmed 247 acres in Goodhue County, demonstrated dairymen's concerns as he detailed his operation. He labeled his farm "neither better nor worse than the average" and noted that it produced 107,225 pounds of milk from 20 cows. His conclusion: "Total loss per cow per day [is] 10¾ cents. In other words, I'm paying $700 per year for the privilege of milking, housing and caring for 20 cows. Does not include depreciation, nor wear and tear on machinery and buildings. Neither have I attempted to give myself any salary as manager in obtaining such 'splendid results.'"[19]

In defense of the Twin Cities Milk Producers' business practices, an independent report from agricultural specialist F. W. Peck explained that the co-op made no profit and only charged a small amount for administrative costs. Milk that could not be sold was sent to six cheese factories, so no surplus was wasted. Milk prices in Minneapolis and St. Paul were among the country's lowest at ten cents a quart. Only Milwaukee had lower prices, at nine cents a quart.[20]

After the hearings, on November 2, 1917, the MCPS issued Order Number 13 regulating milk prices. Its immediate practical goal of cheaper milk was achieved "without treating producers and distributors unfairly" and without "dissolving or regulating them." The order fixed the maximum price charged by milk producers to wholesale distributors at 6 cents a quart and the price which could be charged by wholesalers to consumers at 10 cents a quart. A month later the order was amended upward slightly.[21]

While Order 13 regulated the price of fluid milk, it did not tackle the price of cream, the cash cow of the dairy industry nationally. In Minnesota, butter made from that cream was the coin of the realm. Minnesota's creamery butter attracted national interest, even from "the fastidious New York market" and it was Minnesota's "gold mine." But there was a lot of waste from this gold mine. For every pound of butter made, two and one-half gallons of by-products remained, mostly skim milk. This skim milk was considered "worth but little commercially," and while some farmers simply fed it to hogs or calves, others dumped it.[22]

Soon, however, both farmers and the Food Administration began to see skim milk's potential as a food source. Cottage cheese, in particular, could be made easily and relatively quickly in creameries or on farms. As the *Minnesota Dairy Record* newsletter reported, in 1917, 32 billion pounds of skim milk could be made into nearly 5 billion pounds of cottage cheese, containing "more protein than all the beef eaten in the United States in a year."[23]

"Don't waste skim milk" urged signs at the 1917 State Fair "food training camp." Wartime newspaper articles reported on the hundreds of thousands of dollars worth of skim milk that the Department of Agriculture said was being thrown away in the United States, milk

COTTAGE CHEESE PIE

1 cup cottage cheese	*Meringue:*
(plus ⅔ cup milk—see Note)	2 egg whites
⅔ cup sugar	2 tablespoons sugar
2 egg yolks, beaten—reserve	vanilla
whites for meringue	
1 tablespoon melted butter	
dash salt	
¼ teaspoon vanilla	
unbaked 9-inch pie crust	

Preheat oven to 350° F. Mix first 6 ingredients. (Note: Duplicate the smooth cottage cheese of the World War I era by mixing cottage cheese and milk in a blender or food processor until smooth. Then pour this mixture into a bowl and stir in the remaining ingredients in the order given.) Pour into pie crust and bake until firm in center, about 45 minutes. Remove pie and turn oven down to 250° F while you make the meringue. Beat the 2 reserved egg whites with a mixer until soft peaks form. Gradually add 2 tablespoons sugar, beating constantly at high speed. When peaks are stiff, fold in the vanilla and spread gently over pie. Bake until light brown, about 15 minutes. (Johan D. Frederiksen, *The Story of Milk* [New York, 1919])

With as much protein as many meats, cottage cheese made its way into tasty salads and was even served as a "Boston loaf," baked in combination with beans to resemble meat loaf.

that was high in nutritional value. The *Dairy Record* urged milkmen to "sell skim milk on routes" because it contained "more protein than whole milk" although not as much energy because of the lack of fat. It should be pasteurized and "labeled conspicuously . . . so that the consumer may be fully informed as to its true character."[24]

R. M. Washburn of the University Farm urged farmers to sell the meat they produced on their farms and eat cheese instead. "One and a half pounds of cottage cheese will take the place of one pound of meat. Farmers' wives can make their own dairy cheese. There is almost no outlay for tools needed and the cheese can be made in about an hour." Bulletins and articles urged farm wives to make their own cottage cheese to supplement farm income. "Farmers' wives . . . could make nice pin money by putting a tasty cheese on the local market at 10 cents a pound." Widely published instructions called for cooking soured milk in a water bath, stirring to break it up, draining the curds in a cheesecloth until the whey ran off, and finally working the curds until they were "like mashed potatoes."[25]

There was plenty of skim milk to go around, but butter was scarce. While the federal Food Administration did not specifically restrict use of butter and other fats, it did urge individuals to use less of them. Limits on flour and sugar already meant that homemakers were doing less baking, resulting in savings of butter and other fats, too. The federally approved bread formula for bakeries was also lower in fat than prewar recipes.

Every pound of butter was a valued commodity. Minnesota's prize-winning butter received priority treatment on its trip to the eastern markets. E. A. White of the Pennsylvania Line noted in the *Dairy Record* that "butter shipments got preferential service. Butter concentrated at St. Paul was then shipped to Chicago, New York, Boston, etc. Butter leaving St. Paul landed at New York the sixth morning, and Boston on the seventh."[26]

Much to the dismay of Minnesota's dairymen, however, a butter-competitor spread was making its way west from the factories of large meat processors in Chicago. "Oleomargarine" was a fighting word in barns all across the Upper Midwest. Although the Food Administration urged everyone to make do with substitutes for high-quality animal fats such as butter churned from cow's milk and lard rendered from pig fat, and although an all-vegetable shortening for baking named "Crisco" had been on the market since 1912, this "oleomargarine" or "butterine" was, for some Minnesotans, unpalatable. Unlike today's all-vegetable margarine, World War I–era oleomargarine could combine meat, dairy, and vegetable products. Ingredient lists included beef fat, lard, cottonseed oil, and sour milk. Producers claimed that oleomargarine sometimes even contained the "finest creamery butter" and was "hardly distinguishable from butter." Yet before the war, annual oleomargarine consumption in the United States was a mere two and one-half pounds per person, compared to Europe's 20 to 32 pounds per person annually.[27]

Butter had been drawn into battle. By early 1918, oleomargarine was heavily advertised in national magazines and local newspapers, with meat-packer Armour a major supplier of the alternative spread. In national newspaper releases, Armour noted that national food resources had been reduced to supply the Allies, that dairy exports had increased 1,300 percent, that use of butter alternatives was "imperative," and that Armour was manufacturing oleomargarine on a large scale. Armour claimed it could "protect the public from products compounded from inferior ingredients and produced under conditions where quality has been sacrificed to quantity output." Pointing out its new products, the company promoted Veribest Oleomargarine and Nut-Ola, produced in part with milk "brought in refrigerated cars from the best dairy farms operated under the strict supervision of the Chicago board of health." Armour further promoted a large new factory with "imported machinery and skilled operatives from Holland where oleomargarine manufacture has been brought up to the point of perfection."[28]

Minneapolis-based Northern Cocoanut Butter Company entered the butter *vs.* oleo fray. Beginning in February 1918, it presented its Holiday Nutmargarine in a series of large newspaper ads. "What is Holiday Nutmargarine made of? Four food elements that are in your kitchen in some form: 70 percent coconut oil, 15 percent peanut oil, 15 percent milk, salt. . . . Contains no animal fats and is scientifically prepared in our specially equipped plant—large, strictly sanitary—and already turning out thousands of pounds of this new product every day. Has the exquisite flavor of high-grade creamery butter." The advertisement ended with this strongly worded note: "This product is licensed by the U.S. Food Administration. According to an old law passed before this product was thought of, it must be labeled oleomargarine, but it is not oleomargarine. There is no oleo or other animal fat used in making this wonderful new product."[29]

In April the company's headline quoted an imaginary customer saying, "Certainly I want Holiday Nutmargarine. Everyone in our family likes it best." The ad then claimed that "this remarkable product has taken the place of cow's butter in many thousands of homes." Explaining one remaining problem to homemakers, the ad noted that Nutmargarine "comes to you a creamy white because law requires a tax of 10 cents a pound if we color it, so we supply with each pound carton a capsule of vegetable coloring, the same used in coloring creamery butter."[30]

By the spring of 1918, the tables had turned. Butter prices had increased significantly. Now it cost nearly twice as much as the previously more expensive government-approved fat substitutes. The Nutmargarine company took advantage of its lower price and added a patriotic spin by suggesting that customers also buy Thrift Stamps, a federal war-funding program. As the ad appearing in April noted, "Keep account of your savings with Holiday Nutmargarine. An easy way is to put it in Thrift Stamps, with the result that you will be surprised and pleased as well as patriotic."[31]

Dairy farmers were not about to settle without a fight. In southeastern Minnesota, Farm Bureau dairy councils raised money for pro-butter advertising by charging a levy of one mil per pound. The state's dairy and food department began its 1918 annual report with a salvo against the butter substitutes: "Jealousy and

> **BUTTER SUBSTITUTE**
>
> 1 tablespoon gelatin
> 1 pint milk
> 1 pound butter
> salt
> butter coloring
>
> Dissolve gelatin in milk. Cream butter as if for cake. Add gelatin, salt, and milk slowly, beating with a beater. Keep butter warm while working. Add coloring. Press in a mold. Yield: 2 pounds of butter. (*Park Rapids Enterprise,* March 14, 1918)

STRAWBERRY ICE CREAM

There are always some imperfectly developed berries, especially if the season is dry. These should be sprinkled with sugar, mashed, and squeezed in a cheesecloth until only a ball of seeds is left in the cloth. This juice, combined with twice as much thin cream and more sugar and then frozen, will give the very best strawberry ice cream. When whole or cut berries are put directly into the cream, they are likely to freeze into unpleasant lumps of ice. (*The Farmer's Wife*, June 1917)

trickery, ever zealous in its work of under-mining any successful undertaking, has not overlooked the dairy industry and many so-called butter substitutes have been placed on the market but when the people become educated in the real food value of the genuine butterfat product and the other [products], each will be bought and sold for what it is worth." In Duluth the Palace Market supported local butter makers by adding to its Saturday advertisements the slogan "Today is Butter Day," although the market was compelled to include prices for butter substitutes in their ads as the war continued. Butter-loyal Minnesotans developed their own recipes for extending butter as a table spread by mixing it with milk and gelatin, but these were not useful for cooking.[32]

Consumption of ice cream was another matter of concern during the war. State officials thought children who didn't like to drink milk should eat ice cream, which, despite its name, was made mostly of milk. Dairy commissioner James Sorenson presented a positive opinion on the healthfulness of ice cream: "Milk is not merely a beverage but a food easily assimilated and nourishing and when mixed with cream and a little sugar and flavoring and frozen into ice cream, it is an excellent dessert, nourishing, palatable, and good for sick or well, rich or poor, old or young."[33]

Federal food authorities, however, were less supportive. In December 1917 the Food Administration urged Americans to "eat a little less ice cream. There must be a reasonable margin for conservation in ice cream, for our per capita consumption of this delicacy last year

The Food Administration classifies
Ice Cream as an essential food
Eat it regularly—insisting upon

Crescent Pasteurized
ICE CREAM

Although Herbert Hoover suggested limiting ice cream consumption, many saw this as the best way to eat their milk.

was about 2 gallons. Ice cream is excellent food, but in view of the need for conserving milk and cream and sugar, perhaps a good many Americans could do with a little less of it."[34]

During the 1917 Christmas season, Duluth's Bridgeman-Russell dairy sold a full line of ice cream, including special vanilla with fruits and nuts, as well as orange, pineapple-lemon, and cranberry-mint sherbet at 50 cents a quart. Other cold treats included puddings, French cream, and mousses. Serving-size treats could be purchased in Santa Claus, turkey, Christmas balls, teddy bear, roast turkey, or kewpie shapes.[35]

By early 1918, Bridgeman-Russell trimmed back with ads that still featured weekly ice cream flavors but now contained conservation messages urging Duluth residents to "Eat More Milk." The dairy joined the "cottage cheese brigade" with a large ad touting milk's excellent nutritional and economic benefits. By summer 1918, Bridgeman-Russell returned to reminding customers of their newest ice cream, noting that physicians recommended eating "a plate of Velvet Ice Cream a day to keep healthy."[36]

In the eyes of some social activists, ice cream even offered potential for changing other consumption habits. As the nation moved closer to enacting prohibition against selling alcoholic beverages, the experiences of many Minnesota communities that had already voted to "go dry"—suspend the sale of liquor and close the bars where it was sold—were noted. Sale of ice cream was now a "large and profitable industry" and "buildings formerly occupied by the dispensers of intoxicating beverages" were being converted into ice cream parlors. In this way, appetites that "formerly craved the fiery beverages of the bar are now appeased with this cool palatable substitute, which has real food value as well."[37]

> I just received your money order and bought a dozen eggs and had an old French lady fry them for us. We ate them all for breakfast. You can't imagine how good they tasted. I feel like a different person than I did a few days ago. *David L. Beckman, October 5, 1918*[38]

Egg dishes were frequently recommended by wartime writers as meat-saving main courses. Before the war, many people occasionally ate an egg dish as a main course, but most prewar cookbooks featured very few recipes. The economically minded 1917 cookbook *A Thousand Ways to Please a Husband* featured only five egg dishes. Chronicling the first year of Bob and Bettina's marriage, the book focuses on Bettina's desire to provide inexpensive, well-prepared meals for Bob. Her recipe choices include omelets without fillings, baked eggs, and escalloped eggs with cheese. Bettina serves Eggs a la Goldenrod for dinner, served with potato cakes and cottage cheese, with apple pie for dessert. Food Administration flyers and brochures published many of the same recipes.[39]

While the Food Administration encouraged eating eggs as an alternative to meat, concerns about the available supply lingered. University home economist Josephine Berry explained in a 1917 conservation letter to Twin Cities pastors that "the facts of our low meat production are well known. For this reason and the necessity to share even some of what we have with the Armies of Europe, it will be necessary for us to substitute. . . . It is hoped the efforts to stimulate the increase in the egg production will supply eggs in sufficient quantities."[40]

Like many products from the farmyard, the supply of fresh eggs varied seasonally. Farm wives visiting chicken coops more readily filled their aprons with freshly laid eggs in spring. As one county

DO NOT SELL LAYING HENS

Keep the laying hen

Save the 30 Eggs

—or more—

laid by the average hen from February to May

Food is needed to win the war

Don't sell the laying hen—all spring she will be turning insects, weeds, garbage, and waste into eggs for the Nation

Make 60c. per hen

Those 30 eggs at 24 cents a dozen mean an income of 60 cents per hen— practically all profit, as hens on the farm at this season receive little if any special feed.

2c. a lb. or 2c. an egg?

What if poultry sometimes brings 2 cents more a pound in winter than after the laying season—you would lose only 8 cents on a 4-pound hen, but make 60 cts. on her eggs—gain 52 cts.

IT'S BOTH PATRIOTIC AND PROFITABLE TO KEEP THE LAYING HEN

U. S. DEPARTMENT OF AGRICULTURE

Cooperating with State Agricultural Colleges

Hens generally stop laying eggs in the winter. In normal times, farmers simply got a new laying flock each spring. This poster sets out the economic benefit to keeping those mature hens through their "vacation" and increasing the nation's supply of eggs.

agricultural agent explained, fresh eggs are most expensive "in fall and winter when the hens take their annual vacation. Don't blame the hens—they have always done it and always will." He suggested hatching eggs early in the spring because these chicks would mature and lay later. "If the hens don't want to sit, get broody hens from a neighbor or use an incubator." The more common approach to balancing the egg supply, however, was simply to put eggs into cold storage.[41]

During the war years, Minnesota was a leading producer of eggs. Thousands of small farms had chickens that produced surplus eggs for market. Getting the eggs from those farmyard coops into town and city kitchens was a study in small-town American life. Farmers, or probably more typically farmers' wives earning their "butter and egg" money, would take the eggs into town where the eggs were traded for merchandise or sold for cash. The merchants would then sell the eggs to concentrators to be sorted, graded, packed, and forwarded to large markets in railcar-lot quantities.

Minnesota's hens laid the bulk of their eggs from April through May. Commercial cold-storage facilities purchased spring eggs and held them well into the fall. Eggs stored in the spring had the best shells and were shipped under conditions that were not too hot or cold. One USDA staff member testified in a Congressional hearing that "he would rather have an April egg in January or February" after storage for ten months than an August egg stored only for six months.[42]

Throughout the war, the University of Minnesota poultry experts also conducted a special campaign to increase winter egg production and improve the keeping quality of eggs laid all year. Using the slogan "Beat the Rooster," the initiative sought to prevent fertilization of eggs, since unfertilized eggs kept in good condition longer.[43]

Egg prices remained an issue throughout the war for homemakers trying to beat the high cost of living. In April 1917 Duluth Marine Supply grocery advertised, "Strictly new-laid eggs at 34 cents a dozen." By September they had gone up a penny in price, and by November they were 40 cents a dozen. Accordingly, the store urged shoppers who needed eggs for Christmas baking to buy "Dependable April Eggs" for 42 cents a dozen.[44]

Newspapers, farm bulletins, and food handbooks such as *How We Cook Today* offered tips for homemakers about storing eggs at home for the months ahead. The *Erskine Echo* was one of several Minnesota papers to extend the warning that spring eggs retailing from 20 to 30 cents a dozen would sell for 50 and 60 cents a dozen six months later. The egg-preserving plan noted that "eggs can be carried over until season of high prices at a cost of about 2 cents a dozen" and recommended the use of "water glass" or "liquid glass," a gelled sodium silicate prepared this way: "One quart of water glass mixed with 12 quarts of water that has been boiled and allowed to cool will make enough mixture to preserve about 15 dozen eggs. If the eggs are to be held six or eight months, a stronger solution is better. . . . Clean wholesome eggs are dropped into this solution as gathered each day. The eggs are placed small end down in the water glass. A thin coating of paraffin effectively excludes air and makes replenishing the water glass unnecessary. The jar is stored in a cool cellar."[45]

One popular recipe, appearing in many food conservation cookbooks, sums up the economical and delicious possibilities of new meals combining the products of dairy and coop. Eggs a la Goldenrod was the fancy name for hard-boiled eggs and white sauce over toast. In many versions, a cup of milk and four eggs are stretched to feed six when poured over that many slices of sturdy war bread toast. The "goldenrod" comes from the last fancy touch—sieving the hard-boiled yolks delicately over the top.

My dear boy, I am working every chance I get in the garden. I am going to get six chickens and a rooster next spring, and late in the fall we will eat them up and start fresh every spring. I should have done that this spring. Eggs are 45 cents a dozen now so it will pay to do it. Lovingly, Mama.
Mrs. Cassidy to Gray, July 10, 1918[46]

FOOD WILL WIN THE WAR

You came here seeking Freedom
You must now help to preserve it

WHEAT is needed for the allies
Waste nothing

UNITED STATES FOOD ADMINISTRATION

The Food Administration and Minnesota home economists reached out to immigrant populations with special appeals, classes, and even food conservation recipes translated into dozens of languages, so new Americans could join the battle for freedom overseas.

7

Are You Doing Your Part?

It certainly puts backbone in a man to know that the folks at home stand as solidly behind him as you folks do behind me. It alleviates that sinking sensation in the pit of the stomach when we are requested to travel "a long, long trail a-winding" into no man's land in France, where the shrapnel shells are bursting. *Andrew Glenn, May 9, 1918, Western Front*[1]

War and food conservation restrictions brought out the best in most people, the worst in a few. It allowed some to seek redress for long-held grievances or act spitefully against petty jealousies. Fear motivated some of the worst actions where even those in positions of power acted harshly and shamefully. Yet, for all the stress and uncertainties of the 19 months of war, letters, local newspaper columns, and official reports demonstrate the resolve of most Minnesotans to do their very best, to aid their neighbors, to help with the war effort, and to win the war with food.[2]

Columnist Ada Melville Allen, writing in *The Farmer* in April 1917, addressed women's dedication to the new cause: "You and I may prefer to avoid in our letters and conversations all reference to the War, to the general confusion of the world, to the steady climb of prices, to the increasing difficulty of life in general. But there are times when we should squarely face the issues and each say to herself, 'What is my part in this? How can I help?' It does no good to complain, to preach, to voice fear or anxiety or indignation. Each must do the best she can and do it quietly, simply, trustfully."[3]

None did their part more effectively than A. D. Wilson, Minnesota's food administrator. He traveled the state from top to bottom, explaining, cajoling, pleading, and motivating individuals and groups on the food conservation battlefield. The founding director of the university's extension service, Wilson already knew the state's farmers and the business of farming when he was named in April 1917 to Governor Burnquist's 29-member panel to survey war readiness. Within weeks he was tirelessly attending meetings, making speeches, investigating situations, and sending out press releases to any and all. He wielded his influence and power deftly, and his persuasive speeches were touched with humor. Memos, letters, and press releases were comprehensive and witty. A release issued near the end of the war, for example. cheers the reappearance of sugar for holiday cooking with the salute: "What Ho, the Cranberry."

When Wilson began outreach to the lumberjacks of Minnesota's north woods in November and December 1917, an impressed Bemidji newspaper editor noted, "The United States has her Wilson and so has the state of Minnesota . . . and we're going to . . . tell the people of Bemidji and Beltrami county the reason they don't know him is because he is just about the busiest individual to be found in many moons." The folksy account continued, "He was working like a dock-walloper when others were listening to a radiator sing, and what's more he has been doing just such work with the brass band accompaniment a long way off." Noting Wilson's visit, the editor wrote approvingly, "Sunday, this Wilson fellow was up in the Crookston lumber camps in the dense forests in weather that would make an ordinary mortal steal a red hot stove. . . . We thought like many others that he was a sort of swivel-chair executive with a competent corps of typewriter hammerers and a theoretical knowledge of how to make a snowball serve as a square meal for a chap who works in . . . sub-zero weather, but as we said, We're next to him now."[4]

Wilson's work with lumberjacks underscored their critical role in both the military and home fronts. Jacks were among the first specialized troops sent overseas to prepare camps and roadways through rural France, where they cut timber and finished 12 million board feet of sawn lumber and ties, 15,000 telephone and telegraph poles, 16,000 small poles and pickets, and wood for fuel each month. Lumberjack Robert Shaw wrote from France: "I signed up as the 63rd recruit for the forestry bunch out of Bemidji. . . . Cut logs all day, 77 logs from 7 A.M. to 11 A.M. . . . We are now cutting for

LUMBERJACK'S CONSERVATION CAKE

1½ cups water	2½ cups all-purpose flour
1 cup sugar	½ teaspoon nutmeg
¼ cup butter	¼ teaspoon salt
2½ cups barley flour	2½ teaspoons baking powder

Preheat the oven to 350° F. Combine the water and sugar in a medium saucepan. Bring to a simmer, stirring until the sugar is dissolved. Add butter. While this is cooking, combine the dry ingredients in a medium mixing bowl. Remove the sugar and water from the stove. Pour over the dry ingredients and stir until just blended. Lightly grease and flour 4 miniature loaf pans and bake until cakes are lightly browned on top, about 35 minutes. (*University of Minnesota Farm Press News*, December 12, 1917)

ties. I went to a nearby hotel and had a bowl of bread and milk. I sat at the little table sticky with wine and broke brown bread into the boiled milk."[5]

Lumberjacks were important to war efforts on the home front as well. Men with axes and two-man cross-cut saws felled large trees in sub-zero temperatures. Camp cooks carried noon meals to the work site, and if jacks didn't eat them fast enough, beans could freeze to the plate. The better men were fed, the happier they were and the harder they worked in the brutal winter conditions. Maggie Orr O'Neill described the camp meals she helped her mother and sisters prepare, which included potatoes, beans, rice, dried apples, and salt pork. Jack Leonard Costley remembered eating salt pork, bacon, cold-storage eggs, and a mainstay of flapjacks. Meals included "big kettles of roast beef and brown gravy, and a couple of bushels of boiled potatoes." Costley concluded, "One thing about those cooks in the woods, they were real bakers. . . . White bread, and occasionally, probably once a week, [cornmeal] Johnny cake."[6]

With meals like those it was no wonder the Minnesota Food Administration recognized logging camps "were great sources of food waste." Finding a solution took tact. Wilson realized the lumberjack needed to be well fed and felt that with a direct appeal and

Lumberjacks joined the food conservation movement wholeheartedly. Cooks adapted prewar tables like these filled with flapjacks, doughnuts, and other wheat- and sugar-laden foods to yield significant savings in wheat, meat, sugar, and fats.

explanation of the war conditions the men and their cooks would be willing to join in the sacrifice so that fighting men could be fed. During November and December 1917, Wilson and J. A. Vye, executive secretary of the Food Administration, made weekly trips into the snowbound camps to explain food needs. Despite the fact that "many of these men spoke foreign tongues, the message was transmitted and the response was spontaneous and sincere."[7]

Some cooks from logging camps volunteered to attend cooking conservation classes at the university's farm in St. Paul, and in December 1917 John Raini and Edward Canute, "two woodsmen for life by choice," came to campus to learn recipes and techniques to take back to the north woods. Special courses emphasized using flour substitutes, in particular. After the class, lumberjacks sent back a recipe they developed for Conservation Cake.[8]

Lumber camps' successes were lauded in a report at the end of the war. Camp cooks conserved by reducing their sugar use from the prewar average of 12 to 15 pounds for every 90 meals to a mere 2 pounds per 90 meals in the fall of 1918. Most of the camps "observed meatless days and reduced the quantity of meat used, which had been over a pound per day per man—nearly 25 percent. More fish were served than formerly and the use of vegetables was increased greatly." Prewar use of wheat flour dropped from 26 to 30 pounds per month per man to 14.25 pounds, a "vast savings."[9]

While few camps raised hogs before the war, most "responded when requested. . . . Not only did this provide the camps with fresh pork but over-production enabled a considerable number of hogs to be sold on the market. The logging camps [had] their own gardens. The result was that many clearings were made in the woods and crops were raised where none had grown before."[10]

Lumber camps were not the only communities in Minnesota that required special techniques for food conservation outreach. Nearly 70 percent of Minnesotans were first- or second-generation Americans, and in some neighborhoods English was a second or foreign language.

In Minneapolis and St. Paul, settlement houses already served immigrant families by offering mothers lessons on feeding families with ingredients available in Minnesota. These organizations quickly became a conduit for the Food Administration to reach residents who did not speak English. Recipes in languages including Lithuanian, Yiddish, Swedish, and Finnish offered "a whole dinner in one dish" and advice on making foods that "the youngsters will like. Father will like . . . and your pocketbook will surely like . . . a dish hot and savory—good for work or play." Basic recipes suggested alternate ingredients so that one person's fish chowder might be another's rabbit stew.[11]

In December 1917 MCPS Women's Auxiliary food demonstrator Elizabeth Nickerson worked as a liaison between the government and the northeast Minneapolis ethnic community. She prepared recipes that emphasized healthy cooking and had them translated into Polish. Cooking classes at the settlement house offered demonstrations of the recipes. Nickerson also engaged households at the opposite end of the economic spectrum, noting "I have already talked to a group of the cooks and housemaids of some of the large households and hope to interest them in further gatherings."[12]

Some critics questioned people's consumption of expensive cuts of meat during wartime, but a grocery industry publication asserted that purchase of luxury goods "by households that can afford them is just as important as the consumption of the less expensive merchandise. Hoover says that the largest margin for food savings exists among the 30 percent of our well-to-do population, because 70 percent of our people do not have a very large margin for food savings." The publication then encouraged "judicious promotion of sales along this line" to help the grocer "carry out the true spirit of food savings and also give him the profit balance necessary to make up reduced margins on some of the great staples which are being handled at small profit as his contribution toward winning the war."[13]

Not everyone supported war efforts wholeheartedly. Some people complained about restrictions and shortages, and a few made it their business to offer opinions on how other people could do better. "Do-gooders" were occasionally the subject of humor behind their backs. As reported in the *Farmers Equity News,* published in Alexandria, "New York society women including Mrs. W. R. Vanderbilt, Jr., are touring rural New York in soft-cushioned limousines bearing 'words of advice and encouragement' to women on farms. Some of the slogans are: Can or Collapse, Preserve or Perish, Work or Want." The account noted that farmers and their wives "must ache with laughter as the motors roll by. The farmer leaves his planter for a moment and his wife her thousand and one household duties to read 'Work or Want.' There isn't a farm woman in the whole state of New York who doesn't can more vegetables and preserve more fruit in one year than Mrs. Vanderbilt will do in all her days. Why don't the farmers and their wives run up and down Fifth Avenue with gratuitous advice about canning, preserving, and working? They are too busy *doing* it!"[14]

Families living in cities did not evade scrutiny. Reports from the "Association for improving the condition of the poor" carried in a Winona newspaper suggested that the "menu of the average family of small income was not properly balanced. They ate too much bread and meat." Although it was unclear where this group did its survey, the results noted that "families of varying nationalities did not eat what it had been decided they should eat to meet their food requirements. They almost all exceeded the bread and meat ration. Whenever there was any money on hand, the families plunged in the purchase of meat and bread. . . . All except the Americanized Italians eat meat at least once and often twice a day whenever they have the price. There is great reluctance to use peas, beans and other substitutes for potatoes."[15]

Minnesota cooks of all heritages stepped right up into the food conservation effort. They slipped into their aprons and planned meals without waiting for recipes from federal or state food agencies. Women in Eveleth formed a Hoover Club to develop and test recipes, which they published in the local newspaper. Others sent recipes into magazines or simply shared them with friends on recipe cards passed over the back fence. Mrs. B. B. sent in her own ideas to *The Farmer:* "Good Inexpensive Soup. I serve soup every day. I save what is usually drained away and start it with the water drained from cooked vegetables such as peas, beans, carrots. Then I add a spoonful of left-over gravy, meat stock, milk, a bit of onion or tomato. Watch the leftovers closely and let them do full duty."[16]

Yet, not every recipe printed in newspapers during the first days of the war seemed appropriate for Minnesota kitchens. Many listed ingredients more common in New England than the Midwest. Beginning on June 6, 1917, the *Mankato Free Press* printed the syndicated column "Today's War Recipe," often at the top of the Society column. Recipes included fish cutlets, cheese charlotte, fish pie, bacon soup, stuffed onions, eggplant, and meat pie. Frequently they ended with advice such as "Masticate more and need half as much."[17]

In an August 1917 article, "American Housewives are Frugal and Saving Food," a *Mankato Free Press* reporter interviewed several local homemakers and learned, "There seemed to be unanimous agreement between the women of the moderate and work-a-day homes. 'I don't want any "high-toned" woman coming around here telling me to save,' stated one mother of six who pays the rent and contrives to buy the household necessities and clothes for her family on her husband's magnificent salary of $2 per day." Another woman said,

"We working people don't need to be told to save. We have always saved. There is nothing that goes to waste in our homes." Shortly thereafter the "Today's War Recipe" column stopped appearing in the *Free Press*.[18]

The food-conservation message was inescapable. Public parks and civic buildings were used as large billboards, and every possible medium was pressed into use. Inventive minds came up with similar solutions to get the word out, as seen in this response by Mildred Weigley to a suggestion by Mrs. Charles Thompson of the social service division at Minneapolis General Electric Company: "I have glanced through the little bulletin *What to Eat and Why,* which you compiled, and I think you have done an excellent piece of work. . . . We are in the process of making some poster slips that will fit into envelopes—One Meatless Day a Week and One Wheatless Meal a Day. These slips will carry suggested menus on the back." She continued that there was a possibility of sending these slips out in the monthly electric bills.[19]

FISH CHOWDER

¼ pound salt pork, or 1 tablespoon other fat
1 onion, sliced
2 cups carrots, cut in pieces
9 potatoes, peeled and cut in small pieces
3 tablespoons flour
3 cups milk, or tomatoes
pepper
1½ pound fish (fresh, salt, or canned), or rabbit, fowl, or any meat, boned
   and cut into small pieces

Cut pork in small pieces and fry with the onion for 5 minutes. Add carrots and potatoes, and cover with boiling water. Cook until the vegetables are tender. Mix flour with ½ cup cold milk and stir into the pot to thicken. Add the rest of the milk and the fish. Cook until fish is tender, about 10 minutes. Makes enough to feed a family of 5. (*A Whole Dinner in One Dish,* United States Food Leaflet No. 3, Food Files, Minnesota Historical Society)

This huge billboard in downtown St. Paul, like others posted in public places, made escaping the food conservation message almost impossible.

In Crookston, the U.S. post office began canceling stamps with the phrase, "Food Will Win the War—Don't Waste It." H. J. Titus, superintendent of the dining-car service of the Northern Pacific Railway, did the post office one better when he rubber-stamped this message at the bottom of every letter he sent out: "If each home saves one ounce of meat daily, it means 465,000,000 pounds annually; one slice of bread, 365,000,000 loaves annually; one piece of butter, 114,000,000 pounds annually; and one cup of milk 912,000,000 quarts, or the product of 400,000 cows, annually. Let Us Do Our Part."[20]

In December 1917 the first of the 17,000 Minnesota troops to serve in the war shipped out for the battlefields of France. Informational flyers positioned food conservation as an important part of the holidays and asked people to "add to your gift list the daily savings of wheat, meats, fats and sugar."[21]

By early 1918 it was clear that various food-conservation campaigns were working but that Americans would need to maintain their altered consumption habits at least through the 1918 harvest.

Supplies of critical foods—wheat, some meats, sugar, and fats—
continued to be tight.

New federal regulations continued to make front-page news.
The *Brown County Journal* reported, "More wheatless and meatless
meals sought. Eleven wheatless meals . . . required of patriotic servers of food in America. The only exception to wheatless rules were
communion wafers and Passover matzos. 'Wheatless means wheatless,' according to A. D. Wilson. Serving the new victory bread with
its small percentage of flour other than wheat does not make a meal
wheatless. Whole wheat and graham are not wheatless." Wilson further urged citizens faced with unfamiliar meatless and wheatless
breakfasts: "Goodbye to bacon, roll, and coffee, a highly wasteful
breakfast. You could eat six rolls and all the bacon you would allow
and still not be satisfied. Instead, substitute a corn muffin for the
roll and add a generous dish of locally grown perishables and apples,
potatoes, or hominy grits."[22]

Even the best-intentioned food conservationists found shortages and excesses confusing. Pork, ham, and bacon, for instance,
went from shortage to surplus in six months. In November 1917
bacon-eaters were labeled "traitors" and "ham and eggers just as
bad." Two months later, the *Eveleth News* noted: "Bacon is the soldier's real food friend. He can apparently do more fighting on it than
on anything else. By omitting bacon from home menus, the people
of the community will be doing one of the big things that it rests
with them to do in assistance of the men who have been sent from
the community to do our fighting."[23]

Hoover's Food Administration kept on top of the changing food
supplies and adjusted restrictions and encouraged the use of surplus foods. By the middle of May 1918, however, supplies of bacon
had become so plentiful that Morrell meat-packing company advertised that eating bacon "helps in the conservation of meat. It is
difficult for people who have regularly depended upon meat to get
along without it. By using a little bacon in combination with cereal
and vegetable dishes, many housewives are supplying the desired
meat flavor."[24]

Food Administration appeals, actions, and controls made a positive impact on the high cost of living (H.C.L.) that had plagued

save

1-wheat
use more corn

2-meat
use more fish & beans

3-fats
use just enough

4-sugar
use syrups

and serve
the cause of freedom

U. S. FOOD ADMINISTRATION

Initially, food conservation requests centered on four simple steps everyone could follow.

homemakers from the harvest shortages of 1916 through the first months of the war. General H. C. L. may not have been defeated, but he was on the run. One information innovation helped bridge the gap between homemakers who still had to watch their food dollars and retail grocers who still needed to make a living. Many Minnesota communities followed the Food Administration guidelines and formed "fair price committees." These groups, including a retail grocer and others from the community, set up lists of everyday foods showing the average wholesale price the grocer paid and the highest price that could be charged to consumers. The lists were published in local newspapers.[25]

As the army ranks swelled with draftees, families eager to "do their part" sent home-cooked dishes to tens of thousands of soldiers in distant training camps. The *Cloquet Pine Knot* published this appreciative letter from a soldier: "A while ago five of us had a feast of home made eats. My sister sent me a broiled chicken from New York and we had a beef loaf from Superior, Wis., cake from Aurora, Ill., jam from California, candy from St. Louis and Jacksonville, Fla., another cake from Nebraska, cookies from Brooklyn, N.Y., and two pies made by the cooks here in camp, so you see the U.S. was pretty well covered in our little banquet."[26]

Shipping home-prepared foods across the state and nation, however, put pressure on the U.S. postal service and several railway express companies. In late 1917 the federal government took over operation of these express companies for the duration of the war, and on July 1, 1918, the government consolidated operations, creating the American Railway Express Company. Food reportedly represented half of the bulk of all items shipped, and the company willingly took perishable foods, considering this service "a trust." In St. Paul, the company handled 18,000 waybills a day that included 2,500 full cans of cream and countless personal packages sent from soldier's homes.[27]

By summer 1918 the post office in Minneapolis had developed its own expertise in shipping food. According to the *Minneapolis Journal,* "The refrigerator is working overtime this summer handling large shipments daily of fruit, berries, butter, and eggs, sent to Minneapolis consumers fresh from nearby Minnesota farms." This created challenges because "some perishable articles come through the mails unmarked. . . . Meat can easily be detected because it has a heavy sodden weight distinct from other parcels. . . . A new clerk at the post office started for the refrigerator with a crate of what he believed to be eggs. 'Peep! Peep! Peep!' chirped 50 chicks from inside the box. 'Too late,' he said, thinking they had hatched on their journey." He was told, much to his relief, that new postal regulations permitted sending live chickens through the mail as well as chickens in the making, or eggs.[28]

Despite shippers' best efforts, food sent from farms to cities and from homes to soldiers resulted in wasted food. Eventually the army requested that families stop sending food and do their part for the war in other ways.

Sometimes packed-up food was wasted much closer to home. Mothers were urged to make "conservation lunches" for their schoolchildren. While mothers may have seen this as a convenient way to convert dinner leftovers into a tasty lunch, not all lunches carried to school were actually eaten. Preventing children from wasting food when they were away from mother's watchful eyes was identified as a problem by Harriet Wallace Ashby in *Wallaces' Farmer.* Writing in September 1917, she described meeting a school janitor carrying home a bucket half filled with food. On the top was a fat sandwich of home-baked bread and meat. He told her "The children get in a hurry to play and lots of them will throw out almost their whole lunch. I usually get more than this to take home to my chickens." Ashby noted that "the appetite of a child is capricious but he should bring home what he does not eat. . . . Lunch-bucket leaks will be stopped."[29]

Minnesotans shared more than ideas for saving food. Many shared letters from their soldiers in camp or overseas with the editors of local newspapers. News for one family became information for all. Axel Krohn's letter home was typical of those printed in the *Cloquet Pine Knot:* "I have had my first experience in the trench life, was there for 20 days. I sure would have enjoyed it if it had not been so wet and muddy, and believe me I sure tried hard to get a German while I was there. . . . It makes a fellow think of home the first day when you are in the trenches and hear the big shells going over you singing, 'Home Sweet Home.'"[30]

SUGGESTIONS FOR SCHOOL LUNCHES

1. Sandwiches with sliced meat for filling, baked apple, cookies, or a few lumps of sugar.
2. Slices of meat loaf or bean loaf, bread and butter sandwiches, stewed fruit, small frosted cake.
3. Crisp rolls hollowed out and filled with chopped meat or fish moistened and seasoned or mixed with salad dressing; orange, apple, a mixture of fruit or berries, cake.
4. Lettuce or celery sandwiches, cup custard, jelly sandwiches.
5. Cottage cheese and chopped green pepper sandwiches, or a pot of cream cheese with bread and butter sandwiches, peanut sandwiches, fruit cake.
6. Hard-boiled eggs, crisp baking-powder biscuits, celery or radishes, brown sugar or maple sugar sandwiches.
7. Bottle of milk, thin corn bread and butter, dates, apple.
8. Raisin or nut bread with butter, cheese, orange, maple sugar, baked bean and lettuce sandwiches, applesauce, sweet chocolate. (*Worthington Globe*, April 11, 1918)

Official news releases to the same hometown papers often presented a cheering point of view. In January 1918, the *Pine Knot* reported: "A man is in the front trench under fire, say, two days, and sent back four, or perhaps four days and sent back eight. Usually a brigade is in the 'fire sector' thirty-two days, then sent back to the rest billets [quarters] for an equal time. Here the men are in practically no danger—perhaps an occasional shell. They are together in jolly companionship, having lots of amusements—football, baseball—plenty to do. They are well fed, well equipped, well amused."[31]

Families at home eagerly read reports from community leaders who visited training camps. In November 1918, Rabbi C. David Matt wrote to a Minneapolis paper, "From the moment one arrives at the railroad station of a war camp community to the moment he leaves, he feels the presence of an inclusive, protecting warm bond of fellowship and helpfulness." The rabbi further reported that the American Library Association maintained "a library of books frequently changed, back home newspapers, and books in every language. To what extent the Russian and Italian collections were used, I cannot say, but the Yiddish and Hebrew collections were intelligently selected and, I was told, were read."[32]

People could cooperate across religious lines to support soldiers, but war and the high cost of living also provided opportunities to push for significant societal changes. On the eve of the national prohibition of alcoholic beverages, which would be enacted by Congress in 1919 and take effect on January 1, 1920, many counties in Minnesota were already "dry." In those counties that continued to serve liquor, the rules were changing. In Minneapolis, the first order issued by the Minnesota Commission of Public Safety called for the "closure of all saloons, pool halls and moving picture houses in the Bridge Square and the milling districts." This action was taken in order to control a volatile situation where "rough people do rough work." One of the saloon operators saw the ruling from its policy-developing point of view: "We won't get our licenses back and that's fine with me."[33]

In New Ulm, the war provided cover for an action that local barkeepers welcomed as cost savings to their ongoing business. A front-page article in the *Brown County Journal* was headlined, "No more free lunch in New Ulm bars." It explained that "proprietors of New Ulm thirst parlors will put the lid on free lunch on Tuesday, May 5, 1917. The day will go down in the history of local saloons as an innovation. Hereafter those who desire to enjoy lunch with their glass of amber fluid will have to dig a bit further into their pocket books and pay for the privilege."[34]

Supporters of Prohibition saw the war as an opportunity to close saloons and stop the manufacture of intoxicating spirits. One of the provisions of the Lever Food Control Act, passed in August 1917, called for immediate cessation of the distillation of liquor from grains that could be used for human or animal food; beer brewing was restricted in December. By 1918 brewers were permitted only 70 percent of the previous year's grain, and beer's legal alcohol content was reduced to 2.75 percent.[35]

When saloons continued to sell liquor from existing inventory, irritated citizens who looked forward to nationwide Prohibition

SAVE! SAVE!

FOOD

Needed for the Allies and for our Fighting Men in Europe

FUEL

Needed in the Production of Necessities

MAN POWER

Needed in Army, Navy and Industries

GRAIN, COAL and LABOR
USED IN THE MANUFACTURE OF BEER
ARE WORSE THAN WASTED

CLOSE THE BREWERIES!

Members of the Woman's Christian Temperance Union saw the war as a way to bring about the end of liquor sales in the United States. It was unpatriotic, they argued, to make alcoholic beverages with grains that were needed for food and to keep saloons open when other businesses shut down to conserve fuel.

complained directly to Governor Burnquist. Coal for heating was in short supply, and because manufacturing plants had been ordered to observe "Heatless Mondays," one citizen wrote, it seemed wrong that coal "might be used in heating the saloons. . . . I believe that before this war is won, it will be known as a war for the world's freedom from the liquor traffic. . . . I am not a fanatic or a crank."[36]

Liquor distillers and saloonkeepers were not the only ones singled out for criticism. The Federal Trade Commission accused the nation's biggest meat-packers of monopolistic profiteering, and in response the companies ran a series of newspaper advertisements in the summer of 1918 appealing for fair treatment. One noted, "If you are a business man you will appreciate the significance of these facts. If you are unacquainted with business, talk this matter over with some business acquaintance—with your banker, say—and ask him to compare the profits of the packing industry with those of any other large industry at the present time." An ad in the *Brown County Journal* in August 1918 sponsored by one packer posed the question: "How much do you think it costs to dress beef, cure hides and prepare all the numerous by-products . . . and deliver them to the retailer—sweet and fresh—in less than two weeks after dressing? Swift & Company did all this for you in 1917 at an expense of less than 2½ cents per pound of beef sold, including an average profit of ¼ of a cent per pound."[37]

Although milk producers in the Twin Cities cooperated with the MCPS's investigation and complied with its order establishing the wholesale and retail price of milk, milk producers used the pages of their newsletter to let off steam: "The women's clubs of the cities are there in force to see that the 'millionaire farmers' are throttled in their effort to starve the babies of the cities, and it was hinted by one of the good-natured farmers on the committee that . . . they might do better by spending a little time in an effort to have the babies brought up in the way mother used to. But if this method was adopted, there would not be so much time to attend gatherings of this nature." It continued, "Minneapolis housewives who pay $12 a pair for fine kid boots and turn down good wholesome milk at 12 cents a quart would rather display robust calves than 'kids.'"[38]

Some dairies had problems with their customers, who did not return milk bottles promptly. The city of Cloquet appealed to residents, "Don't use the bottles for kerosene containers because when they are sent back to the dairy, it spoils the rest of the milk. The dairy men should, on the other hand, wash the bottles freely and if possible sterilize them before putting in fresh milk."[39]

Keeping enough cows in production so all those bottles could be filled was a significant problem in the fall of 1917 and 1918. Farmers and dairymen were asked to change their time-tested ways of operation to meet the increased demand for milk and milk products. Milk supplies usually decline in the fall and winter as farmers cull their less productive animals and cows produce less milk until they deliver their next calf.

A severe shortage of hay—the winter feed used by most Minnesota dairymen—combined with the usual seasonal factors to put the now-essential milk supply in jeopardy. With milk and cheese taking the place of meat and with butter in high demand, Minnesota dairy farmers and their cows needed help to survive and produce over the winter. The short-term solution was to use straw as a feed and to ask fellow farmers across the state to share their hay. Reported the *Worthington Globe,* "In many parts of Minnesota the hay crop is short. . . . They may not have a large supply of rough feed this fall. . . . When hay sells at $12 to $ 15 per ton, straw is easily worth $4 to $5 per ton for feed. This year, when the attempt is being made to save every possible kind of foodstuff, it would be well to give special attention to the straw crop."[40]

University extension and Food Administration posters went up at feed and grain stores and other small-town meeting places. Rallying networking beyond neighborliness, these graphic messages urged cooperative help for dairy herds and the beef cattle being raised in drought-stricken northwestern Minnesota, North Dakota, and Montana.

Farming was already a cooperative venture, with neighbor helping neighbor in times of plenty as well as in times of trouble. One poster suggested, "Help your fellow farmers! Help the nation!" In response, farmers in southern Minnesota sent straw and hay to their northwestern fellows. Railroads were asked to provide special freight rates and, it was noted, they "will doubtless comply."[41]

Another flyer pleaded, "Don't sell cows or heifers unless absolutely necessary—Europe is contracting for American live stock to be delivered after the war, and this demand will continue." The flyer also described how nonfarmers could aid the cause: "Commercial interests must help. Bankers, Merchants, Farmers must assist in this plan. It will pay! It will help to win the war!"[42]

University dairy specialist Arthur McGuire had anticipated the feed problem and promoted a long-term solution. During the summer of 1917 he accompanied farmers on "silo tours" in several counties. Near Staples, more than 200 people in 72 cars viewed concrete-block and wooden-stave silos. In August, the Pipestone newspaper discussed the value of silos, noting that the county agent advised farmers, "Feed will be scarce and very high the coming winter. The value of a silo is not only in the feed it produces, but also due to the fact that the stock-carrying capacity of the farm is increased. It is the amount of stock kept on a farm that determines the amount of fertilizer left on the farm each year."[43]

As grain and other plant material are stored in a silo, the material compresses and, in a fermentation process, is converted into a succulent, nutrient-rich feed. As the Strandell Cement Products Company of Crookston advertised in the *Erskine Echo* on August 16, 1918, "you save 40 percent of your entire corn crop which you otherwise would lose if you store your corn in a cement stave silo. The whole crop—60 percent corn and 40 percent stalk—is turned into succulent feed." This was why, the ad continued, the Hubbard County agricultural agent advised farmers, "Every farm having 10 cows or its equivalent should have a silo. It is the cheapest feed grown and furnishes succulent feed during the winter months and helps out pastures during a dry spell in the summer."

By 1918, silo construction in the Minnesota countryside had increased. Renville County farmers alone put up 31 new silos, according to one report. But for those who had not yet invested, dairy agent McGuire wrote a forceful article warning, "If the war continues, it is possible that the price of cows next spring will be double

Silos changed the rural landscape. Plant material stored in the airtight tower is converted from indigestible roughage into succulent feed, especially important in Minnesota where cows can graze only during the four or five months pastures are filled with green grass.

what they were last spring. It is a public duty for you to keep them. The small farm without cows is . . . without sufficient means of helping the country in its time of greatest need."[44]

Another of McGuire's modernization efforts pitted the actions and interests of small farms and towns against big dairies and cities. McGuire was a strong proponent of cooperative creameries. Located in rural Minnesota, these businesses operated in a number of ways, but essentially they took in the cream from farmers and churned it into high-quality butter. Some also made and sold ice cream and other milk products. At the start of the war there were some 800 cooperative creameries. There were also 1,600 cream-buying stations. And that was the problem.

In many small towns farmers simply took their cream into town and sold or traded it for merchandise at a number of stores. The complaint was that these cream buyers did not have the proper storage facilities to keep the cream cool and wholesome before they shipped it on to a large creamery in St. Paul, for example.

James Sorenson, commissioner of the state's dairy and food department, wrote to the MCPS, calling the commission's attention to "wasteful practices" at cream-buying stations: "1,600 or more men are now engaged in this apparently non-essential work. Many of these stations . . . encourage the production of sour and old, stale cream. . . . There is also considerable loss in shipping cream long distances. . . . The successful prosecution of the war depends largely on food, manpower and transportation, and it would seem to be only our plain duty to eliminate waste of these war-time necessities."[45]

The operator of the Montgomery Cooperative Creamery Association wrote the MCPS the same month that "there are at present 7 cream buyers in town. One only handles cream and eggs; two handle cream & eggs, a little feed and flour and substitutes; 4 grocery & general stores also buy cream. Neither of these buyers have any ice nor a cool place to keep the cream, and the cream is taken in all day long. . . . The cream that gets in Sat. stays in the store until Monday morning 8 A.M. without being cooled."[46]

The labor engaged by these stations also came under fire. A letter from the state creamers, cheese factory operators, and managers association observed "that at the present time with all help so badly

Nothing was wasted. Pits from fruits were ground for Allied soldiers' gas-mask filters.

needed in the successful prosecution of the war, a Cream Buying Station is about as essential as a well in the bottom of a lake."[47]

Taking the other side, the cashier of the Borup bank in northwest Minnesota opposed any move by the MCPS to close local independent cream stations. He explained that "several farmers tell me that if this order should go into effect, they would have to quit the dairy . . . as the hauling of the cream cans to the creameries would take up too much time for them to do. . . . A clean sweep hail storm would not do as much damage to us at this time as an order of that kind."[48]

Ultimately, the matter of regulating or eliminating cream stations must have been too complicated for the MCPS to sort out. While letter writers received polite replies from the MCPS and the commission seemed to take the matter seriously, it did not act.[49]

Farmers must always compete with animals for the fruits of

their fields, but the pressures of war escalated that battle. In the conflict between nature and growing food crops, some Minnesotans thought animals should be on the losing end. When asked in April 1917 for suggestions that could improve food production, the agent for Lac qui Parle County suggested "killing rabbits that now destroy fruit trees and using the rabbits as food."[50]

Town dwellers living next to families who raised chickens expressed another grievance, with battle lines formed across backyard property lines. The *Erskine Echo* reported, "Of all the petty, irritating annoyances of neighborhood life, doubtless the predatory chicken is the greatest. Nothing eatable or destroyable is safe from its industrious bill and claws. . . . Thousands of people have planted war gardens in the two-fold hope of piecing out household expenses and of relieving the world shortages of food. It is with these gardens that the roaming fowl play havoc." The *Echo* continued, "The owner of chickens who permits his fowls to become a nuisance to his neighbors is greatly lacking the spirit of patriotism that should govern all our people in these strenuous times. . . . Pen the chickens at least till the gardens are out of the way."[51]

The *Mankato Ledger* editor offered a light look at the problem:

"Are you sure this chicken is tender?" asked the customer in the market.

"Yes, I think it is, sir," replied the market man.

"And do you know that it is fresh killed?"

"Oh yes, sir."

"Why are you so positive?"

"Because I caught it in my war garden only yesterday."[52]

As the months of war passed, eyes watching for wasted food and resources seemed to be everywhere. An anonymous article in the *Brown County Journal* got down to basics when it observed, "The greatest cause for food wasting is overeating. Four persons out of five eat too much. . . . The appetite is not always a safe guide. . . . Overeating and eating foods that are hard to digest are the causes of the largest part of our illnesses."[53]

Even the U.S. Army was on the lookout, following Hoover's first request to reduce waste at every meal. One news release commented on soldiers whose eyes were bigger than their stomachs: "The pig table is the newest institution at the mess hall at the Army Mechanics Training School on the University Farm Campus. Soldiers who indulge in piling more on their plates than they can eat sit there as an example." Noting that nothing was permitted to go to waste at the school, the release added that meat and bone scraps were sold to packers who rendered out the grease and the bone for chicken feed. Leftover fats were used for cooking, and bread crumbs from the 80 loaves of bread served at each meal were converted into dressing or back into the baking of breads. Leftover rice and oatmeal were added to bread.[54]

Minnesotans were bombarded at every turn with war news, Red Cross and war bond appeals, and ever-changing food conservation requests. Every avenue of interaction became a medium for motivation, information, and influence. As rural and city citizens adjusted to the changes thought essential for victory, they grasped the possibilities for the future as well. Silos, gardens, and other war-created changes—even simple waste-reducing measures—would set the state, and the nation, on a path for long-term success, with everyone playing a part.

One woman owned a somewhat pampered cat that often, because of some whim or for want of appetite, left his breakfast untouched. Before the war it had become the custom to consign this untouched breakfast to the garbage pail, but the thrifty housekeeper declared this could not be allowed in a time of food shortage, and so Puss, much to his chagrin, now found his discarded breakfast dished up for dinner. And as he, made hungry by his long fast, mincingly ate the dose, he was lectured by his mistress: "Eat it, Tom, or Hoover won't like you. We've all of us got to stand by Hoover."
From "Hamline in the Great War"[55]

8

Every Spud a Soldier!

Potato week in Park Rapids was a decided success. Handed out recipes and made up new dishes which were very good, even if they were original. All growers are enthusiastic over the lowly potato. *May V. Coppernall, food conservation chair, Hubbard County, May 21, 1918*[1]

For every soldier on K.P. duty serving up a mountain of spuds, there were Minnesota farmers looking to make a handsome crop, and homemakers urged to follow recipes using the humble potato in all sorts of unexpected ways. While the idea to stretch wheat and meat supplies by encouraging Americans to eat more potatoes seemed an ideal solution, there were a few bumps along the spud's road to serving as a "pota-triot." Home economist Josephine Berry of the University of Minnesota advised Minnesotans to increase potato consumption from an estimated 250 grams a day to 375 grams. This was equivalent to eating two fist-sized potatoes a day, adding up to 24 pounds (two-fifths of a bushel) per month. For a family of six, this amounted to a whopping monthly consumption of 144 pounds of potatoes, or two and one-half bushels.[2]

In spring 1917, however, Minnesotans hardly had enough potatoes to go around. The fall 1916 crop had been a dismal failure, about half of a normal harvest. Potatoes sold for three and four times the typical bushel price. In Pipestone the local paper jokingly reported that potatoes had become "a sign of great wealth. It is said that many wealthy people are now placing a thin coating of gilt over potatoes and placing them in conspicuous positions on their dressers, pianos, etc. The editor of this paper still remembers the good old times when potatoes were used as food."[3]

While it looked as though the potatoes planted in 1917 would

No vegetable did more to win the war than the lowly potato. In short supply in the spring of 1917, potatoes were planted by the bushel in home gardens, bringing a bountiful harvest of the sturdy spuds beginning in midsummer.

yield a normal crop, food writers started recommending other starches to fill the breach. As a writer in *The Farmer's Wife* suggested, "it would be well to make new food combinations and learn to use foods we have not hitherto included in our bills of fare."[4]

In the years before World War I, Minnesota was potato country, the fourth-largest producer in the nation, close behind New York, Michigan, and Wisconsin. Some areas of the state were "the best natural potato soil of any," according to I. W. Haycroft, who moved to Beltrami County from Texas to help farmers raise the highly profitable Bliss Triumph seed potato suited to the former forest country's "rich, fluffy, fine, sandy loam with a heavy mixture of decayed timber vegetation." It was ironic that the university's home economists needed to issue a 1917 release headlined, "Conservation of Potatoes and Wheat: Use Rice."[5]

WHEATLESS SUGAR-SAVING POTATO CHOCOLATE CAKE

2 potatoes
2 ounces unsweetened baking chocolate squares
½ cup milk
½ cup butter
1 cup sugar
2 eggs
½ teaspoon salt
4 teaspoons baking powder
1½ cups barley flour (you may use regular unbleached wheat flour)

Preheat the oven to 350° F. Cook the potatoes in their skins. Peel and put through a potato ricer or coarse sieve. Measure 1½ cups by lightly placing into measuring cup. Do not pack; you will lose the fluffiness of the grains and have too much potato. Melt the chocolate in the milk and set aside to cool slightly. Cream the butter and sugar. Beat in the potato and eggs. Add the salt, baking powder, and half the flour. Mix well. Stir in the milk and chocolate and then the last of the flour. Stir until well blended. Grease and flour two 8- or 9-inch round cake pans. Spoon the batter into the pans. Bake until the cake begins to pull away from the sides of the pans and is firm in the center, about 20–25 minutes. Cool and frost if desired. (adapted from Mrs. H. C. Hotaling, Blue Earth County Coordinator, to Mildred Weigley, 1917[?], Food Files, Minnesota Historical Society)

Far from being a staple in Upper Midwest kitchens, white rice was usually considered a southern food. Recognizing that this unfamiliar starch might not be easily accepted by cooks and their families on its own, Minnesota home economists sent out careful directions for cooking rice properly, wrote tasty recipes, and even suggested extending mashed potatoes by adding an equal amount of cooked rice.

By May 1917, the push to plant more potatoes and to plant them efficiently hit Minnesota potato country. A Given Hardware store advertisement from May 10, 1917, printed in the *Bemidji Pioneer,* reminded farmers that potatoes still could be planted in 20 or even 30 days because "it has become the question of feeding 231,000,000 people." Given Hardware also promoted the Hoover one-man potato planter, citing the experience of Frank Pierson: "Frank is a hustler when it comes to clearing up his farm and in getting up-to-date machinery. He claims his planter is *absolutely* accurate and that he is there to show anyone who doubts it. . . . He also says that with his planter and a sprayer and a digger, he can raise 10 acres easier than he could three-fourths of an acre the old way." Givens said the machine was well worth the investment of $85.[6]

On June 15, 1917, the *Bemidji Pioneer* reported the first local "harvest." "Martin Lonballa Monday brought to the *Pioneer* office three new potatoes, about the size of hickory nuts, dug from his garden. The plants were started inside and transplanted a short time ago. The small spuds look healthy and would make an ideal scarf pin if set in gold and platinum." Later that summer, Josephine Walezak, a proud young "soldier of the soil," wrote to T. A. Erickson, head of the Boys and Girls Clubs at the university, about her three-eighths-acre potato patch. When the potato bug emerges "in his striped uniform," she promised to take action, "I hear that every potato bug helps the Kaiser, so I will keep the potato bugs off."[7]

Potato-bug attacks were front-page news in Eveleth on August 23, 1917: "A green bug has been found in large number on many potato fields. . . . The insects live by sucking the sap out of the stems." Agricultural instructor C. J. Skrivseth provided a home-brew remedy: "⅔ ounce soap, 1 teaspoon 40 percent solution nicotine extract, and

1 gallon of water. Spray on the plant, being sure to strike the insect with the solution as it kills by contact."[8]

Once the year's crop seemed to be growing well, Minnesotans turned attention to assuring a profitable harvest. Because farm laborers were in short supply—young farmers and seasonal hired help were being drafted into the army—a good hand was welcomed wherever it could be found. Troop 69 of the St. Anthony Park Boy Scouts combined a hiking and camping adventure with an opportunity to do a good deed and earn their way. As reported in the July 14, 1917, issue of *Minnesota Farm Review,* the boys headed out with two pushcarts full of gear: four tents, cooking utensils, and plenty of food. Their first stop was Boiling Springs near Shakopee, then Lake Minnetonka, Osseo, Robbinsdale, and finally Brooklyn Center, where 80 acres of potatoes awaited digging.

Many people planted potatoes in their 1917 war gardens for home use and for sale. The university's Agricultural Extension Service's Special Bulletin No. 14 helped people new to growing potatoes understand the steps to assure a good crop. The report said in Minnesota potatoes should remain in the ground for seven to ten days after the vines have died and be protected from freezing at night and from sunburn during the day. If immature, potatoes should be allowed to "sweat and dry out on the barn floor or other dry place with good ventilation." Then they could be graded by size and bagged in "uniform 2½ bushel sacks weighing 151 pounds." City dwellers who grew potatoes and other root vegetables in their backyard for personal use received

COLCANNON

2 cups mashed potatoes, divided
1 cup cooked chopped greens such as spinach, beet, or turnip
1 tablespoon fat
½ teaspoon salt (or to taste)
½ teaspoon paprika (or to taste)

Preheat the oven to 350° F. Mix 1 cup of the mashed potatoes with the greens. Add the fat and seasonings. Spread in a lightly greased baking dish. Cover with remaining mashed potatoes and bake until browned. Serve very hot. (*The Farmer,* May 4, 1918)

information from the Food Administration on the proper way to set up a storage area in their basement, including partitioning off "a small room as far as possible from the heating plant. . . . Two of the walls should be outside walls."[9]

Minnesotans begin harvesting commercially grown potatoes in August, but home gardeners dug small "new" potatoes earlier to combine with other garden produce in meat-saving dishes. The 1917 crop was full of promise, and A. D. Wilson reported on its progress in his weekly market letters as though he were writing about a horse race nearing the homestretch. These frequent news releases, issued by the Markets Division of the Minnesota Committee of Food Production and Conservation, gave growers information so they could judge the best time to bring their crop to market. On July 20, 1917, the state's potato yield was projected at 35 million bushels, more than double the 16.8 million bushels harvested in 1916.[10]

Wilson's market reports fluctuated over the next six week in their projections on the success of the harvest. In early October, a sharp drop in the temperature brought increased producer prices. Sacks of potatoes sold at $1.35 to $1.40 per bushel, putting "thousands of dollars into the pockets of producers who had dug their stock and placed it under cover. Reports as yet are uncertain as to frost damage on potatoes in hills, but the stock in the fields that was dug and not gathered has undoubtedly suffered large damage," wrote Wilson.[11]

The *Bemidji Pioneer* on October 15 gave firsthand reports to its potato-raising readers. "Severe weather visited Bemidji and vicinity Tuesday. Heavy frost being reported, and this morning crops have a most dejected look. Acre after acre of promising potatoes badly wilted and turned a sodden green hue." The paper commented that there were "many heavy hearts in Bemidji and the country surrounding" but hoped that "the potatoes will pull along with favorable weather and the loss not as severe as anticipated."

Some farmers seem to have tried to sell their freeze-damaged potatoes before they rotted, but dairy and food commissioner James Sorenson noted on October 19 that "a frozen potato is not food quality. A frozen potato means a rotten potato. It is easy to distinguish.

When you pierce the skin, there is not the same resistance encountered as in a good spud." He identified 97 bushels of dud spuds and said they were to be "subjected to a bath of kerosene to make them unsalable." At the end of the 1917 harvest season, Wilson's October 29 market letter reported a surplus of frost-damaged potatoes as well as a shortage of cars to transport good potatoes to market. Further complicating matters, shippers were reluctant to take stock "not up to grade."[12]

Professor R. A. Gortner of the University of Minnesota's agricultural biochemistry department saw an opportunity. Not only did potatoes freeze in the fields, he realized, they also frequently froze on railroad sidings while waiting for transport. A newspaper photo showing boxcars full of potatoes being tossed into a Chicago dump moved him to action. As Gortner wrote to food administrator Wilson, "The food value of a frozen potato is exactly the same as that of an unfrozen potato, the only difference being that the frozen potato can not be peeled and cooked in the usual manner." Gortner urged that freezing be seen as the first step in a process. "It would be a great savings in transportation if all potatoes which are at the present time being shipped were to be first frozen and then passed through presses in which the surplus water could be squeezed out of them, the final product being marketed as potato meal or flour. . . . It is in the form of potato flour that the great bulk of potatoes are consumed in Germany, especially in their war breads."[13]

Thinking along these same lines, backyard inventor Lars Eriksson from Eriksenville, near Onamia, wrote Gortner: "I have made a potato grinding mill here to grind not only good potatoes but frozen potatoes to flour. . . . Too bad the farmers should lose so much potatoes, just now when everything so well needed. I can make potato mills to run by handpower or with gasoline engines. P.S. My little mill runned by Gasoline engine can grind one bushel of potatoes in 1 to 1½ minutes." Gortner forwarded the letter on to Wilson with the comment: "He is apparently applying the methods of the old country to Minnesota problems, and while his English is at fault, there is nothing the matter with his patriotism." Gortner also suggested that frozen potatoes might replace corn in the manufacture of alcohol. In the end, Minnesota starch factories bought up most of the year's frozen potatoes for conversion into nonfood-grade starch. Wilson wrote Gortner, "I believe they are paying fifty to sixty cents per hundred," about one-quarter the rate of potatoes sold at normal market rate.[14]

Home cooks did add mashed or riced potatoes to their breads and other baked goods. While A. D. Wilson had hoped to restrict the 1917 Boys and Girls Club baking contests to recipes for potato breads, advisors decided this would be unfair to the youngsters who had been practicing the preparation of standard white loaves all year long. However, the wheat-saving recipe for potato bread handed out by Agricultural Extension Service was demonstrated at the 1917 State Fair and used as the only recipe for the 1918 Boys and Girls Club baking competitions.[15]

By the end of the 1917 growing season, farmers across the United States had harvested almost 304 million bushels of potatoes, with Minnesota farms contributing 10 percent. Potatoes stood ready to serve as hearty, wheat- and meat-saving dishes. The Food Administration spread the word, encouraging people to eat more of them, with flyers and even displays in retail store windows. One plan for a fact-based tableau had signs in front of bushel baskets of spuds demonstrating that German people ate an impressive 16 quarts a week while Americans had a mere 2.3 quarts. A flyer released by the university's extension service similarly encouraged, "Potatoes are Perishable—Eat Them Today."[16]

As the *au gratin* evenings of winter 1917 slipped toward the potato salad days of spring 1918, it quickly became evident that the United States had more than enough spuds to go around. With meat and wheat consumption limited and fresh vegetables just being planted, the U.S. Food Administration launched

COTTAGE PIE

Preheat oven to 350° F. Line a greased baking dish with 3 cups mashed potatoes. Fill center with 1 cup minced leftover meat. Season with onions or celery, salt, and pepper. Moisten with ½ cup gravy or cream. Cover with another cup of mashed potatoes and place in oven until heated through and brown over the top. (Undated and untitled leaflet, U.S. Food Administration, Missouri Division, Food Files, Minnesota Historical Society)

Declaring "Every Spud a Bullet" in the war for food conservation, this display in St. Paul's Golden Rule store urged passersby to "Eat potatoes by the bushel, not the peck." Recipes abounded for new ways to use the now overly plentiful spuds in everything from main dishes to desserts.

a major potato-saturation campaign. War volunteers planned cooking demonstrations and placed articles and recipes in local newspapers. Patriotic campaigns urged people to buy potatoes "by the bushel, not the peck." Department store windows featured potatoes attired in paper military uniforms under inspiring slogans such as "Every Spud a Bullet against the Kaiser," and prepared dishes from the oven joined bushel baskets overflowing with the brown tubers.

News releases and articles urged farmers and gardeners to continue to grow more potatoes for harvesting in the fall. One Farm Bureau worker wrote to the state administrator that government promotions for growing more food had "increased interest in home gardens and market gardens in the vicinity of Duluth to a great extent." He continued that a high-school agriculture teacher had been cooperating in collecting potato exhibits for a meeting in Brainerd with the understanding that the exhibits would then help farmers breed new seeds.[17]

Potatoes began appearing in centerpiece one-dish meatless

meals and even in desserts. Recipes suggested potatoes could be used to make any cake by substituting one cup of mashed potatoes for a half cup milk and a half cup flour. A Food Administration news release manipulated guilty feelings by suggesting, "When you complain, think of France. Whatever [a French woman] gives up for the sake of her loved ones at the front means just so much less for her to eat herself. There are no other foods for her to use as substitutes. We, on the other hand, need suffer no privation. The biggest sacrifice we are asked to make, that of giving up all our wheat, does not necessitate our even going without our desserts."[18]

In May 1918 the Food Administration sent newspapers another guilt-inducing release noting that America had fallen behind in shipping food to Europe and that eating the plentiful potato would release wheat. It asked Americans to get "such an enthusiasm for potatoes that next year's production will beat this year's. . . . The men crippled in fighting our battles, the women widowed for our freedom, the children orphaned to make the world safe for future children . . . stretch their pitiful hands to us across the seas. . . . No able-bodied true American will object to potatoes as a substitute at the noon or evening meal."[19]

On May 20, 1918, food administrator Wilson reported that Minnesotans were eating potatoes and that the campaign to reduce the winter's ten-million-bushel potato inventory had worked. Wilson urged the continuing use of potatoes "every day and in every meal

---

WHITE POTATO CUSTARD

2 cups riced baked potato	⅓ cup fat
4 eggs lightly beaten	¼ cup top milk
1 cup sugar	juice and rind of one lemon

Preheat oven to 400° F. Mix ingredients in order given. Beat hard for 5 minutes and pour into a greased baking dish. Bake for 20–30 minutes or until custard is delicately set. Or make two pies. ("When You Complain, Think of France," news release IV-3, U.S. Food Administration, April 1918, Food Files, Minnesota Historical Society)

Once again, children could be at the forefront in the "potato patriot" efforts. The Food Administration sent out classroom lesson plans featuring potato facts, contests, and recipes. In Minnesota many young farmers grew their first profitable crop when they planted potatoes aided by a "growers loan" from Successful Farming *magazine.*

as a vegetable, as an ingredient in bread, and camouflaged in various ways to tempt the appetite."[20]

Schools joined the campaign. In a leaflet for schools published in March, the Food Administration urged school lunches serving potatoes, cooking classes with potato recipes, handwriting practice with potato recipes, and essay contests about the value of potatoes. A set of "Five Lessons on Potatoes for Elementary Grades" could culminate in a Potato Day program including a contest for the biggest potato grown, displays of the five best potatoes for home use, readings of essays about how to use potatoes and save wheat, a story about the life of a potato, patriotic recitations, and singing of "The Star Spangled Banner."[21]

Overseas and at home, potatoes were lifesavers and life builders.

After several days near the German front lines, Ingvald Smith had been away from an army kitchen and hot meals. He and a companion took matters into their own hands. He wrote in his diary, "Sunday July 28th On awakening this morning I decided to go on a vigorous campaign for something to eat. While searching the woods Reisdorf and I discovered in an open space a plot of potatoes belonging to civilian people. We helped ourselves to a sufficient amount which we carried back to camp with these potatoes also some hard tack and coffee we were fortunate in procuring we managed to prepare a satisfactory dinner considering that we had missed three consecutive meals."[22]

Several young Minnesota farmers got their start in life by planting potatoes during the war. Harvey Scoville wrote to *Junior Soldiers of the Soil,* "On June 19, I planted my potatoes with a hand planter. In about ten days my potatoes came up. And I dragged them with a spike tooth drag. On July 3, I sprayed my potatoes with Paris green, and on July 25 I sprayed again. During this time I cultivated three times and once after this. I did not do anything more until I dug them. On October 25 I took them to market, receiving $1.10 a bushel for them, making a total value after cost of work and other things of $86.55." Another youngster, George Butler of Benton County, expressed gratitude for a small "growers loan" and enclosed a money order for $10.60, the amount of the loan plus interest. "I bought potatoes with the money and they yielded three hundred bushels per acre. Thanking you for the loan and my start in life."[23]

Dear boy, This Thursday evening I will write you a short letter as I have little news to write. We rec'd no mail today. I am digging potatoes every evening—I get home about 4 o'clock and change clothes and start with two sacks, bushel basket, and spading fork. I have now dug about 8¼ bushels and will have 1½ or 2 bushels yet. I think not a good crop but it will help some. Your father,
W. B. Core, Minneapolis, October 15, 1918[24]

9

The Sweetness of Life

Dear Women's Club members, I want to make a special appeal to you on food conservation. Far too many of us still think of it as a "fad" or a comparatively trivial matter, [but] France is on a ration of 20 pounds of sugar a year for each person. We are using 90. Now France is notifying us that unless *we* can supply her needs, she will have no sugar at all this winter. . . . If the old saying that an American family wastes enough to feed a French family is true, we ought constantly, when we live according to our old-fashioned standards of wasting foods, to say to ourselves: "There goes another French family hungry" or "Now I am making another Belgian child starve." *Woman's Club of Minneapolis, September 28, 1917*[1]

Among the first official documents issued by the U.S. Food Administration in August 1917 was the simply titled *Seven Ways to Save Sugar*. It harkened back to Puritan values with advice such as "Use fresh fruits. Cook dried fruit without sugar. Can fruit without sugar. Use less sugar in tea and coffee—you will soon learn to like it better. Avoid sugar luxuries—candy, cake, sweet drinks and sodas. Use honey, maple syrup and syrups, and other sweeteners. Cut out all desserts or other sweets that require sugar."[2]

During the first months after the April declaration of war against Germany, life in Minnesota towns and cities appeared to go on as usual. People attended weddings and church picnics, curling tournaments, and baseball games. Local newspapers reported relatives' visits and residents' vacation trips, event decorations, and guest lists for anniversary and birthday parties as though nothing much had changed. But the war and food conservation touched every aspect

HOLIDAY SWEETS COCONUT BALLS

3 teaspoons vanilla   3 cups shredded coconut
¼ cup peanut butter

Mix vanilla and peanut butter. Stir into coconut, kneading with your
hands until well blended. Form into small balls, about ¾ of an inch in
diameter. Place on waxed paper and put in refrigerator to firm. Store in a
covered container in a cool place. (Adapted from Pearl Bailey Lyons, *The
Farmer's Wife*, November 1918)

of life; the strands that knitted American and Minnesota society
together wound tighter and took on heavier burdens.

The St. Paul Boy Scouts were ready when the war began in April
and saw an opportunity for service. "If the Mayor calls on us, we will
be prepared to respond with at least 500 scouts to do their bit in the
city." The national scout office added, "We are able to render first aid
to the injured, to do signaling, and serve as messengers. Some of us
have bicycles, motorcycles, automobiles, motor boats, sail boats, trek
carts, tents and other equipment which are at your service and the
services of our country."[3]

Similarly, female students at St. Olaf College in Northfield signed
a College Women's War Work Pledge to maintain "the highest standards of womanhood, physical, intellectual, social and spiritual" and
"give up the use of candies and ice cream, keep lunches to an absolute
minimum," and participate in Red Cross work. Women's social clubs,
study groups, and church circles turned their meetings to war work.
Some groups converted part of their meeting spaces into clean spaces
where they could put on their all-white Red Cross uniforms and fold
bandages, essential for treatment of wounded soldiers overseas. The
Minneapolis Woman's Club offered Red Cross service opportunities
three days a week, and the Hamline College Auxiliary included men
and women at an evening meeting where they folded an impressive
total of more than 60,000 dressings.

Red Cross work mattered. Mrs. L. H. Rice, speaking in Park Ridge, dramatized its importance: "When a wounded man dies the Red Cross is to blame."[4]

Another report was more specific: "In France, for lack of better dressings, sterilized burlap, it is reported by a Minneapolis doctor, are being used at times to bind up wounds. . . . All hospital supplies and shipments of clothing will be sent to France without delay by the Red Cross and will be distributed to the French as well as our own units abroad."[5]

Women knitted sweaters, sleeveless jackets, mufflers, wristlets, and socks during club meetings, which they gave to the Red Cross for distribution to soldiers and sailors. One soldier, Normal Lawrence, wrote the *Cloquet Pine Knot* that his nearly 80-year-old mother knitted 30 pairs of socks plus numerous sweaters and mittens for the Red Cross, working on Sundays although she had never before done that. The *Pipestone Leader* provided instructions for knitting officially approved gray navy wristlets, noting, "It takes 500 of these sets for one battle ship, 20 for a submarine."[6]

In another specific appeal, Mrs. James G. Swan, chairman of the Minnesota Federation of Women's Clubs, urged club women across the state to keep knitting socks, "as the average soldier wears out one pair of socks a week when on the march."[7]

Women attending club meetings who knitted while they conducted business faced an additional change in their prewar customs: the lack of sweet treats. After the Food Administration requested that people eliminate their "fourth meal" of the day, many clubs decided to serve tea or coffee without dainty cakes and pastries for their regular refreshments.

Sugar and sweets might have been the easiest national sacrifice requested by the Food Administration, since sugar was essentially unnecessary in people's diets, a university bulletin explained. Sugar is a "splendid stimulant for men doing muscular work," but too much sugar "is likely to bring on disease. Let us be patriotic, save sugar for the armies and improve our own health."[8]

In an October 1917 speech in Argyle, food administrator A. D. Wilson discussed sugar conservation in personal terms: "I have a little boy [with] a decided sweet tooth. He likes lots of sugar and it has been a source of anxiety to his mother and me to see him dip into the sugar

Women all over Minnesota gave up treats at meetings and turned to Red Cross war work. Knitted socks, sweaters, and wristlets supplemented basic soldier and sailor uniforms. Some clubs, such as this one in St. Paul, even invested in table-mounted knitting machines to speed the process.

bowl and keep dipping and putting sugar on everything he eats. His mother finally conceived the idea that he might save some sugar for a soldier. There is something appealing and romantic about a soldier and it struck his fancy. . . . I wish that every child under 80 in the state of Minnesota might do just the same thing."[9]

While the idea of conserving nonessential sugar seemed simple, Americans had quite a sweet tooth. Consumption had doubled between 1880 and 1916. Coca-Cola, formulated by Atlanta's John Pemberton in 1886, shipped 12 million gallons of sugar-based syrup to soda fountains and bottlers in 1917—enough to make one and one-third billion glasses of Coke each year. Pharmacists had discovered that soda fountains lured customers into their retail stores. Ice cream parlors and soda fountains on town squares across the state sold temperance-friendly refreshments to young and old alike. Clip-clopping horse sounds mixed with the *ah-ooog-ah* of Model T horns punctuated by clanging streetcar bells as suspendered swains pulled out wrought-iron chairs to seat their Gibson-girl coiffed friends at marble-topped tables before ordering the newest tasty novelty sweets.[10]

A 1917 soda menu from St. Croix Drug Company in Stillwater offered seven pages of phosphates, sodas, frappes, sundaes, and egg drinks. Among their 157 specialties were a Mutt and Jeff Sundae, Oriental Parfait, Siberian Freeze, Silver Fizz, Frosted Egg Coffee, and the Stillwater Breeze. Competing Starkel's Fountain offered 149 treats, and both stores featured fine fresh chocolates. In late May 1917, Ellis Andrews, proprietor of New Ulm Candy Kitchen, invited *Brown County Journal* readers to "join the crowd during these hot days and evenings" for specials like Sweet Navy Boy, Midnight Sun Delight, or Peg O' My Heart, while Hofmeister's Orchestra played on Sunday afternoon and evening. Corner bakeries tempted passersby with cakes, dainty tea biscuits, cookies, and muffins. Creameries sold ice cream. In Eveleth, a new creamery opened its doors in May 1917, announcing "dairy lunches and ice cream in the parlor" along with bakery goods.[11]

Treats and temptations abounded despite restrictions that first suggested, then required, that businesses use less sugar. The Food Administration offered advice for patriotic sweets such as this: "Popcorn has Power. Popcorn is very valuable as a food. Give children popcorn balls made with honey or corn syrup. The children will be happy and satisfied, and you will be helping your country."[12]

Mothers could also follow directives on sweets published in popular magazines, such as this advice from Dr. Emelyn Coolidge in the *Ladies Home Journal:* "Since we must use less sugar, a little pure maple syrup or even molasses on bread or cereal may be given the children occasionally. One or two teaspoonfuls of honey spread on bread may be allowed sometimes *at the end* of a meal *after* the other

GINGER SNAPS

1 cup sorghum syrup or
  molasses—black-strap
  molasses will not do
½ cup white sugar
1 cup nice drippings [or
  butter]
2 eggs, well beaten
dash salt
½ teaspoon each ginger,
  cloves, cinnamon
2 teaspoons baking soda
5–6 cups rye flour
½ cup white flour

Mix first 3 ingredients
and boil slowly for about
10 minutes. Cool and then
add eggs, spices, and soda.
Stir in 5 cups of the rye
flour, then turn out and
knead in sixth cup. Must
be very stiff. Roll very thin,
using white flour when rolling; about a ½ cup is all that
is necessary. These cookies
require careful watching
for they burn quite easily.
Recipe makes at least
11 dozen snaps. (*Eveleth
News,* March 7, 1918)

articles have been eaten. If sweets
are allowed with the first course, it
will be much more difficult to get
the children to eat the more stable
articles which they so much need."
Coolidge presented a week's menu
on a wheel-shaped chart a mother
could cut from the magazine. Each
day suggested a single ginger snap,
ginger cookie, or piece of ginger-
bread for supper dessert, except
for wheatless Wednesday, when a
baked apple topped off the meal.
(After the war, Herbert Hoover
quipped that parents took advantage of sugar and food restrictions
"to impose upon their children
the disciplines which had been the
griefs of their own youth—and
blamed it on me.") Women reading Red Lake County's *Oklee Herald* learned that on average each
American consumed seven pounds
of sugar each month in cooking and
table use. The paper didn't mince
words: "Your grandmother's cookbook may furnish some good tips,
for a century ago they knew nothing of ordinary white sugar."[13]

The Food Administration's search
for a solution to the sugar problem was not as simple. Managing the
sugar supply was the most complex commodity challenge encountered
by the federal agency. Sugar is refined from two plants—sugarcane
grown in countries such as Cuba and Java and sugar beets grown in
the United States and Europe, as well as other areas. These several
sources of international supply and overseas and domestic demand
called for extraordinary measures.[14]

Sugar industry executives had thought supplies would be adequate. The president of the American Sugar Refining company initially suggested in May 1917 that "the housewife who wants to 'do her bit' for the country can do it by buying only normal quantities of sugar." But pleas for voluntary reduction in sugar use were not as effective as the government had hoped. Wartime employment brought higher wages for many working people, and some people who formerly could not afford luxuries now could buy sweet treats. The United States had a sugar shortage.[15]

Recognizing the normal economic rules of lower supplies and increased demand would drive up prices, Hoover's Food Administration met with sugar growers and refiners. The resulting voluntary International Sugar Committee, organized in October 1917, set the price for all sugar and brought a lowered and stable price to homemakers across the nation.[16]

After months of rising prices for all kinds of foods, these lower sugar prices tempted homemakers to buy more than they needed. But the supply was still short. It fell to grocery wholesalers and stores to control possible hoarding by limiting purchases. The *Brown County Journal* warned in stern tones on its front page, "If people hoard sugar, the candy makers and pop manufacturers will be put out of business here." They explained local candy establishments and the New Ulm Bottling Works depended on people not hoarding sugar, which appeared to be happening. More

HONEY FRUIT CHOCOLATES

1 12-ounce package raisins, steamed until tender
1 8-ounce package dates
⅔ cup figs
1 cup nuts
grated rind of half an orange
2 tablespoons orange juice
2 tablespoons honey
⅛ teaspoon salt
dipping chocolate such as melted semi-sweet chocolate chips

Put fruit through food chopper and add nuts coarsely chopped. Add orange rind, orange juice, honey, and salt, and mix. Form into balls and set aside in refrigerator until firm. Dip fruit balls into chocolate and drain on waxed paper. (*How to Save Sugar* [Medina, Ohio, 1918?])

sugar had been sold in October than during the height of the canning season, when cooks usually purchased the pounds of sugar essential to turning fruits into jams and jellies. The article described how local stores were taking control of the situation: "Grocers can purchase a limited amount each month [from wholesalers]. Local stores are now refusing to sell sugar by the sack. This measure was taken to curtail hoarding. It is said that many people have two and three and even more sacks of sugar on hand. All that has been stopped and sugar will now be sold to the consumer as it is consumed."[17]

In October 1917 the Food Administration issued a set of rules for commercial eating establishments. Along with requirements for wheatless and meatless days, the measures specifically addressed the matter of sugar bowls: "*No* public eating place shall use or permit the use of the sugar bowl on the table or lunch counter. Nor shall any public eating place serve sugar or permit it to be served unless the guest so requests, and in no event shall the amount served to any one person at any one meal exceed one teaspoonful or its equivalent."[18]

John Jager, superintendent of the bee and honey exhibit at the Minnesota State Fair, saw sugar conservation as an opportunity to raise interest in the occupation "which to my notion is the most interesting and paying business one can enter." Jager had an important story to share and the State Fair was a key place to reach and influence Minnesotans. "The United States wastes $19,000,000 in honey each year due to lack of bee keepers. Honey is one of nature's purest foods and it is a shame to see so much of it actually go to waste merely because there are not enough bee keepers to take care of it. There is a fine chance for attention by those who are working for the conservation of food and I look for added interest in the bee business."[19]

The Food Administration was all abuzz about bees, too. They reached out to the nation's public libraries with a series of "Food Notes" newsletters with ideas for public outreach and displays. They suggested libraries ask their patrons to "spend some time this winter advising those of your acquaintance that have time—and flower gardens—to keep bees. Locate the sugar maple trees in your district, and see that attention is called to their possibilities." The "Food

Notes" suggested using honey, maple syrup, molasses, and brown sugar instead of granulated sugar, because "we cannot ship the first three commodities, as they require too much shipping space; we cannot ship brown sugar, as it ferments. Use these commodities at home so that granulated sugar may be sent abroad."[20]

Sugar and soldiers were inextricably linked, and not only in the mind of A. D. Wilson's young son. Products containing sugar were essential to soldiers' survival and morale, and soldiers ate far more sugar than people back home. Chocolate bars were issued to troops for emergency rations, and YMCA volunteers ferried cookies, candy, and tobacco from safe staging areas to canteens and depots just behind the battle lines. Sweet treats and satisfying food helped men remember what they were fighting for.[21]

Soldier Frank Street wrote home to Minnesota from France describing the scene at one YMCA canteen where people worked to bring comfort to soldiers "with maximum efficiency. I am sitting in a little room at the end of one section of the building. The main room is filled with men, some buying candy, tobacco, and cookies. They serve hot chocolate until three. The men are all enthusiastic over it. There are some delightful middle-aged women behind the counter. Believe me, it makes things home-like after the rough army life. The YMCA sells some delicious ginger cakes—three for one franc. You ought to hear the men *parlez vous*. About the only word any know is "Good day," and they say that to everybody."[22]

Back home at the close of 1917, Elizabeth Nickerson, home demonstration agent for the MCPS Women's Auxiliary office in Minneapolis, recruited 500 students from East High School. The young people promised to give up sugar candy during December and January so that men overseas could enjoy some comforts.[23]

After the 1917 Christmas holiday season, the federal Food Administration instituted more restrictions on sugar, limiting each American to three pounds of sugar a month through voluntary actions. Bemidji's newspaper commented, "The average household does not use in excess of three pounds per capita per month. It is said in many homes there is an excessive use of sugar through the making of candies and other sweets. The new regulations will stop this practice in great extent. The grapefruit market is expected to

Separating Americans from sugar was the most complicated effort of the Food Administration. In the end there were price controls, an honor system of rationing, and direct appeals like this one.

be hard hit as this variety of fruit requires a large amount of sweetening." Verna Mikesh, a young girl at the time, remembers the dramatic impact of this announcement in her home. Her father picked up their nearly empty glass sugar bowl, read the words "Made in Germany" on the bottom, and threw the bowl with all his might out the back door into the woods.[24]

The American Sugar Refining Company, maker of Domino sugar, explained the underlying problem in the country's sugar supply in a January 1918 advertisement in the *Bemidji Pioneer*. "The sugar crop of Java is like unmined gold. It is there, but we can't get at it, as the ships needed to transport it are essential for troop transport." American Sugar commended housewives' efforts to preserve fruits: "Every jar of fruit preserved adds that much to our insurance of victory, adds that much to hasten the end of this conflict." The company then pledged to keep refineries working as long as there was raw sugar to process, mentioning its new packaging in "convenient cartons and small cotton bags to make it easy for groceries to limit sales to actual needs and prevent hoarding."[25]

Life changed all over Minnesota and the nation as more and more men were called up and sent off to training and action in France.

Food wasn't the only thing that needed to be conserved. Money and resources were tight, too, while the imperative for home-front support increased. Communities changed. In Eveleth the Masinter brothers were both drafted on November 11, 1917, and had to close their men's clothing store, as there was no one who could take it over, before they left in mid-December. Farmers had to sell their land as they, too, were drafted and there was no one to work the farm. Homeowners put their houses up for rent as the husband went off to war and his wife moved in with her parents or her in-laws.

Although wages were increasing for essential workers staying at home, money was tight for many soldiers' families. Some Minnesota companies, including the Oliver mining company and the Donaldson department store, did pay partial wages to soldiers serving overseas, but many families found it hard going without the regular paycheck from husbands or sons.[26]

Soldier's pay was delayed and some, still in training, had their own expenses. Air corpsman Granville Gutterson wrote home from Texas on April 3, 1918. "We got paid for Feb! and were notified that our pay is reduced (all over the U. S. for all cadets) to $75.00 a month. With buying all your clothes and 40 cents a day for meals we're trying to figure out if a private who gets $33 and all clothes and eats doesn't come pretty near to getting the best of us."[27]

Wives and mothers did what work they could for additional income. The Minneapolis Woman's Club combined war work and food conservation with community assistance. They publicized their efforts in their January 1918 newsletter. "The Commission Shop has had its formal opening. . . . That this is a real war work and offers a much needed market to women who must earn money in their homes, is proved to us every day. Considered in this light, the shop deserves the support of every woman of The Woman's Club. . . . A darning business is being established. Several worthy women, who do excellent work, are now listed on the books of the shop. The work will be done at 20 cents an hour, with ten per cent added as commission. For the food conservationists, orders are being taken for bran bread, brown bread and Red Cross cake. The Cookery Committee is expecting to work up an order business of regular weekly customers. We are constantly on the lookout for new consignors in

RED CROSS WAR CAKE

2 cups brown sugar
2 cups hot water
2 tablespoons lard
1 teaspoon salt
1 teaspoon cloves
1 teaspoon cinnamon
1 package (8 ounces)
  raisins, chopped
1 teaspoon baking soda
3 cups flour

Preheat oven to 350° F.
Put everything but soda
and flour into a 2-quart
pot. Bring to a boil over
medium heat, stirring
frequently. Boil 5 minutes
after it bubbles, then cool.
Stir in soda and flour.
Put batter into 2 lightly
greased mini-loaf pans.
Bake 45 minutes. Cake
keeps fresh for a long time
and can be sent to men at
the front. (*Conservation
Recipes* [Minneapolis:
Women's Committee of
Minnesota Commission
of Public Safety, 1917],
Minnesota Historical
Society)

this department. As yet no one has been found who will make us the much demanded baked beans."[28]

There were causes to support at every turn. In addition to regular fund-raising efforts on behalf of the YMCA and the Red Cross, half the cost of the war was financed by a series of five Liberty Loan bond issues, sold by volunteers in campaigns managed by the Federal Reserve Bank. Their efforts raised $24 billion. Individuals could purchase these 30-year bonds in denominations between $50 and $100,000. The bonds paid interest of between 3.5 and 4.75 percent, varying with the campaign. A Thrift and War Stamp campaign encouraged regular savings in small amounts between 25 cents and $4.25.[29]

The 27 boys in St. Paul Boy Scout troop #76 sold more Second Liberty bonds than any other troop in the United States. They raised $1,805,100 from 785 donors.[30]

Social events across the state went to war, too, as the 1,200 Red Cross chapters in Minnesota found novel fund-raising methods. They put on plays or concerts and held conservation dinners and sales. Some combined food conservation with fund-raising by selling their own conservation cookbooks. Eleanor Nutchell of St. Cloud described their work: "We have sold these for fifty cents, forty cents going to Red Cross.... 'High Finance' I call that, but I think too that people are more likely to seriously

Half the cost of the war was financed by the sale of a series of interest-bearing war bonds. Parades, rallies, and direct appeals continued the drumbeat for victory both on the battlefield and in the treasury.

consider the things they have to pay for. . . . They are selling fast and I do hope will keep up the interest in food conservation."[31]

The Park Rapids Red Cross day-long picnic culminated in an auction that was an unusual success. "One gift that received special attention of the crowd was a 3 × 6 foot flag donated by Atty. Woolley. It was first sold at $27; then handed back for sale again and this was repeated until the flag had brought $304. The last time it was offered for sale it was bid in by H. W. Krause whose property it became."[32]

All the money supported Red Cross nurses and hospitality facilities for soldiers. It also purchased supplies for Red Cross projects. The St. Paul chapter completed more than 166,000 hospital supplies such as patient gowns, 3.5 million surgical dressings, 54,000 knitted articles, and nearly 20,000 refugee garments. Minneapolis Red Cross volunteers were similarly hard working. In addition to the hospital supplies they installed knitting machines on which a skilled knitter could make a pair of socks in 40 minutes.[33]

This drive and energy to do all that could be done for the war effort spread to the drive to make use of alternatives that could be grown or found nearby and converted to sweeten life in all kinds of ways. Newspapers across Minnesota urged farmers to produce alternative sweeteners, and professors associated with the University Farms and agricultural biochemistry division promoted a variety of crops for farmers to "grow their own sugar." Although both sugar beets and sorghum had been raised on Minnesota farms, the war increased demand for seeds and for information and expanded opportunities. Early in the war the Minnesota Sugar company of Chaska had made arrangements in Mankato to build a sugar beet dump to handle the immense crop of sugar beets harvested in the area, thereby eliminating the need to shovel beets into railcars and "save a stupendous amount of labor and time." Most of America's supply of sugar beets had "finished in Germany, but the war cut off the supply, making it imperative that this deficit be made up at home."[34]

In early 1918 an article by Professor R. A. Gortner urging farmers to produce their own sugar substitutes went out to local papers and farm journals. The response was immediate. Farmers from all over the state sent in requests—penciled on penny postcards, formally penned on stationery, and sometimes typed—for copies of the free bulletins on how to make sugar beet, sorghum, and maple syrups. Gortner put the value of the campaign into perspective in a letter to R. B. Greeley of Menahaga: "If you can give publicity to this campaign in any way, I feel you will be doing a patriotic duty. There is no farmer in Minnesota who cannot raise ⅘ of the sugar which his family requires, and the more sorghum or sugar beet syrup that is raised, the more [cane] sugar will be released for war work. I also feel that there is a handsome profit coming to the farmers who will go to the trouble to manufacture sorghum syrup."[35]

In a letter to Benjamin Waltner of Jackson in March 1918, Gortner cited the success of a Waconia sorghum factory, which "last year made something over 100,000 gallons of sorghum syrup and sold it all before the plant was in operation . . . on prior orders without a bit of advertising." He suggested, "The thing for you to preach is cooperative sorghum plants where a number of farmers go in together."[36]

While converting sorghum to syrup efficiently required economies of scale, making sugar beet syrup could be a farmyard project. As Professor Gortner explained to K. S. Bergstad of Lake Park, the process was a simple one. "The roots . . . should be sliced with a kraut cutter or with a Sterling Rotary Slicer No. 10 . . . at $2, the extra cost of the slicer made up in time saved. The slices should be cut rather thin, and 10 gallons of boiling water added to each bushel of beets used. The best container for the beets and water would be a hardwood barrel, which could be covered with a heavy piece of canvas to keep in the heat." After an hour or so, Gortner continued, "the water is drained off through cheesecloth and boiled slowly until the syrup is thickened. Ten gallons of drained liquid would yield 1 gallon of syrup." The leftover sliced beets, Gortner noted, would not be wasted because "the extracted slices make a valuable food for livestock or chickens."[37]

In response to another letter about whether beet syrup could be used for canning, Gortner wrote that while "it is not practicable to make beet *sugar* on the farm . . . you could use beet syrup for canning purposes, providing you don't mind if the juice is a little bit darker than ordinary. It would work perfectly well with blackberries,

SOUR MILK MAPLE SYRUP PIE

2 tablespoons cornstarch

¼ cup cold water

1 cup buttermilk, sour milk,
  or sour cream

¾ cup maple syrup

2 beaten egg yolks

1 lemon, juice and grated rind

1 tablespoon melted butter

baked 9-inch pie crust

Meringue:

2 egg whites

¼ cup maple syrup

½ teaspoon vanilla

Preheat oven to 325° F. Mix cornstarch with water and combine with milk in top of a double boiler. Cook over simmering water, stirring frequently, until mixture is thickened. Stir in other ingredients and pour into baked pie crust. In clean bowl, make meringue by beating egg whites until stiff. Gradually add syrup, then vanilla. Continue beating until meringue holds stiff peaks. Spread meringue over pie. Bake pie until lightly browned, about 25 minutes. Refrigerate leftovers. (*The Farmer,* August 10, 1918)

strawberries or anything of that sort, but the juice from peaches and pears would have a brownish tinge. . . . For sweetening in all general purposes . . . it will answer perfectly well. I have used it . . . and find it perfectly satisfactory."[38]

Some Minnesotans interested in making a sugar substitute without having to plant a crop tried making maple syrup, a staple in the diets of the area's Dakota and Ojibwe people for centuries. Gortner received inquiries about how to make maple syrup and its sugar from city dwellers with several maple trees in their yards, from the owner of a grove of 1,500 trees in northern Minnesota, and from plenty of farmers in between. He wrote back to H. F. Wharton of Minneapolis about the relatively simple process, suggesting that after tapping the trees, taking care that rain or snow did not enter the bucket, the gathered syrup "should be evaporated to probably 219 degrees F., preferably in a copper sugar-evaporating pan, but large kettles or wash boilers will answer fairly well. . . . The finished syrup should boil 9 degrees F. higher than the boiling point of water. . . . The finished syrup should weigh 11 pounds per gallon. . . . The returns per 100 trees are about 300 pounds of sugar, or 40 gallons of syrup." The boiling down would take some time, Gortner wrote in another letter, because the sap boils down "at the ratio of about 40 gallons of sap to 1 gallon of syrup."[39]

Despite the enthusiasm for varied approaches to sugar independence, none of these alternatives significantly impacted Minnesota's farming practices. Although some individual farmers tried to "grow their own sugar," Minnesota did not produce enough to rank in agricultural statistics for sugar beet or maple sugar production during the war years.

Most Minnesotans continued to purchase sugar, a practice that the Food Administration continued to cast in a dim light. "The American people last year spent enough money for candy to feed all Belgium for two years," noted one article. In its "Food Questions Answered" release sent to newspapers in summer 1918, the Food Administration noted that the voluntary agreement between producers and retailers had stabilized sugar prices, but it warned that "hoarding is having on hand more than is needed for a reasonable length of time. You should not fail to return an unused balance of sugar purchased for canning purposes." Hoarders were "selfish, cowardly and unpatriotic . . . at a time when all Americans should be on the same footing." Sugar was not necessary in the diet, and syrups, honey, and fruits worked just as well.[40]

In May 1918, *Wallaces' Farmer,* known for its straight talk, took a clear stand on sugar and canning. "The submarine has forced fighting Europe to a very strict sugar ration and compelled America to look the situation squarely in the face. There is only so much sugar, there are certain definite needs, and the problem before us is finding a practical plan of distribution."[41]

In July 1918, Hoover decided the sugar situation needed a stern hand to control the supply and to manage the demand. With the approval of President Wilson, Hoover used five million dollars of Food Administration funds and established the United States Sugar Equalization Board to "equalize the cost of various sugars and secure better distribution." In essence, the Food Administration controlled the entire sugar supply for the country's use.[42]

Hoover acted just in time. The first fruits of summer 1918—strawberries and raspberries—came in simultaneously with the serious sugar problem. In July the *Bemidji Daily Pioneer* carried a front-page article about a "sugar famine" for canning. The article explained that stores were allowed to sell customers no more than five pounds in cities and towns, or ten to the farm trade. Hotels, boarding houses, and restaurants could buy 25-pound lots, provided the stores could determine that commercial customers were neither reselling it nor purchasing more than a week's supply on the basis of three pounds per capita per month. "If you think a person is trying to evade this rule by purchasing from several dealers, ask for a signed statement to protect yourself."[43]

Controlling the supply of sugar in the spring and summer of 1918 finally led to a program of out-and-out rationing. While the government's system of voluntary restrictions with fines had worked for flour, it did not work for sugar. Enforcement still relied upon trust. Retailers whose July 1918 supplies were limited to one-third of their total sales for April, May, and June could only sell sugar two pounds at a time in cities and five pounds to customers who lived in the country. The monthly allotment was three pounds for each person in the family. On August 1, that amount dropped to two pounds. The *Minnesota Official Food News* explained that this amounted only to "six level teaspoons a day, three for beverages and three for cooking." More sugar was allowed for canning jams and jellies, but those allotments were strictly supervised. Like those who had hoarded wheat flour by amassing more than a 30-day supply, the names of individuals who cheated were published in the newspapers. Fines were to be paid to the Red Cross.[44]

Behind this restriction was an underlying system of verifying certificates and public trust. Manufacturers, wholesalers, and retailers certified to the state food administrator the amount of sugar they had used or sold in 1917, then received certificates for 80 percent of that amount. Every time they purchased sugar, they submitted certificates from their allotment which were sent up to the food administrator who had issued them, so all purchases could be tracked. Grocery stores sold sugar to consumers on trust. However, homemakers who wanted larger amounts for canning—up to 25 pounds—needed to fill out certificates saying they needed the additional sugar to put up foods. In Mankato, the newspaper criticized hoarding's effect on the community. Addressing the certificate system, an article noted pointedly, "People must secure a card from the food administrator before he can buy sugar for canning. Just because there are a few hogs in this community, the rest of us who want to play fair have to suffer the inconvenience."[45]

Some groceries took special initiative to manage their fresh fruit and sugar inventory, as the *Pipestone Leader* reported. "The J. W. Hilliard Co. wholesale fruit and groceries have the right idea in food conservation. Last week they had quite a quantity of cherries for which there was no demand on account of the scarcity of sugar. Rather than let the cherries spoil, cans were purchased, steam was piped from the power house, and about 200 half-gallon glass jars were canned by the no-sugar hot pack method. . . . It might be a good plan for housewives."[46]

Public awareness and pressures on the sugar supply continued into late summer and fall 1918. At the 1918 State Fair, billed as a "War Exposition," no pies, cakes, or fancy pastries were exhibited because "altogether too much sugar, lard and other ingredients needed elsewhere in winning the war are required for pie and cake," said Bertha Dahl Laws, superintendent of the Woman's Work Department.[47]

"Patriotic travelers" complained to A. D. Wilson and other state food chairmen that they had seen open sugar bowls in the dining cars on trains passing through Minnesota, Montana, and South Dakota. Traveling salesmen had grown accustomed to sugarless hotel and restaurant tables, but some trains refused to take sugar bowls off their tables, declaring they were not subject to state laws. They eventually bowed to public pressure, however, and removed the bowls.[48]

By late fall 1918, letters from soldiers continued to carry messages about the importance of sweets and food. Alonzo Carlisle, serving with the YMCA, hand delivered extra food packages to troops near the front lines, and after a battlefront mishap, he said, "I arrived back, minus my reserve rations of two boxes of hard tack, a can of salmon, and some chocolate which fell out of my haversack when I

*After 19 months of war, Minnesotans celebrated the coming of peace earned by
a nearly universal participation in conservation efforts and sacrifices.*

fell. . . . It was the start of a nine-hour barrage and very close to us.
We did not sleep but laid there huddled close to keep warm with our
fingers in our ears to keep out the noise. For breakfast we had coffee, bread and syrup which tasted mighty good. . . . Since my arrival
over here, I have distributed thousands of packages of cigarettes,
chocolate and cookies."[49]

As hopeful news of Allied battlefront victories filled the newspapers, so did rumors of an end to sugar restrictions before Christmas
1918. One printed in the *St. Cloud Daily Times* suggested that sugar
conservation had been required because so much of the supply had
been sunk at sea and that the "sugar famine" would last only until
the middle of November. The paper praised compliance with sugar
restrictions: "Enough sugar in sight. People have been very good
about observing the sugar regulations."[50]

The end to sugar rationing did come very quickly. On November 1 the per-person monthly limit was raised to three pounds; it was raised again on November 13 to four pounds and eliminated on November 27, 1918. A. D. Wilson greeted the news by sending out a press release celebrating the use of sweeteners on traditional holiday cranberries.

On the 22nd of October rolled packs and started towards the front lines about 2 o'clock. . . . We went on up into a woods where the Germans had been only a short time before at last we stopped and got ready to spend the night. . . . We got up early and ate some hard bread and salmon which we carried with us everywhere now.

There was no such thing as sleep for the shells were falling all around us. . . . A big shell hit about 50 feet from me. . . . The shell must have wounded a couple of men close by me for I could hear someone moaning all night. . . . When daylight came 3 other boys and I took a litter and went out to find them. . . . We had a mile to carry him to get to the first aid station. This was very hard on us for we were nearly all in ourselves from lack of sleep and nothing to eat for we had been going for 3 days. . . .

When we started over the top we had 60 men, now we only had 14, the rest being killed or wounded at this time. It was hard to get anything to eat but our sergeant had managed to get a gallon of syrup and a half sack of bread so we sat down and ate that. [Later] we found our kitchen in a woods, where we got a good cup of coffee, the first I had had for 5 days. . . . At 6 o'clock on Monday morning orders came in that they would cease firing at 11 hour of the 11 day of the 11 month and our division, which was the 90th was on the front lines when the Armistice was signed.
Lester Allen McPherson[51]

The PRESIDENT says

"Hunger does not breed reform; it breeds madness and all the ugly distemper that makes an ordered life impossible .... The future belongs to those who prove themselves the true friends of mankind"

Save Food
Don't Waste It

UNITED   STATES   FOOD   ADMINISTRATION

Settling Up Accounts

> If the folks at home could only see the socks they knit-
> ted! We fill one of a pair and stick the other inside of it; we
> put nuts, candy, gum, and one little present, knife, game
> or something of the sort, Khaki handkerchief, package of
> cookies and a cake of chocolate in each one . . . filling 1,500
> socks for our hospital. . . . About 3:00 A.M. we began hang-
> ing the socks on the beds which was more fun than I have
> ever had. The boys did not hear us although we did get
> giggling fits. . . . It was one of the best Christmases I've ever
> had. *Charlotte Manson*[1]

The Christmas of 1918 was one that Hamline Red Cross nurse
Charlotte Manson would never forget, celebrated in a field hospital in Toul, France. Six weeks after the end of the war, wounded
soldiers were still being cared for in French Red Cross hospitals.
Soldiers and civilians were hospitalized on this side of the Atlantic,
too, as they fought for their lives against a most dangerous enemy that knew no national boundaries. The Spanish influenza
threatened especially the young and otherwise healthy in the fall
of 1918. Beginning in military camps in August, it spread like wild-
fire during the last months of the year and into 1919. Hundreds of
Minnesota newspaper notices announced that club, school, civic,
and religious gatherings were "cancelled due to the flu." The pandemic claimed 2,000 people in the Twin Cities and another 6,000
across the state.[2]

One of those soldiers was Minnesota airman Granville Gutterson.
A gifted pilot and flight instructor, "Granny" wanted passionately
to take his flying skills to dogfights in the French battle zone. After
spending months in Texas learning to fly and then training others, he finally received his order to ship out. He got as far as New

Banner headlines once again brought international news into the homes of Minnesotans. On the pages of papers across the state, people read all about the success and the work yet to be done.

York just as the Armistice was declared. A disappointed Gutterson packed up and followed his orders back to Texas, but somewhere on his journey he met the influenza virus. He died within a few days, losing the only battle he ever fought. He was among the more than 118,000 Minnesotans in uniform during World War I, of whom 4,799 were wounded and 3,480 lost their lives to battle or disease before and after the Armistice.[3]

The work and the words continued after silence fell on the battle-ground and the cheering stopped. Returning soldiers brought their own visions home with them. Gray Cassidy wrote home in September, "You'll never get me out of the old US again. This is an awful pretty country . . . but it isn't America. I heard a boy say that if he owned France he'd trade the whole thing for a city lot in the US." The possibility of America filled the minds and hearts of women in Europe who embroidered over the printing on flour sacks as a gift to Hoover or who wrote letters of appreciation to women's clubs that had sent money and food to support their fatherless children. American citizens took pride in their rapid accomplishments that changed the world.[4]

American sacrifices and food policies had won the war to end all wars. Now it was time to assure the peace. Minnesota's food administrator A. D. Wilson wrote powerfully of the road ahead. "Peace will bring added responsibilities to America as the food source of the world. . . . Now we must feed hundreds of millions. . . . We must realize that it is our duty as well as our privilege to share and share alike with those who have fought our battles for world peace . . . and to share our food with the hungry Germans as readily as with any other suffering humans."[5]

The nation's farmers were up to the task. A billion more pounds of meat were shipped in 1919 than in 1918. Dairy-product and grain exports were up significantly as well.[6]

Distribution of food, which was stockpiled in surpluses, shifted from the government to charitable organizations in Europe. American markets stabilized and largely returned to prewar operations.[7]

The Food Administration, which had shaped public opinion and guided consumption habits for many months, was dismantled as quickly as it had been created. Food administrator Herbert Hoover expressed gratitude to the "millions of our farmers and our women, without whose patriotic devotion and self-sacrifice the winning of the war would have been impossible."[8]

But while American life returned to prewar normalcy, it was also different. The Eighteenth Amendment to the Constitution banned the manufacture, sale, or transport of liquor, making legal drinking of alcohol a thing of the past. By another constitutional amendment women received the right to vote in every election.

It would be another decade before Americans faced a serious national challenge. The Great Depression began with the stock market crash of October 1929, less than a year after Herbert Hoover's election to the presidency. His term ended under the shadow of thousands of desperate World War I veterans camping out in Washington, D.C., seeking payment of a promised military bonus.

A thorough analysis of crops, cooking, and conservation in the years between the two world wars is the topic for another book, but pages from *Wallaces' Farmer* in the early 1930s shed some light on the lasting impact of World War I's food programs and how midwesterners used those lessons to meet the new hardships. This time, the task was to feed our own people when businesses closed, jobs disappeared, and Dust Bowl conditions swallowed up crops. Farm wives frequently described bartering farm products for doctor visits and town necessities. Some suggested that "no one who reads these pages will go hungry" because of its recipes for stretching summer's bounty through the winter and ideas for thrifty use of now expensive meats. One World War I recipe stood the test of time well into the 1930s. "War Cake" appeared frequently in community cookbooks under names such as Hoover Cake, Red Cross Cake, Canadian War Cake, and Eggless Butterless Cake. And, once again, the frugal French were held up as an example in the pages of *Wallaces' Farmer*: "To the thrifty French woman, what seems like economy in this country appears the wildest extravagance."[9]

These economic challenges were not fully overcome until the military and industrial buildup for World War II, when Germany was again the aggressor and the people of the United States stepped up once again to fight for world peace on battlegrounds across the oceans and to sacrifice on the home front so people would be fed.

In my mind's eye, I see them, these Minnesota soldiers and the soldiers of the soil, the homemakers who fought kitchen campaigns against waste and battled through shortages. I see the innovators and educators who saw opportunity in the midst of war. As the pressures of war disappeared and peace was fed, these Minnesotans

HUMAN STATUE OF LIBERTY
18,000 OFFICERS AND MEN
AT
CAMP DODGE, DES MOINES IA.
COL. WM. NEWMAN, COMMANDER
COL. RUSH S. WELLS, DIRECTOR

This living Statue of Liberty, photographed on August 22, 1918, from the top of a 40-foot tower, is made up of 18,000 soldiers at Camp Dodge, Iowa. Soldiers in white shirts form the detail outlines. The perspective 400 yards into the distance required 12,000 men to make up the flame, 2,800 for the torch, 1,200 for the right arm, and 2,000 forming the head, body, and base.

returned to building a successful and progressive state with the energy, insights, and skills honed in this intense experience.

The United States became a world power through its military might, its economic strength, and the generosity of its citizens toward people in need an ocean away. The lasting lesson of the World War I experience can be found in President Wilson's vision for world peace, quoted on a Food Administration poster issued at the end of the war: "Hunger does not breed reform; it breeds madness and all the ugly distemper that makes an orderly life impossible. The future belongs to those who prove themselves the true friends of mankind."[10]

Acknowledgments

L ois Hendrickson at the University of Minnesota Archives has been a remarkable asset to my research. I would not have had as clear an understanding of the impact of the university's staff and departments without her thorough understanding of the College of Agriculture and her guidance toward the best archived documents to search. Karen Klinkenberg and other University Archives staff generously gave continuing support to this project. Matthew Schaefer, archivist at the Herbert Hoover Presidential Library, provided early insights to Hoover and food conservation.

At the Minnesota Historical Society, Debbie Miller and Hamp Smith provided equally astute insights and helped me unearth hidden treasures from that rich collection of documents. Thank you also to Wendy Freshman of the society's program department, and to Anne Kaplan, editor of *Minnesota History,* for their early support for the project, and to Gregory Britton, former director of the Minnesota Historical Society Press, who first suggested turning an article into a book. Many others at MHS Press helped bring this complex work forward, in particular Ann Regan and Shannon Pennefeather. I am grateful to cover designer Brad Norr, page designer and compositor Wendy Holdman, and proofreader Lis Trouten for their contributions to the book. My friend Kay Culton first sent me a copy of the remarkable "Statue of Liberty" photograph. I would not have known of this image without her. And last, but certainly not least, my deepest appreciation to editor Marilyn Ziebarth. Marilyn was able to track down the source of that photo and find many of the others that help tell the story. I am most grateful for her insights and kind considerations. She has improved this work immeasurably.

University of Minnesota Liberty Breads

University of Minnesota home economists under the visionary leadership of division chief Josephine Berry quickly developed recipes for meat- and potato-saving main dishes and wheat-saving breads. Mildred Weigley, assistant professor in foods and cookery, began experiments in the spring of 1917, and by early August she and her assistants had developed a number of "man-pleasing" recipes for quick and yeast breads "whereby Americans, through Liberty bread, might save a bigger portion of wheat for European war breads."

YEAST CORN BREAD

1¼ cup combination of milk and
    water or water alone
⅔ cup cornmeal
1 to 2 teaspoons salt (optional)
1 tablespoon cold butter or other fat
1 package instant dry yeast

¼ cup warm water
2 tablespoons sugar
2⅓ cups bread flour
1 tablespoon soft butter
nonstick cooking spray

In medium saucepan, bring milk or water to a slow simmer. Sprinkle in the cornmeal and salt, stirring constantly. Cook until thickened, about 5 minutes. Cool slightly and add the cold butter. Allow to come to lukewarm, and put into a large mixing bowl. Combine the yeast, warm water, and sugar in a measuring cup. Stir to mix and let stand until the mixture bubbles. Stir into the cornmeal. Knead in 2 cups of the bread flour, adding the remaining ⅓ cup if necessary to make a smooth dough. Spread the soft butter over the dough and put in a warm place to rise until double. Punch down and knead until smooth. Lightly spray a standard-sized loaf pan with nonstick spray. Place the dough in and allow to rise again in a warm place until doubled. Preheat oven to 325° F. Bake the bread until loaf is browned on top and sounds hollow when tapped, about 45–50 minutes. Remove from pan and set loaf on its side to cool. (*Minnesota Farm Review*, August 4, 1917)

OATMEAL MUFFINS

2 cups old-fashioned oats, uncooked
1½ cups milk
2 tablespoons melted butter
1 egg

2 tablespoons sugar
3 teaspoons baking powder
½ teaspoon salt (optional)
1 cup flour

Mix the oatmeal and milk in a medium bowl and let stand a half hour. Preheat oven to 350° F. Stir the melted butter and then the egg into the oatmeal and milk mixture. Mix very well. Add the remaining ingredients and stir until just blended. Spoon batter into lightly greased muffin cups and bake until lightly browned on top, 25–30 minutes. Cool in tins 5 minutes and serve or remove to continue cooling on wire rack. Makes 36 gem-sized muffins or 12 ¾-cup muffins. (*Minnesota Farm Review,* August 4, 1917)

RICE CORN BREAD

1 cup boiling water
1 cup yellow cornmeal
1⅛ cup softly cooked regular white rice
1 tablespoon melted fat

1 egg
1 cup milk
2 teaspoons baking powder
½ teaspoon salt

Pour the boiling water over the cornmeal, stir to mix thoroughly, and allow to stand until cooled. Preheat oven to 425° F. Combine the rice, fat, egg, and milk in a food processor or blender. Pulse until the rice grains are finely chopped. Stir in the baking powder, salt, and cornmeal. Pulse till just combined. Pour into a well-greased 9 × 9-inch pan. Bake until bread is firm in the center, about 15 minutes. Serve warm. (*Minnesota Farm Review,* August 4, 1917)

RICE AU GRATIN

1½ tablespoons butter
1 tablespoon flour
1 cup milk
½ cup grated cheese

¼ teaspoon paprika
2 cups boiled rice
½ cup grated stale bread crumbs
2 tablespoons butter

Preheat oven to 350° F. In a medium saucepan, melt the butter and add the flour. Stir until combined and then slowly add the milk. Cook over medium heat until mixture is thickened, stirring frequently. Stir in the cheese and paprika. Lightly grease a 2-quart casserole. Put in the cooked rice and pour the cheese sauce over. Combine the stale bread crumbs and melted butter and sprinkle over the top. Bake, uncovered, until crumbs are browned, about 30 minutes. (Bulletin No. 5, Food Files)

Cost of Living in 1917–18

Selected salary and expense listings taken from sources of the time suggesting wartime costs and prices.

WAGES AND SALARIES

Carpenters building Camp Dodge:

62½ cents an hour, 11-hour days, or $6.87 a day. Double wages for Sundays and holidays. Unskilled laborers $3.85, teamsters $7.50.

(*St. Cloud Daily Journal Press,* October 6, 1917)

Annual salaries of university teachers:

Incoming with a Ph.D. assistant professorship: $1,600 to $1,800

(Letter to Chas. W. Stoddart, March 16, 1918, Agricultural Biochemistry Records, Collection 584, University Archives)

REAL ESTATE

Homes for sale in Minneapolis

New Homes for sale Columbus Avenue between 38th and 39th streets. Two-story house, frame exterior or stucco eight rooms $5,800.

3825 Park Ave. with garage $5,000.

(*Minneapolis Journal,* May 6, 1917)

Farm in Cloquet

Splendid garden farm 2½ acres next to school farm. Nearly all cleared and ready for the plow. City water, electric light and telephone—all that will make a beautiful home. $350.

(*Cloquet Pine Knot,* July 5, 1918)

GOODS

Icycle Refrigerator, 33 inches wide, 19¼ inches deep, 47 inches
high, ice capacity 110 pounds. $26.95
(*Minneapolis Journal*, May 1, 1918)

Span of young mares weighing about 1,150 pounds. Set of
buggy harnesses. $280 for all.
(*St. Cloud Daily Journal Press*, October 17, 1917)

The Ford Motor Company of Minneapolis has cut its production. Order now. Touring car $360. Runabout $355.
(*Brown County Journal*, July 21, 1917)

Men's Milwaukee wooden-soled shoes. Cheaper than all-
leather. Keep feet dry and warm. 15-inch boot. $3.75.
(*The Dairy Record*, June 20, 1917)

ENTERTAINMENT

Barnum and Bailey—Greatest Show on Earth. 1,400 people,
780 performers, 50 clowns, 41 elephants, 89 railroad cars,
20 acres of tents. One 50-cent ticket admits to all.
(*Brown County Journal*, July 21, 1917)

ICE

Ice delivered this summer to homes will be $15 for the season or
60 cents per hundred pounds.
(*Oklee Herald*, May 17, 1917)

GROCERIES

Sorghum, 1-lb tins, 90 cents
Case fancy apples, $2.00
Barley flour, 10 lbs, 65 cents
Dried prunes, 50-lb case, 10 c per lb
Dried peaches, 25-lb case, 11 c per lb
Cider vinegar, gallon, 35 cents
Dried loganberries, 1 lb, 50 cents
Coffee, reasonable good, 7 lbs, $1.00
Coffee, special grade, 19 cents per lb
(*Bemidji Daily Pioneer*, May 17, 1918)

Timeline

JUNE 28, 1914
Archduke Franz Ferdinand, heir to the Austro-Hungarian throne, is assassinated, upsetting already uneasy alliances among European nations.

AUGUST 1914
Germany declares war on Russia and France; England declares war on Germany. Herbert Hoover establishes volunteer organization that becomes the Commission for Relief in Belgium, an organization that provides essential food supplies to civilian populations caught in war zones.

JANUARY 1915
William C. Edgar, editor of *Northwestern Miller,* accompanies a shipment of 7,000 tons of relief wheat sent from Minnesota to Europe.

MAY 17, 1915
German U-boat sinks the British ocean liner *Lusitania,* killing more than 1,000 people, including 128 Americans.

FEBRUARY 1917
Germany declares unconditional submarine warfare against all ships in the North Atlantic.

MARCH 1917
Herbert Hoover meets with President Woodrow Wilson to discuss the role food supply will play if America enters the war.

APRIL 6, 1917
United States declares war on Germany.

APRIL 12, 1917
University of Minnesota professor and head of extension service A. D. Wilson calls for state's farmers to increase yields.

APRIL 15, 1917

President Woodrow Wilson calls upon all Americans to become "citizen-soldiers" who supply abundant food to the common cause.

MID-APRIL 1917

Minnesota Governor J. A. A. Burnquist appoints the 29-member Committee on Food Production and Conservation (Food Committee), headed by A. D. Wilson.

Minnesota legislature establishes the Minnesota Commission of Public Safety with sweeping powers to protect public safety.

MAY 1917

President Wilson appoints Herbert Hoover to head United States' food efforts to reduce waste and use of wheat. Wake up America patriotic rallies and parades are held across Minnesota and the nation.

MAY 18, 1917

U.S. Congress passes conscription legislation.

MAY–JUNE 1917

University of Minnesota home economists develop recipes for breads using less wheat and send news releases to newspapers across the state.

SPRING–SUMMER 1917

Hoover and the U.S. Department of Agriculture call on Americans to conserve food, reduce waste, and plant war gardens.

JUNE 5, 1917

Men between ages of 21 and 30 register for the draft.

SUMMER 1917

University of Minnesota Extension division offers courses on making "war breads" and home canning of garden produce on campus and across the state.

JULY 1917

First men are called up in the draft

AUGUST 1917

U.S. Congress enacts the Food and Fuel Control Act, known as the Lever Act, providing funding for Hoover's Food Administration as well as establishing wide-ranging price controls. The legislation gives price guarantees to farmers, establishes structure to provide penalties for hoarding and speculation, sets trade margins, and permits full control over sale of essential foods such as wheat and sugar.

Minnesota State Fair focuses on war-related food production and conservation.

SEPTEMBER 1917

Men whose draft numbers have been called in July report for service.

Americans are asked to sign the Food Pledge.

OCTOBER 1917

Food Administrator Hoover calls for eating one meatless and one wheatless meal each week.

Sugar bowls are removed from tables in restaurants and other commercial eating establishments to limit use.

NOVEMBER 1917

MCPS establishes bread store in Minneapolis as an experiment to lower the price of bakery-made bread across the state.

DECEMBER 1917

U.S. Food Administration issues bread formula requiring use of less wheat, fats, and sugar.

FEBRUARY 1918

U.S. Food Administration restricts use of wheat flour in bakery-produced goods and asks home bakers to comply with the "50/50 Rule" requiring use of alternative grains (such as cornmeal) equal to every pound of wheat flour purchased. Hoover calls for strictest food conservation of the war: of 21 weekly meals, 7 should be wheatless, 7 meatless, 4 without meat and wheat, and 3 unrestricted.

LATE WINTER–SPRING 1918
Bountiful supply of potatoes floods the state, and people are urged to make "every spud a soldier."

MARCH 1918
Meatless restrictions are lifted, but Hoover urges limits on amount of meat served.

SPRING 1918
U.S. Food Administration continually adjusts wheatless and meatless restrictions to balance supplies and surpluses of limited commodities.

SUMMER 1918
Volunteers in small towns across the state help farmers harvest their small grain crops. Severe shortage in sugar supply leads to limits on sales of three pounds per person per month or three tablespoons a day. Individuals needing sugar for home canning may sign request at their grocery store and receive an extra allotment.

NOVEMBER 11, 1918
Armistice declared. World War I ends.

Notes

The following abbreviations are used within these notes:

MHS   Minnesota Historical Society

UA   University Archives, University of Minnesota Twin Cities

Ag. Ext. files   Agricultural Extension Service files, 935 (4), box 63, UA

Food Files   Federal Food Administration and State Conservation Commission files, Minnesota State Archives, MHS

MCPS Files   Minnesota Commission of Public Safety Records, Main Files, Minnesota State Archives, MHS

Wilson War Letters   A. D. Wilson, War Letters in Agricultural Extension Service Records, Collection 935, UA

NOTE TO "APPETIZER"

1. William C. Mullendore, *History of the United States Food Administration, 1917–1919* (Stanford, CA.: Stanford University Press, 1941), 41.

NOTES TO CHAPTER 1

1. Here and throughout this chapter, all letters to and from Tracy Gray Cassidy in Tracy Gray Cassidy and Family Papers, Minnesota Historical Society (hereinafter, MHS), St. Paul (hereinafter, Cassidy Papers).

2. Franklin F. Holbrook and Livia Appel, *Minnesota in the War with Germany* (St. Paul: MHS, 1932), 1:97–107, 123–24, 374. A second registration occurred in June 1917 for men who had turned 21, and a third took place in September 1918 for men ages 18 through 45.

3. Virginia Brainard Kunz, *Muskets to Missiles: A Military History of Minnesota* (St. Paul: Minnesota Statehood Centennial Commission, 1958), 136, 150; Holbrook and Appel, *Minnesota in the War*, 1:68–75, 93–94.

4. Holbrook and Appel, *Minnesota in the War*, 1:307–31; *St. Cloud Daily Journal Press*, Oct. 6, 1917, 6; Kunz, *Muskets to Missiles*, 157.

5. *Eveleth News*, July 19, 1917, 1; Holbrook and Appel, *Minnesota in the War*, 2:13. In this book, I frequently refer to organizational and staff subdivisions within the University of Minnesota's Department of Agriculture, which included the College of Agriculture and Home Economics, the Central School of Agriculture, the Agricultural Extension Service, and the Agriculture Experiment Station. Dean A. F. Wood used this structure in his 1916–17 report that appears in the 1918–19 President's Report in the *University of Minnesota Bulletin*.

6. *Brown County Journal*, Sept. 29, 1917, 1; Louis Berger Papers, MHS.

7. University of Minnesota, *University of Minnesota Pocket Guide to Food Conservation*, May 1918; data from *Brown County Journal*, Feb. 1, 1918, 1.

8. According to Holbrook and Appel's 1928 study, 104,416 Minnesotans served in the army; 1,319 were killed or died of wounds received in action, 2,024 others died from unspecified causes, and 4,480 were wounded but not mortally. Another 11,236 Minnesotans served in the navy; 8 were killed in action, and 137 died of disease and other causes. Of 2,845 marines from Minnesota, 105 were killed or died of wounds received in action, 14 died of disease or other causes, and 319 were wounded. Holbrook and Appel, *Minnesota in the War*, 1:374.

9. Cassidy Papers.

NOTES TO CHAPTER 2

1. Merrill Family Papers, MHS.

2. Archie Dell Wilson and Eva Ward Wilson, *Agriculture for Young Folks* (St. Paul: Webb Publishing Co., 1910), 134.

3. "Belgian Relief Efficient," *New York Times*, Apr. 29, 1915, and "Northwest's Flour Landed for Belgians," *Minneapolis Journal*, in Newspaper Clippings 1909–19, and William Edgar to "My dearest little Annie," Feb. 28, 1915, all in William Edgar and Family Papers, MHS.

4. Data from U.S. Census 1920, 507; Carl H. Chrislock, *Watchdog of Loyalty: The Minnesota Commission of Public Safety During World War I* (St. Paul: MHS Press, 1991), 20, 286; Kathleen Neils Conzen, *Germans in Minnesota* (St. Paul: MHS Press, 2003), 68–69.

5. *New York Times*, Mar. 23, 1917, 1; President Wilson's second inaugural address, Mar. 5, 1917; see also www.thisnation.com/library/inaugural/wilson2.html (accessed Sept. 2009).

6. President Wilson's address found at http://www.firstworldwar.com/source/doyourbit.htm (accessed Sept. 2009).

7. Chrislock, *Watchdog of Loyalty*, 47; U.S. Census 1920, 520–24; various issues of *Brown County Journal*.

8. Herbert Hoover, *Memoirs* (New York: Macmillan, 1952), 1:225; T. A. Erickson memo, Apr. 20, 1917, Food Files; Herbert Hoover, in Introduction to Mullendore, *History of the U.S. Food Administration*, 9.

9. *Minnesota Farm Review*, Sept. 8, 1917, 1.

10. *St. Cloud Daily Journal Press*, Apr. 10, 1917, 1.

11. *Brown County Journal*, June 2, 1917, 6; Mullendore, *History of the U.S. Food Administration*, 114–16.

12. *The Farmer's Wife*, May 1917, 290.

13. *Duluth Herald*, Apr. 13, 1917, 1.

14. A. D. Wilson, War Letters (hereinafter, Wilson War Letters), in Agricultural Extension Service Records, Collection 935, University Archives, University of Minnesota–Twin Cities (hereinafter, UA).

15. David F. Houston, quoted in Ida Clyde Gallagher Clarke, *American Women and the World War* (New York: D. Appleton and Co., 1918), 63.

16. *Ramsey County Times*, Apr. 27, 1917, 1.

17. War letters 1, 2, and 3, Wilson War Letters. The Food Committee's subcommittees included crop production, livestock, labor mobilization, marketing, finance and credits, home economics, and publicity.

18. Chrislock, *Watchdog of Loyalty*, 68, 89, 98, 108; Minnesota Commission of Public Safety (hereinafter, MCPS) to Prof. W. P. Kirkwood, May 5, 1917, MCPS Files, 103.L.8.4 (F), MHS.

19. War Activities sheet, Records of Governor J. A. A. Burnquist, 148.6.17.4 (F), Minnesota State Archives, MHS.

20. Hoover remarks: Henry W. Wolff, *The Future of Our Agriculture* (Westminster, London: P. S. King & Son, Ltd., 1918), 463.

21. Hoover, *Memoirs*, 1:249.

22. Mullendore, *History of the U.S. Food Administration*, 9, 130.

23. Mullendore, *History of the U.S. Food Administration*, 238.

24. *The Farmer's Wife*, Aug. 1917, 54.

25. Hoover, *Memoirs*, 1:244.

26. *Eveleth News*, Nov. 8, 1917, 1.

27. Clarke, *American Women and the World War*, 63; Holbrook and Appel, *Minnesota in the War*, 1:156.

28. Mildred Maddocks, *Good Housekeeping*, Sept. 1917, 74.

29. *Brown County Journal*, Nov. 10, 1917, 1.

30. Mullendore, *History of the U.S. Food Administration*, 96–97.

31. William C. Edgar, *The Minneapolis Club: A Review of Its History* (Minneapolis: The Minneapolis Club, 1974); commemorative menu, Builders Exchange of St. Paul, Sixteenth Annual Dinner, Jan. 23, 1918, Menu Collection, MHS.

32. Mullendore, *History of the U.S. Food Administration,* 112–15.

33. Mullendore, *History of the U.S. Food Administration,* 342–45.

34. Hoover, *Memoirs,* 1:270.

35. *St. Paul Pioneer Press,* June 17, 1917; *Refrigerators and Cooling Rooms* (St. Paul: Manteuffel Refrigerator Co., 1919), 11–13.

36. *Everybody's Best* (Howard Lake, MN: Howard Lake Library and Improvement Society, 1917).

37. *Cloquet Pine Knot,* May 18, 1917, 5; *The Farmer's Wife,* July 1917, 28.

38. Mildred Maddocks, "Electrical Cooking Minimizes Heat," *Good Housekeeping,* June 1916, 807; Anita de Campi, "Home Harmonious," *Minneapolis Journal,* May 13, 1917, women's sec.

39. Woman's Club of Minneapolis, *Bulletin,* Jan. 1918.

40. *Brown County Journal,* Aug. 3, 1918, 1, and Aug. 10, 1918, 3.

41. Louis D. H. Weld, "Current Problems, Number 4, Social and Economic Survey of a Community in the Red River Valley," University of Minnesota, 1915, UA; A. M. Daniels, "Electric Light and Power in the Farm Home," in *Yearbook of the United States Department of Agriculture* (1919): 223–38.

42. Cotton to J. A. A. Burnquist, Dec. 21, 1917, Burnquist Records, 148.6.17.4 (F); J. D. Denegre to Kenneth G. Brill, Apr. 11, 1918, Brill Family Papers.

43. Mullendore, *History of the U.S. Food Administration,* 88–89.

44. *Pipestone Leader,* Sept. 6, 1917, 6.

45. *St. Cloud Times,* Oct. 13, 1917, 4.

46. Frank W. Street Papers, MHS.

NOTES TO CHAPTER 3

1. Letter, Mar. 1918, Granville Gutterson Papers, MHS; Grace V. Gray, *The Farmer's Wife,* June 1918, 6.

2. Mullendore, *History of the U.S. Food Administration,* 5.

3. *Mankato Daily Free Press,* Apr. 18, 1917, 1.

4. Ag. Ext. files.

5. War letter, Apr. 21, 1917, Wilson War Letters.

6. *St. Paul Pioneer Press,* Apr. 3, 1917; *Minnesota Farm Review,* Sept. 8, 1917, 3.

7. Greg Kimmet, agricultural statistician, Minnesota Department of Agriculture, interview by author, Apr. 19, 2005; *Yearbook of the United States Department of Agriculture* (1919):745; *Minnesota,* U.S. Railroad Administration booklet (Jan. 1, 1919), 19.

8. *Duluth Herald,* Apr. 13, 1917, 1.

9. Bulletin No. 5, Food Files.

10. *Bemidji Daily Pioneer,* Dec. 9, 1917, 12.

11. "Report and Plans of the Minnesota Committee of Food Production and Conservation," June 5, 1917, MCPS Files, 103.L.11 2 (F).

12. Berry Report, Food Files; *Northwestern Miller,* June 13, 1917, 755; "Conservation of Potatoes and Wheat: Use Rice," Bulletin No. 5, typescript in Food Files.

13. *Mankato Daily Free Press,* Apr. 18, 1917, 1.

14. Mildred Weigley files, Food Files.

15. *Northwestern Miller,* June 6, 1917, 687.

16. *Minnesota Farm Review,* Sept. 8, 1917, 1; Mullendore, *History of the U.S. Food Administration,* 26.

17. *Northwestern Miller,* June 13, 1917, 755.

18. Mullendore, *History of the U.S. Food Administration,* 115.

19. Hennepin Avenue Methodist Episcopal Church, *Culinary Guide* (Minneapolis, n.d.), MHS.

20. *Minnesota Farm Review,* Sept. 29, 1917, 2.

21. Here and below, Weigley files, Food Files.

22. *Junior Soldiers of the Soil,* June 1919, 9.

23. Elizabeth Condit and Jessie A. Long, *How to Cook and Why* (New York: Harper & Brothers, 1914), 40.

24. *Junior Soldiers of the Soil,* June 1919, 7.

25. Mullendore, *History of the U.S. Food Administration,* 164.

26. "Report I Bread Shops," Aug. 28, 1917, MCPS Files, 103.L.11.2 (F); *Eveleth News,* Aug. 2, 1917, 2.

27. "Report I Bread Shops"; Chrislock, *Watchdog of Loyalty,* 209; Lind to "March," Jan. 17, 1917, 8, in "Report I Bread Shops."

28. *Brown County Journal,* Dec. 14, 1917, 8.

29. *Brown County Journal,* Dec. 22, 1917, 6.

30. *Brown County Journal,* Dec. 29, 1917, 1; interview with Charles Ritz, chairman of the board, International Milling Company, Lake Minnetonka, MN, Aug. 1, 1962, Flour Milling Oral History files, 4, MHS; *Pillsbury's 40 Wartime Recipes,* MHS.

31. Interview with Rose Holub, Edina, MN, July 8, 1958, 17, Flour Milling Oral History files.

32. *Norwegian American,* Feb. 22, 1918, 1.

33. Maxcy Robson Dickson, *The Food Front in World War I* (Washington, DC: American Council on Public Affairs, 1944), 41.

34. W. W. Loveless advertisement, *Worthington Globe,* Feb. 2, 1918; *Duluth News Tribune,* Aug. 17, 1918, 1.

35. *Bemidji News Tribune,* Mar. 6, 1918, 3.

36. *Le Sueur News,* May 30, 1918, 8.

37. *Eveleth News,* May 30, 1918, 5.

38. Letter from Clara A. Hale, Ramsey County Women's War Organization, to MCPS, Feb. 23, 1918, and Mrs. A. W. Strong to Mrs. Hale, Feb. 25, 1918, both MCPS Files, 103.K.7.10 (F).

39. Letter, June 12, 1918, Food Administrator for Hennepin County (WPD) to Mrs. W. A. Strong, Woman's Committee Council of National Defense, MCPS Files, 103.K.7.10 (F).

40. *Minneapolis Journal,* May 2, 1918, 7.

41. *Minneapolis Journal,* May 5, 1918, editorial sec., 14.

42. U.S. Food Administration, "To All Active Workers Farm Enrollment Campaign," Oct. 22, 1917, Food Files.

43. *Erskine Echo,* June 14, 1918, 2.

44. Memo, July 15, 1918, Meeker County Threshermen's Organization, Farm Bureau Records, Collection 935, box 63, UA.

45. *Crookston Times,* Aug. 17, 1918, 2.

46. *Crookston Times,* Aug. 31, 1918, 2.

47. F. E. Bahlmer files, Farm Bureau Records, Collection 935, box 63, UA.

48. Diary, Ingvald D. Smith, 68–70, MHS.

NOTES TO CHAPTER 4

1. Diary, Maybelle [Jackobson] Brekken, MHS.

2. War letter 4, Wilson War Letters.

3. *Crookston Weekly Times,* Apr. 14, 1917, 3.

4. *Crookston Weekly Times,* Feb. 7, 1917, 3.

5. *Crookston Weekly Times,* May 2, 1917, 1.

6. *Eveleth News,* May 3, 1917, 1; May 17, 1917, 1; and May 25, 1917, 1.

7. *Pipestone Leader,* Apr. 19, 1917, 1.

8. Typescript recipes, Weigley files, Food Files.

9. *Winona Weekly Leader,* May 4, 1917, 1.

10. *Duluth New Tribune,* Apr. 28, 1917, 4.

11. B. B. Jackson to L. S. Donaldson, Apr. 14, 1917, and Donaldson to Jackson, Apr. 16, 1917, Correspondence files, 1917, L. S. Donaldson Company Records, MHS.

12. *St. Cloud Daily Journal Press,* Apr. 12, 1917, 5; *Crookston Weekly Times,* May 5, 1917, 8.

13. *Farmers Equity News,* June 12, 1917, 3.

14. *Erskine Echo,* May 4, 1917, 1.

15. *Erskine Echo,* May 11, 1917, 3.

16. *Crookston Weekly Times,* May 12, 1917, 3.

17. War letter 4, Wilson War Letters.

18. R. S. Mackintosh, "A Garden for Every Home," University of Minnesota Agricultural Extension Division, Special Bulletin No. 11, May 1917, 103.L.12.1 (B), MHS.

19. *Crookston Weekly Times,* Apr. 14, 1917, 3.

20. "Vegetable Gardening in Minneapolis," A. W. Hasselberg, pub., Minneapolis Garden Club, 1914[?].

21. *Crookston Weekly Times,* Apr. 28, 1917, 2.

22. *Oklee Herald,* Apr. 26, 1917, 3.

23. *Minneapolis Journal,* Apr. 15, 1917, sec. 2, 12; *Minneapolis Journal,* May 19, 1917, editorial sec., 14.

24. *Crookston Weekly Times,* May 5, 1917, 7.

25. *Mankato Ledger,* May 9, 1917, 1.

26. *Oklee Herald,* July 21, 1917, 4.

27. *St. Paul Pioneer Press,* June 17, 1917.

28. *Mankato Ledger,* July 10, 1917, 1.

29. *St. Cloud Daily Journal Press,* Apr. 15, 1917, 5; Minneapolis Public School record cards, MHS; *St. Cloud Daily Times,* Oct. 12, 1917, 5.

30. *Eveleth News,* Sept. 1, 1917; *University Farm Press News,* Dec. 5, 1917, 1; *The Visitor,* Dec. 1917, Division of Agricultural Education, Department of Agriculture, University of Minnesota, UA.

31. "Storing Vegetables at Home," USDA news release, Fall 1917, Weigley files, Food Files.

32. *The Farmer's Wife,* June 1917, 6.

33. *St. Cloud Daily Times,* Oct. 16, 1917, 5.

34. *Bemidji Daily Pioneer,* Nov. 9, 1917, 8.

35. *Worthington Globe,* Aug. 2, 1917.

36. Arthur McGuire diary, A. J. and Marie McGuire Papers, MHS; "Seed Corn Selection a Patriotic Duty," MCPS Files, 103.L.9.6 (F).

37. Mullendore, *History of the U.S. Food Administration,* 342–45.

38. *Mankato Daily Free Press,* Dec. 22, 1917.

39. Here and below, see Market Basket column, *Duluth News Tribune* weekly edition, 7, 8, varying dates through winter 1917 and spring 1918.

40. *Weekly Bulletin: Trade and Technical Section,* Public Information Division, U.S. Food Administration, Dec. 15, 1917.

41. "Grow Vegetables That Will Keep for Winter Use," *Minneapolis Journal,* May 2, 1918, 11; *Bemidji Daily Record,* Apr. 11, 1918, 3.

42. "How's Your War Garden?" USDA Bulletin, Spring 1918, Food Files.

43. *Mankato Daily Free Press,* Apr. 22, 1918.

44. *Eveleth News,* May 23, 1918, 7.

45. *St. Cloud Daily Times,* July 6, 1918, 3.

46. *Minneapolis Journal,* May 19, 1918, news and city sec., 15.

47. "Vegetable Time," USDA news release, July 16, 1918, Food Files.

48. *The Farmer's Wife,* May 1918, 288.

49. *The Farmer's Wife,* Oct. 1918, 100.

50. *Minneapolis Journal,* July 18, 1918, 1.

51. Charles Lathrop Pack, *The War Garden Victorious* (Philadelphia, PA: Lippincott Co., 1919), 3, 15.

52. *1919 Annual Report of Boys and Girls Club,* Boys and Girls Club files, Collection 17, box 29, UA.

53. *The Farmer,* Apr. 28, 1917

54. *The Farmer's Wife,* June 1917, 6.

55. *Minneapolis Journal,* May 3, 1917, 1.

56. *Brown County Journal,* July 26, 1917, 7.

57. *The Farmer,* July 14, 1917.

58. *Minnesota Farm Review,* Sept. 8, 1917, 1.

59. *Minnesota Farm Review,* July 28, 1917, 2.

60. *Brown County Journal,* Sept. 15, 1917, 1.

61. *Junior Soldiers of the Soil,* May 1919, 5.

62. Weigley files, Food Files.

63. Weigley files, Food Files; *Minneapolis Journal,* May 31, 1918, 4.

64. Holbrook and Appel, *Minnesota in the War,* Oct. 9, 1918, 4.

65. *1919 Annual Report of Boys and Girls Club.*

66. *Minnesota Creameries, Ice Cream and Canning Factories* (1918 Annual Report, St. Paul: State Dairy and Food Department, 1919), 88–90, MHS.

67. *Minnesota Farm Review,* mid-July 1917.

68. Catherine Dean Cummings, *Making Food Conservation Interesting* (N.p.: Simmons Hardware Company, 1918 [?]).

69. "Can All Food That Can Be Canned," Pack, *The War Garden Victorious,* 17.

70. *Minnesota Farm Review,* July 28, 1917, 2.

71. David L. Beckman Papers, MHS.

NOTES TO CHAPTER 5

1. Raymond Brunswick Papers, MHS.

2. Ida C. Bailey Allen, "Three Meals a Day," *Good Housekeeping,* Apr. 1916, 229–39; other cookbook sources.

3. *Good Housekeeping,* Jan. 1916, 106.

4. *Everybody's Best,* 6–12.

5. Mullendore, *History of the U.S. Food Administration*, 232.

6. *Duluth News Tribune*, Aug. 18, 1917, 5.

7. *Brown County Journal*, Sept. 8, 1917, 1.

8. *Eveleth News*, Mar. 15, 1917, 1, and May 10, 1917, 6.

9. *Brown County Journal*, May 26, 1917, 8; *Duluth News Tribune*, May 5, 1917, 5.

10. *Mankato Daily Free Press*, Apr. 11, 1917, 6.

11. *Duluth News Tribune*, May 5, 1917, 5.

12. Cummings, *Making Food Conservation Interesting; Wallaces' Farmer*, Nov. 9, 1917, 1533.

13. *Wallaces' Farmer*, Nov. 9, 1917, 1533.

14. *Crookston Weekly Times*, May 5, 1917, 4.

15. U.S. Census for Minnesota 1920; *Minneapolis Journal*, Apr. 12, 1917, 20; *Mankato Ledger*, June 20, 1917, 1.

16. *Mankato Ledger*, June 29, 1917, 4.

17. John C. Culver and John Hyde, *American Dreamer: A Life of Henry A. Wallace* (New York: W. W. Norton, 2000), 47–48.

18. Culver and Hyde, *American Dreamer*, 47–48; Mullendore, *History of the U.S. Food Administration*, 264.

19. Data from USDA Economic Research Service, http://www.ers.usda.gov (accessed Sept. 2009), including *Food Review January 2000* and Judy Putnam, *Major Trends in U.S. Food Supply 1909–1999*.

20. *Erskine Echo*, May 18, 1917, 3.

21. *Crookston Weekly Times*, May 5, 1917, 3.

22. *Cloquet Pine Knot*, Nov. 23, 1917, 6.

23. *Long Prairie Leader*, quoted in *St. Cloud Daily Times*, Oct. 13, 1917, 3.

24. *Crookston Weekly Times*, Jan. 17, 1918, 3.

25. *Minneapolis Journal*, Dec. 17, 1913, 7; *Western Magazine*, Oct. 1917, 133.

26. *St. Cloud Daily Times*, Oct. 11, 1917, 6; *Eveleth News*, June 21, 1918, 6.

27. *St. Cloud Daily Times*, Oct. 13, 1917, 3.

28. *Duluth News Tribune*, Nov. 10, 1917, 12.

29. "Minnesota Lakes are 'Helping Hoover,'" *Western Magazine*, Nov. 1917, 134; *Eveleth News*, June 21, 1918, 6.

30. *Bemidji Daily Pioneer*, Nov. 24, 1917, 1; Nov. 13, 1917, 1; Nov. 15, 1917, 8.

31. *Oklee Herald*, Feb. 28, 1918, 1.

32. *Brown County Journal*, Jan. 4, 1918, 2; *Eveleth News*, May 9, 1918, 8.

33. *Eveleth News*, Sept. 13, 1917, 8; *Brown County Journal*, Sept. 15, 1917, 4, and Sept. 22, 1917, 4; *Bemidji Daily Pioneer*, Nov. 13, 1917, 1.

34. *Bemidji Daily Pioneer*, Nov. 1, 1917, 1; *Le Sueur News*, Oct. 17, 1917, 7.

35. "'Club Service' for Hotels," *Weekly Bulletin: Trade and Technical Section,* Nov. 10, 1917, 1:12.

36. *Winona Weekly Leader,* Oct. 26, 1917.

37. U.S. Food Administration food flyers, Food Files; USDA Food Thrift Series No. 5, "Wheatless Meals," 3, Food Files; *Minnesota Farm Review,* Sept, 19, 1917, 1.

38. *Duluth News Tribune,* Nov. 17, 1917, 12; *Brown County Journal,* Nov. 10, 1917, 1.

39. *The Farmer's Wife,* Nov. 1917.

40. *Mankato Daily Free Press,* Nov. 28 and Dec. 1, 1917, 1.

41. *Brown County Journal,* Dec. 22, 1917, 6.

42. "Camp Cody," *Brown County Journal,* Dec. 1, 1917, 1.

43. *Pipestone Leader,* Feb. 7, 1918, 1.

44. Division of Home Economics, *Conservation Recipes and Suggestions* (St. Paul: Minnesota Farmer's Library, Feb. 1918), Agricultural Extension bulletin 64, UA.

45. *Bulletin of the University of Minnesota,* Northwest School and Experiment Station, Crookston, MN, Oct. 1917.

46. Merrill Family Papers.

47. Brunswick Papers.

48. Letter, Jan. 25, 1918, Andrew Glenn Papers, MHS.

49. Letter, Mar. 1918, Zens Smith Papers, MHS.

50. *Minneapolis Journal,* May 3, 1918, 8, 12.

51. Mullendore, *History of the U.S. Food Administration,* 114–16; *Minneapolis Journal*, May 3, 1918, 8, 12; *Bemidji Daily Pioneer,* May 18, 1918, 1.

52. *Winona Weekly Leader,* July 12, 1918, 6.

53. *Brown County Journal,* Aug. 3, 1918, 5.

54. *St. Paul Union Stockyards Annual Report 1917* and *1918;* also typescript report of 1914, all MHS.

55. *St. Paul Union Stockyards Annual Report 1917* and *1918;* also typescript report of 1914, all MHS.

56. *Eveleth News,* Apr. 12, 1917, 7; Apr. 18, 1918, 3.

57. *Le Sueur News,* May 20, 1918, 8.

58. *Northrup King Seed Catalog* (1918), 18, 55; *St. Cloud Daily Times,* July 8, 1918, 4.

59. *Minneapolis Journal,* May 26, 1918, women's sec., 8.

60. *Brown County Journal,* Sept. 21, 1918, 1.

61. *Oklee Herald,* Feb. 28, 1918, 1, and May 30, 1917.

62. Undated news release from office of A. D. Wilson, Food Files.

63. Mullendore, *History of the U.S. Food Administration,* 102.

64. Undated news release, Wilson, Food Files.

65. *Oklee Herald,* Jan. 3, 1918, 4.

66. *Bemidji Daily Pioneer,* May 21, 1918, 7.

67. *Eveleth News,* Mar. 14, 1918, 1.

68. *Brown County Journal,* Aug. 24, 1918, 1; Oct. 6, 1918, 1; Nov. 10, 1917, 2.

69. *Le Sueur News,* Nov. 29, 1918, 7.

70. Letter, Jan. 6, 1918, Gutterson Papers.

NOTES TO CHAPTER 6

1. Letter, Mar. 1918, Gutterson Papers; Grace V. Gray, *The Farmer's Wife,* June 1918, 6.

2. *Yearbook of the United States Department of Agriculture* (1919), 663, 710; Hoover, in *History of the U.S. Food Administration,* 13.

3. *Minnesota Creameries,* 1917 annual report, 4.

4. Open letter to the Board of Regents, undated, McGuire Papers.

5. "Henry Schroeder's Dairy," *Ramsey County History* 21.1 (1984): 10.

6. Johan D. Frederiksen, *The Story of Milk* (New York: Macmillan Company, 1919), 44–46; "How to Use Skim Milk," *The Dairy Record,* July 4, 1917, 32–33.

7. Frederiksen, *Story of Milk,* xix.

8. Mary Swartz Rose, *Feeding the Family* (New York: Macmillan Co., 1916), 139; Louise Eleanor Shimer Hogan, *Diet for Children* (New York: Bobbs Merrill, 1916), 16, 72.

9. Hogan, *Diet for Children,* 16. Today's milk is pasteurized much faster. The pasteurization process heats milk to 161° Fahrenheit (63° centigrade) for 15 seconds; see http://www.fcs.msue.msu.edu/ff/pdffiles/foodsafety2.pdf.

10. Undated news release, Wilson, Food Files; "Milk for the Children," *The Farmer's Wife,* Feb. 1918.

11. Quaker Creamery, Colfax and Western Aves, Minneapolis, Dec. 8, 1917, MCPS Files, 103.L.8.4 (F); *Duluth News Tribune,* Aug. 18, 1917, 5, and Aug. 24, 1917, 9.

12. "Memorandum Regarding the Twin Cities Milk Producers Association," Sept. 13, 1917, MCPS Files, 103.L.11.2 (F); Frederiksen, *Story of Milk*, 152.

13. *Twin City Milk Producer's Bulletin* 3:8; *Brown County Journal,* May 26, 1917, 2.

14. Costs from the notes from Special Food Committee Meeting, Sept. 26, 1917, MCPS Files, 103.L.8.4 (F).

15. *Duluth News Tribune,* Oct. 26, 1918, 8.

16. "Milk, A Cheap Food," *The Dairy Record,* July 25, 1917, 8.

17. Chrislock, *Watchdog of Loyalty,* 89; U.S. Census 1920; letter to J. A. A. Burnquist, July 24, 1917, Correspondence 1916–19, Burnquist Records, 103.L.8.4 (F).

18. Kildee Report, Aug. 11, 1917, MCPS Files, 103.L.8.4 (F).

19. John O. Lysne to MCPS, Aug. 29, 1917, MCPS Files, 103.L.8.4 (F).

20. Memorandum, Twin Cities Milk Producers, Sept. 13, 1917, MCPS Files, 103.L.8.4 (F).

21. MCPS Order No. 13, 3, MCPS Files, 103.L.8.4 (F).

22. *Minnesota Creameries,* 1918 annual report, 6, MHS.

23. *Minnesota Creameries,* 1918 annual report, 6; Frederiksen, *Story of Milk,* 48; *Dairy Record,* Feb. 2, 1918, 15.

24. *Oklee Herald,* July 5, 1917, 3; *Dairy Record,* July 7, 1917, 28.

25. "Home Made Cheese Meat Substitute," *Erskine Echo,* June 8, 1917, 11; University of Minnesota Agricultural Extension Division, Special Bulletin No. 12, "Farm Dairy Cheese," UA; *St. Cloud Journal Press,* Apr. 19, 1917, 3.

26. *Dairy Record,* July 14, 1917.

27. Frederiksen, *Story of Milk,* 80; *Mankato Daily Free Press,* Apr. 3, 1918.

28. *Mankato Daily Free Press,* Apr. 3, 1918.

29. *Duluth News Tribune,* Feb. 23, 1918, 11.

30. *Duluth News Tribune,* Apr. 20, 1918, 7.

31. *Duluth News Tribune,* Apr. 20, 1918, 7.

32. "The War Activities of the Department of Agriculture," typescript, University of Minnesota, Apr. 1917–Aug. 1, 1918, 14, UA; *Minnesota Creameries,* 1917 annual report, 6.

33. *Minnesota Creameries,* 1917 annual report, 5.

34. *Weekly Bulletin: Trade and Technical Section,* 1, Dec. 15, 1917.

35. *Duluth News Tribune,* Dec. 22, 1917, 10.

36. *Duluth News Tribune,* Aug. 17, 1918, 9.

37. *Minnesota Creameries,* 1918 annual report, 78.

38. David L. Beckman Papers, MHS.

39. Louise B. Weaver and Helen C. LeCron, *A Thousand Ways to Please a Husband* (New York: A. L. Burt Company, 1917), passim.

40. Josephine T. Berry to pastors of the Twin Cities, July 29, 1917, Food Files.

41. *Duluth News Tribune,* Apr. 28, 1917, 5.

42. *Cold Storage Legislation Hearings before the Committee on Agriculture, House of Representatives, Aug. 11–26, 1919* (Washington, DC: GPO), 177–85.

43. "War Activities," UA; *Minnesota Creameries,* 1917 annual report, 17.

44. See, for example, *Duluth News Tribune,* Apr. 14, 1917, "Market Basket" 5.

45. *Erskine Echo,* May 18, 1917, 3.

46. Cassidy Papers.

NOTES TO CHAPTER 7

1. Letter, May 9, 1918, Glenn Papers.

2. For a full account of the MCPS's controversial actions to defend the state from perceived economic and political enemies, see Chrislock, *Watchdog of Loyalty.*

3. "Waste Not Want Not," *The Farmer,* Apr. 28, 1917.

4. *Bemidji Daily Pioneer,* Dec. 11, 1917, 2.

5. David A. Clary, "The Biggest Regiment in the Army," *Journal of Forest History,* Oct. 1978, 183; Robert C. Shaw, "Minnesota Lumberjack in France," typescript, 69, 101, and 102, MHS.

6. Interviews with Julius Joel, June 30, 1953, Leonard Costley, Aug. 3, 1957, and Maggie Orr O'Neill, Oct. 1, 1955, Forest History Society, comp., "Interviews with Pioneer Lumbermen 1953–1957," MHS.

7. Personnel Reports, Benjamin Finch file, Food Files.

8. Personnel Reports, Benjamin Finch file, Food Files; *University Farm Press News,* Dec. 12, 1917.

9. Personnel Reports, Benjamin Finch file, Food Files.

10. Personnel Reports, Benjamin Finch file, Food Files.

11. Recipes in Food Files.

12. Elizabeth Nickerson to Elizabeth Lange, emergency home demonstration agents, University Farms, Dec. 17, 1917, MCPS Files.

13. *Weekly Bulletin: Trade and Technical Section,* Dec. 15, 1917.

14. *Farmers Equity News,* June 15, 1917.

15. *Winona Weekly Leader,* June 8, 1917, 8.

16. "Mrs. B. B. in Minn.," letter, *The Farmer,* Sept. 8, 1917.

17. *Mankato Daily Free Press,* June 27, 1917, 5.

18. *Mankato Daily Free Press,* Aug. 3, 1917, 5.

19. Mildred Weigley to Mrs. Charles Thompson, Social Service Division, Minneapolis General Electric Company, Oct. 24, 1917, Food Files.

20. *Weekly Bulletin: Trade and Technical Section,* Jan. 12, 1918.

21. "Food Notes for Public Libraries," Nov. 1917, 23, copy in Wilson Library, government documents, University of Minnesota–Twin Cities.

22. *Brown County Journal,* Feb. 2, 1918, 1; *Minnesota Farm Review,* Sept. 29, 1917, 1.

23. *Eveleth News*, Jan. 31, 1918, 3.

24. Morrell Company advertisement, *Eveleth News*, May 19, 1918.

25. Mullendore, *History of the U.S. Food Administration*, 222.

26. Letter from Corp. Norman W. Lawrence, Camp Sevier, SC, *Cloquet Pine Knot*, Mar. 29, 1918.

27. T. B. Harrison, "Our Relations with the Government," *The Express Messenger* (newsletter of the Railway Express Company), July 1918, 3–4, Aug. 1918, 18, Nov. 1918, 71, Dec. 1918, 85.

28. *Minneapolis Journal*, July 7, 1918, 10.

29. Harriet Wallace Ashby, "Lunch Bucket Leak," *Wallaces' Farmer*, Sept. 23, 1917.

30. "Cloquet Boy in the Trenches," *Cloquet Pine Knot*, Nov. 19, 1917.

31. *Cloquet Pine Knot*, Jan. 11, 1918.

32. *American Jewish World*, Nov. 8, 1918.

33. Chrislock, *Watchdog of Loyalty*, 97.

34. *Brown County Journal*, May 10, 1917, 1.

35. Mullendore, *History of the U.S. Food Administration*, 107–9.

36. J. G. Durrell, Blood Broom Manufacturing Co., to J. A. A. Burnquist, Feb. 8, 1918, Correspondence 1916–19, and War Activities sheet, Burnquist Records, 148.6.17.4 (F).

37. *Brown County Journal*, Aug. 17, 1918, 7.

38. *Twin Cities Milk Producers Bulletin* 1.2:2.

39. *Cloquet Pine Knot*, July 12, 1918.

40. *Worthington Globe*, Aug. 2, 1917.

41. Posters and flyers, MCPS Files, 103.L.9.6 (F).

42. Posters and flyers, MCPS Files, 103.L.9.6 (F).

43. Agricultural Extension Division Weekly Report, June 25, 1917, Agricultural Extension Service Records, Collection 935, box 4, UA; calendar entries for summer 1917, McGuire Papers; *Pipestone Leader*, Aug. 8, 1918, 1.

44. Undated article [late summer or early fall 1917], McGuire Papers.

45. Here and following, letters to MCPS, Sorenson to Commission, July 20, 1918, MCPS Files, 103.L.8.4 (F).

46. Donney to Commission, July 26, 1918, MCPS Files, 103.L.8.4 (F).

47. Minnesota State Creamers & Cheese Factory Operators & Managers Association District Unit No.12 to Commission, Aug. 7, 1918, MCPS Files, 103.L.8.4 (F).

48. Kittleson to Commission, Aug. 1, 1918, MCPS Files, 103.L.8.4 (F).

49. Correspondence files, MCPS Files, 103.L.8.4 (F).

50. Agricultural Extension Service Records, UA.

51. *Erskine Echo,* July 26, 1918, 4.

52. *Mankato Ledger,* July 19, 1918, 8.

53. *Brown County Journal,* July 7, 1917, 3.

54. Undated news release, Wilson, Food Files.

55. Mary D. Akers, "Hamline in the Great War," typescript notebooks, 1:46, MHS.

NOTES TO CHAPTER 8

1. Weigley files, Food Files.

2. Food Files.

3. *Pipestone Leader,* May 9, 1917, 8.

4. *The Farmer's Wife,* June 1917.

5. I. W. Haycroft, "Potatoes in Minnesota," typescript, MHS; Rice recipes, typescript, Food Files.

6. *Bemidji Pioneer,* May 5, 1917.

7. *Minnesota Farm Review,* July 21, 1917.

8. *Eveleth News,* Aug. 23, 1917, 1.

9. Here and below, University of Minnesota Agricultural Extension Division, Special Bulletin No. 14.

10. War letter 11, Wilson War Letters.

11. War letters 22 and 13, Wilson War Letters.

12. *Bemidji Pioneer,* Oct. 23, 1917, 1; War letters 32 and 39, Market letters 15 and 19, Wilson War Letters.

13. Letter from R. A. Gortner to A. D. Wilson, Nov. 5, 1917, University of Minnesota Department of Agricultural Bio-chemistry files, UA (hereinafter cited as Ag. Bio-chem. files).

14. Eriksson to Gortner, Nov. 19, 1917, Ag. Bio-chem. files.

15. *Minnesota Farm Review,* Aug. 4, 1917, 1.

16. Mar. 1918, Food Files; War Activities sheet, Burnquist Records, 148.6.17.4 (F).

17. St. Louis County agent Hostetter to F. E. Blamer, Dec. 10, 1917, Farm Bureau files, UA.

18. Food Administration News Release, Spring 1918, Food Files.

19. Food Administration News Release, May 1918, Food Files.

20. *Bemidji Daily Pioneer,* May 20, 1918, 1.

21. Food Files.

22. Diary entry, Ingvald D. Smith.

23. "Made Money from Potatoes," *Junior Soldiers of the Soil,* Jan.

1919; "Three Hundred Bushels Per Acre," *Junior Soldiers of the Soil,* June 1919, 12.

24. Letter, Louis Core Papers, MHS.

NOTES TO CHAPTER 9

1. Woman's Club of Minneapolis, *Bulletin,* Oct. 1917.

2. U.S. Food Administration, *Official Food News,* Sept. 1, 1917.

3. *St. Paul Pioneer Press,* Apr. 10, 1917, 1; *Boy Scouts of America Eighth Annual Report* ([New York City: National Council of Boy Scouts of America, Mar. 25, 1918]), 21–22.

4. *Park Rapids Enterprise,* Mar. 21, 1918, 5.

5. Woman's Club of Minneapolis, "Hospital Relief Work," *Bulletin,* Oct. 1917; Akers, "Hamline in the Great War."

6. *Minneapolis Journal,* May 13, 1917, society sec., 2; *Cloquet Pine Knot,* Aug. 20, 1917; "How to Knit Sleeveless Jackets, Mufflers and Wristlets," *Pipestone Leader,* May 17, 1917, 11.

7. *Minneapolis Journal,* May 13, 1917, society sec., 2.

8. *Guidelines for Farm Women's Clubs and Resources for Meetings of Women of Farmer's Clubs,* Special Bulletin No. 20, Agricultural Extension Division, Food Conservation Program, Feb. 1918, University of Minnesota, UA.

9. A. D. Wilson, speech typescript, Oct. 23, 1917, box 935 (63), UA.

10. Mark Pendergrast, *For God, Country and Coca-Cola* (New York: Charles Scribner's Sons, 1993), 9, 64, 130; Colin Emmins, "Soft Drinks," in Kenneth F. Kiple and Kremhild Coneè Ornelas, eds., *Cambridge World History of Food* (New York: Cambridge University Press, 2000), 707–9.

11. Menus from St. Croix Drug Company and Starkel's Fountain in Stillwater, pamphlet collection, MHS; *Brown County Journal,* May 26, 1917, 2; *Eveleth News,* May 17, 1917, 1.

12. Frederic J. Haskin, *War Cook Book for American Women: Suggestions for Patriotic Service in the Home* (Washington, DC: U.S. Food Administration, 1918), 10.

13. "Wartime Feeding Chart for Children from Two to Eight Years," *Ladies Home Journal,* June 1918; Hoover, *Memoirs,* 1:250; *Oklee Herald,* Nov. 29, 1917, 1.

14. Mullendore, *History of the U.S. Food Administration,* 170.

15. *Minneapolis Journal,* May 2, 1917, 20; *Mankato Free Press,* Sept. 19, 1917.

16. Mullendore, *History of the U.S. Food Administration,* 171.

17. *Brown County Journal,* Oct. 27, 1917, 1.

18. *Le Sueur News*, Oct. 17, 1917, 7.

19. *Oklee Herald*, Aug. 9, 1917, 2.

20. *Food News Notes for Public Libraries* (Washington, DC: U.S. Food Administration, Nov. 1917), 1:23, copy in Wilson Library, government documents, University of Minnesota–Twin Cities.

21. Mullendore, *History of the U.S. Food Administration*, 110.

22. Street Papers.

23. Letter from Elizabeth Nickerson to Elizabeth Lange, Dec. 17, 1917, MCPS Files, 103.K.7.10 (F).

24. *Bemidji Daily Pioneer*, Feb. 27, 1918, 1; author interview with Verna Mikesh, May 2007.

25. *Bemidji Daily Pioneer*, Jan. 10, 1918, 12.

26. "Oliver Will Pay Soldiers," *Eveleth News*, July 19, 1917, 1; Men in Service 1916–18, Box 3, 149.D.13.9 (B), L. S. Donaldson Company Records.

27. Gutterson Papers.

28. Woman's Club of Minneapolis, *Bulletin*, Jan. 1918.

29. Holbrook and Appel, *Minnesota in the War*, 2:190–223; Milton Friedman and Anna J. Schwartz, *A Monetary History of the United States, 1867–1960* (Princeton, NJ: Princeton University Press, 1963), 221.

30. *Boy Scouts Eighth Annual Report*, 27; bronze medallion, North Star Museum of Boy Scouting and Girl Scouting, North St. Paul, MN.

31. Weigley files, Food Files.

32. *Park Rapids Enterprise*, May 16, 1918, 1.

33. Holbrook and Appel, *Minnesota in the War*, 2:94–107.

34. *Mankato Daily Free Press*, Apr. 18, 1918; *Mankato Ledger*, July 18, 1917, 5.

35. R. A. Gortner to R. B. Greeley, Mar. 1918, Ag. Bio-chem. files.

36. Gortner to Benjamin Waltner, Mar. 4, 1918, Ag. Bio-chem. files.

37. Gortner to K. S. Bergstad, Feb. 28, 1918, Ag. Bio-chem. files.

38. Gortner to Mrs. Charles Paine, Mar. 16, 1918, Ag. Bio-chem. files.

39. Gortner to H. F. Wharton, Mar. 2, 1918, and to R. S. Mackintosh, Mar. 12, 1918, Ag. Bio-chem. files.

40. *Cloquet Pine Knot*, Aug. 2, 1918, 3.

41. *Wallaces' Farmer*, May 10, 1918, 788 (16).

42. Mullendore, *History of the U.S. Food Administration*, 179.

43. *Bemidji Daily Pioneer*, July 11, 1918, 1.

44. Mullendore, *History of the U.S. Food Administration*, 113–14; *Minnesota Official Food News*, Aug. 1, 1918, 1.

45. Mullendore, *History of the U.S. Food Administration*, 112; *Mankato Ledger*, July 10, 1918, 1.

46. *Pipestone Leader,* Aug. 8, 1918, 1.

47. *Worthington Globe,* Sept. 8, 1918, 4.

48. *Mankato Ledger,* July 10, 1918, 1.

49. Letters, Oct. 3 and 22, 1918, Alonzo Carlyle Papers, MHS.

50. *St. Cloud Daily Times,* Oct. 19, 1918, 2, and Sept. 21, 1918, 2.

51. Lester Allen McPherson Papers, MHS.

NOTES TO "SETTLING UP ACCOUNTS"

1. Akers, "Hamline in the Great War," 1:83–84.

2. By June 1919, about 1,131 people in Minneapolis and 898 in St. Paul could be counted as excess deaths from the Spanish flu or pneumonia. (Mortality statistics for the state are unreliable, but this standard source suggests that between September 1918 and June 1919, about 8,500 people in Minnesota died from influenza and pneumonia.)

3. Kunz, *Muskets to Missiles,* 157; Holbrook and Appel, *Minnesota in the War,* 1:374.

4. Sept. 2, 1918, Cassidy Papers.

5. *Official Food News,* Nov. 15, 1918, 1.

6. *Yearbook of the United States Department of Agriculture* (1919), 11–12. Exports of meat were 3.3 billion pounds in 1919 and 2.3 billion pounds in 1918. Dairy products went from 592 million to 781 million pounds, and aggregated cereals went from 162 million pounds for the five-year average preceding the war to 448 million pounds in 1919.

7. Mullendore, *History of the U.S. Food Administration,* 43.

8. Mullendore, *History of the U.S. Food Administration,* 43.

9. Various issues of *Wallaces' Farmer,* 1930–31; "Potato Water Wisdom," *Wallaces' Farmer,* Aug. 22, 1931.

10. Poster, National Archives, NWDNS-4-P-98, http://firstworldwar. com/posters/usa.htm (accessed Sept. 2009).

Bibliography

Much of the information for this work came from letters and documents housed in two repositories, the Minnesota Historical Society, St. Paul (MHS), and the University Archives, University of Minnesota, Minneapolis (UA). The following books provided helpful information, perspectives, and insights.

Carl H. Chrislock, *Watchdog of Loyalty: The Minnesota Commission of Public Safety During World War I* (St. Paul: MHS Press, 1991)

Ida Clyde Gallagher Clarke, *American Women and the World War* (New York: D. Appleton and Company, 1918)

Elizabeth Condit and Jessie A. Long, *How to Cook and Why* (New York: Harper & Brothers Publishers, 1914)

Alfred W. Crosby, *America's Forgotten Pandemic: The Influenza of 1918* (Cambridge, MA: University Press, 1989)

John C. Culver and John Hyde, *American Dreamer: A Life of Henry A. Wallace* (New York: W. W. Norton and Company, 2000)

Maxcy Robson Dickson, *The Food Front in World War I* (Washington, D.C.: American Council on Public Affairs, 1944)

Johan D. Frederiksen, *The Story of Milk* (New York: Macmillan Company, 1919)

Milton Friedman and Anna J. Schwartz, *A Monetary History of the United States, 1867–1960* (Princeton, NJ: Princeton University Press, 1963)

Frederic J. Haskin, *War Cook Book for American Women: Suggestions for Patriotic Service in the Home* (Washington, D.C.: U.S. Food Administration, 1918)

A. W. Hasselberg, *Vegetable Gardening in Minneapolis* (Minneapolis: Minneapolis Garden Club, 1914)

Louise Eleanor Shimer Hogan, *Diet for Children* (New York: The Bobb-Merrill Company, 1916)

Franklin F. Holbrook and Livia Appel, *Minnesota in the War with Germany*, 2 vols. (St. Paul: Minnesota State Historical Society, 1932)

Herbert Hoover, *Memoirs of Herbert Hoover* (New York: Macmillan Company, 1952)

Virginia Brainard Kunz, *Muskets to Missiles: A Military History of Minnesota* (St. Paul: Minnesota Statehood Centennial Commission, 1958)

William C. Mullendore, *History of the United States Food Administration, 1917–1919* (Stanford, CA: Stanford University Press, 1941)

Mark Pendergrast, *For God, Country and Coca-Cola* (New York: Charles Scribner's Sons, 1993)

Mary Swartz Rose, *Feeding the Family* (New York: Macmillan Company, 1916)

United States Department of Agriculture, *Yearbook of the United States Department of Agriculture 1919* (Washington, D.C.: Government Printing Office, 1920)

Louise Bennett Weaver and Helen Cowles LeCron, *A Thousand Ways to Please a Husband* (New York: A. L. Burt Company, 1917)

Recipe Index

For more World War I food conservation recipes, see the author's blog, "Food Will Win the War," at http://foodwillwinthewar.blogspot.com.

Subject Index

Page numbers in *italic* refer to figures

Illustration Credits

The image on page 22 is courtesy the Herbert Hoover Presidential Library and Museum, Hoover Online website.

The photograph of soldiers in Statue of Liberty formation, page 209, is courtesy the Iowa Gold Star Military Museum, Camp Dodge.

The posters on pages 69, 146, and 172 are from *Posters of World Wars I and II* (Minneola, NY: Dover Publications, 2005).

All other illustrations are from the Minnesota Historical Society, St. Paul, Minnesota.